Thomas Jefferson
LAWYER

Thomas
Jefferson
LAWYER

FRANK L. DEWEY

University Press of Virginia
Charlottesville

Drawing of Thomas Jefferson by Benjamin Henry Latrobe.
(Courtesy of the Maryland Historical Society, Baltimore.)

THE UNIVERSITY PRESS OF VIRGINIA
Copyright © 1986 by the Rector and Visitors
of the University of Virginia

Third printing 1987

Library of Congress Cataloging-in-Publication Data
Dewey, Frank L., 1906–
  Thomas Jefferson, lawyer.

  Bibliography: p.
  Includes index.
  1. Jefferson, Thomas, 1743-1826—Career in law.
2. Lawyers—Virginia—Biography. I. Title.
KF363.J4D48 1986   349.73'092'4 [B]   85-26571
ISBN 0-8139-1079-X   347.300924 [B]

Printed in the United States of America

To Eleanor Powell Dewey
and Mary Lewis Dewey Grow

Contents

Foreword

*Having on several occasions had the opportunity of discussing
this study with the author as his research and writing progressed,
I am especially gratified to see it published as the accomplished
piece of work that I think it is. Frank Dewey has brought two
qualities in particular to the task of completing it. One is a
scholarly curiosity of the highest order that has enabled him to
pursue his investigation with energy and discipline. The other is
his own long experience as an attorney. Much of the strength of
the present work stems directly from Dewey's grasp of the precise
meaning of critical details in his evidence that concern legal
questions.*

*The result is a book that in numerous ways adds to our under-
standing of Thomas Jefferson and his milieu. As the author
correctly notes, Jefferson's career as a practicing attorney was
brief, spanning only eight years at the beginning of his adult life,
and was quickly overshadowed by his later accomplishments. Yet
this phase of his life marked the completion of his formal education and his introduction to public affairs. Although the number
of excellent biographical studies of Jefferson that we have might
seem to leave scant opportunity to add anything to what we know
of this inadequately documented part of Jefferson's life, Dewey is,
in fact, able to correct some details, expand upon others, and
above all help us see more clearly the nature of Jefferson's law
practice.*

*Jefferson's example illustrates, too, the more prominent role
that an emerging group of professional lawyers were assuming in
a court system that had long been dominated by county justices of
the peace and members of the General Court who lacked formal
training in law. While Dewey's method is not to present us with
explicit generalizations about this development, his close examination of Jefferson's experience tells us a great deal.*

The eight years in which the young Jefferson conducted his

*practice—1767 to 1774—coincided, too, with a critical period
in the developing crisis between Britain and its colonies. The year
1774 marked the passage of Jefferson the lawyer into the ranks
of philosophers of the Revolution. During June and July he
penned two well-known documents for the first Virginia convention in August—the Albemarle County resolutions and* A Summary View of the Rights of British America. *During that
same period, Dewey tells us, he wrote another document, not so
well known, but demonstrating the influence of legal training on
his political views—his "opinion" in the dispute that arose in
1774 over the failure to renew legislation establishing the structure of fees for various actions in the courts of the colony. Jefferson sided with those outspoken revolutionaries who argued that
the lack of a new law required closing the courts, a measure that
would have the additional effect of blocking suits by British
creditors against their Virginia clients who were in default. The
issue was a complex one, ultimately decided in favor of closing
the courts in civil cases and more on political than legal grounds.
Dewey's careful account of the controversy is indispensable for
understanding what was a significant turning point in the revolutionary movement in Virginia.*

*In his analysis of Jefferson's fee bill opinion as in so many
other parts of the book, the author succeeds, then, by his careful
attention to detail and his close reading of law both in directly
addressing Jefferson's work as an attorney and in clarifying some
broader themes in the history of late eighteenth-century Virginia.
Its exposition of the more technical legal aspects of the study is,
moreover, always lucid and never obscure. Frank Dewey has in
my judgment made an enduring contribution—a greater one
than his own modesty would ever permit him to claim—to the
literature on Thomas Jefferson and colonial Virginia.*

THAD W. TATE

Preface

This book has a modest objective—to enlarge our understanding of the eight years Thomas Jefferson spent as a practicing lawyer. He took his first case in February 1767, when he was twenty-three years old, and gave up his practice in August 1774 just in time to assume a role on a larger stage. Clearly the Jefferson who wrote the Declaration of Independence in the early summer of 1776 owed much to the forensic and drafting skills he had acquired as a lawyer, and this makes it important to know more about the experience that nurtured those skills. Strangely enough, however, except for Judge Edward Dumbauld, writers have largely neglected Jefferson's law practice. There have been perhaps two reasons for this neglect. First, it is not one of the most fascinating aspects of Jefferson's career. Second, published source material is scarce and manuscript material fragmented. Judge Dumbauld's book *Thomas Jefferson and the Law* makes valuable contributions to the subject, but Jefferson's law practice is not its primary focus. A book devoted to his practice seems justified and desirable—perhaps eventually more than one book, because this one does not pretend to offer an exhaustive treatment.

Many relevant documents in Jefferson's handwriting survive, from notebooks to scraps of a page or less. The most important are his memorandum books consisting of legal diaries and personal accounts. Next in importance is his case book. Each of these sources gives only a few lines to any one case, largely brief notes made at the time Jefferson was retained. Other documents, listed in Appendix D, reveal more bits and pieces of information. The process of fitting the fragments together is a tedious one, rather appropriate for a retired lawyer like myself, with a consuming interest and plenty of time.

The study of Jefferson's law practice has been my principal

occupation for the past eight years. I began with no experience in historical research, and my acquaintance with Jefferson was only that of the average person. Fortunately, during most of those eight years I lived in Williamsburg, where Jefferson and his contemporaries still walk the streets. There I frequented the research library of the Colonial Williamsburg Foundation, a good environment for the beginner. It is rich in colonial materials, including dissertations and theses, manuscripts on microfilm (from other collections as well as its own), and bound copies of the *Virginia Gazette*. John Hemphill II, who has an inexhaustible knowledge of Virginia history, was my chief mentor. He introduced me to the Parker-Steuart correspondence and other sources too numerous to mention. Available at both Colonial Williamsburg and the Marshall-Wythe School of Law were collections of old lawbooks, and at the Swem Library at the College of William and Mary was all that one would expect in a fine college library plus St. George Tucker's books and papers. Individuals who gave much-needed and appreciated advice and assistance in the early stages of my work included William M. E. Rachal, E. Lee Shepard, W. Hamilton Bryson, and George M. Curtis III.

A year and a half ago I moved to Richmond, where the resources are as rich though more widely scattered. My chief reliance has been on the excellent facilities of the Virginia Historical Society, but I have also made use of the Virginia State Library and the law library at the University of Richmond. In Charlottesville I have made use of the manuscript treasures of the University of Virginia Library, rare books at the Arthur J. Morris Law Library, and Jeffersoniana at Monticello. Farther afield, I have visited more than once the Library of Congress, the Massachusetts Historical Society, and the libraries of Harvard Law School and Wellesley College. In addition, various of these libraries, and others not listed above, have assisted by correspondence. I am grateful to one and all.

Thanks to microfilm and photocopy devices, I have copies of most of the manuscript material relevant to Jefferson's law practice. The originals are in the Library of Congress, the Massachusetts Historical Society, and the Huntington Library (see Appendix D for details). I am obliged to them for furnishing copies or permitting me to have them made from copies held by others. I have found it necessary on occasion to consult original manuscripts at both the Library of Congress and the Massachusetts Historical Society. It is an awesome experience to hold these priceless documents in one's hand.

An important ingredient in historical research is luck, and I was especially blessed early in my Jefferson labors to encounter James A. Bear, Jr., then resident director of the Thomas Jefferson Memorial Foundation. He was in the process of editing Jefferson's memorandum books for publication and provided me with copies of his typescripts. Without them my constant resort to these documents would have been infinitely more time-consuming. Moreover, the typescripts are sprinkled with informative footnotes. Mr. Bear and his associate, Lucia S. Goodwin, are familiar with all Jefferson sources, published and unpublished, and have been continually helpful. I am much in their debt.

My study of Jefferson has led to many unexpected results, among the most pleasant of which has been friendship with Dumas Malone, whose scholarship and graceful prose are the envy of all who follow the trail of Jefferson. He has repeatedly urged me to write a book, and I hope he will be pleased with this one. My book owes much to two other friends, Paul C. Nagel and Thad W. Tate, both of whom have read substantial parts of the manuscript and have given invaluable advice. Nelson D. Lankford has skillfully examined the entire manuscript, blue pencil in hand. One result of his help has been a drastic rearrangement of chapters and appendixes. Last but not least, my wife has read multiple drafts of each chapter and has made helpful comments and suggestions.

The first four chapters of this book sketch the background of Jefferson's practice and describe the general nature of his work. The last chapter examines his reasons for abandoning his legal career. In between are detailed accounts of some facets of his work, selected in most instances because sources were found to supplement the bare outline provided by Jefferson's records.

Chapters 5 and 6 appeared in slightly different form in the *Virginia Magazine of History and Biography* 90 (1982): 165–76 and 91 (1983): 39–53 and are reprinted by permission of the publisher. Chapter 7 is a modified version of two articles: "Thomas Jefferson and a Williamsburg Scandal: The Case of *Blair* v. *Blair*," *Virginia Magazine of History and Biography* 89

(1981): 44–63, and "Thomas Jefferson's Notes on Divorce," *William and Mary Quarterly,* 3d ser., 39 (1982): 212–23. I wish to thank Margaret Cook of the Swem Library, College of William and Mary, John Hemphill II, and Thad Tate for calling my attention to additional material which has been incorporated into the revised chapter.

Thomas Jefferson
LAWYER

1

The Legal Profession in
Virginia in Jefferson's Time

Thomas Jefferson was admitted to the bar of the General Court of colonial Virginia at its October term in 1766 and for the next eight years was an active member of that bar.¹ Being a lawyer in those days meant being a trial lawyer. A Virginia lawyer might draw an occasional deed, will, or contract, but that kind of work was incidental. From time to time he might write an opinion. If he did, it probably concerned bringing a suit or defending one. The bulk of his business was preparing cases for trial or appeal and appearing in court. It was not unusual for one client to have several cases pending at one time, and the most successful lawyers had inventories of hundreds of cases at various stages of the long journey from initiation to final disposition.²

There were two classes of trial lawyers in colonial Virginia. The first and more numerous consisted of those who practiced in inferior courts—the county courts and the hustings courts of Williamsburg and Norfolk. The number of lawyers practicing in any one inferior court was small.³ Typically, a county court lawyer would practice in several contiguous counties, "riding the circuit." With a few exceptions, such as Albemarle and Augusta, where the court sat only quarterly, county courts sat monthly for a day or two or three, depending on the amount of business to be dealt with. To accommodate the lawyers, court days in neighboring counties were arranged to avoid conflicts. For example, John Aylett practiced in Botetourt, Pittsylvania, Bedford, and Amherst counties.⁴ Pittsylvania's court began its session on the last Thursday of January, April, July, October, and December, while the others met, respectively, on the second Tuesday, fourth Monday, and first Monday of each month.⁵

The second class of Virginia lawyers practiced in the General Court, in which most important litigation was begun. It was also the court to which decisions of the inferior courts could be appealed. The bar of the General Court was small. When Jefferson began his practice, the active members were Edmund Pendleton, George Wythe, Attorney General John Randolph, Thomson Mason, John Blair, Jr., and James Mercer.[6] Robert Carter Nicholas, recently appointed the treasurer of the colony, was taking no new clients but occasionally participated in one of the large number of his cases still pending before the court.[7] Richard Bland was also a member of the General Court bar, though his activity, like Nicholas's, was limited.[8] Peyton Randolph had just quit the bar to become speaker of the House, and John Mercer, James's father, had just retired.[9] As a result, Jefferson gave the group some badly needed reinforcement.

The General Court bar that Jefferson joined was also a young group. Aside from Bland, who was sixty-three, Pendleton was the eldest at forty-five; Wythe, Randolph, and Nicholas were about forty; Blair was thirty-five; and Mason and Mercer were in their early thirties. Of this youthful band, Jefferson at twenty-three was by far the youngest. It was a politically powerful group as well. All were members of the House of Burgesses, and Bland, Pendleton, and Wythe were among its most influential leaders.[10] John Randolph was the brother of the new speaker of the House, and Blair was the son of the senior member of the governor's council.

In Jefferson's time General Court lawyers who were not barristers could not practice in the inferior courts. A 1748 statute making such dual practice illegal was repealed in 1757 but reinstated in 1761.[11] The result was that lawyers who, like Peter Lyons, were not barristers and who had practiced in both General Court and county courts in the period between 1757 and 1761, had to choose one or the other forum. Lyons chose to give up his General Court practice and to work at the county court level.[12] Among Jefferson's brethren at the General Court bar, John Randolph, John Blair, Jr., and Thomson Mason were barristers and remained free, even after 1761, to practice at both levels; but Pendleton, Wythe, Nicholas, Bland, and James Mercer were not. Robert Carter III wrote Benjamin Tasker of Maryland on 30 May 1767 that certain lawsuits that Tasker had entrusted to George Wythe and John Blair, Jr., were being handled by Blair in the county court, "for only barristers can practice in the general and county courts, and the former gentleman is not one."[13] In accordance with this rule, Jefferson never practiced in an inferior court, although many authorities have mistakenly asserted that he did.[14]

Wythe, Randolph, Nicholas, and Blair lived in Williamsburg where the General Court sat.[15] Pendleton, Mason, and Mercer, like Jefferson, commuted to Williamsburg for the semiannual sessions in April and October. Pendleton lived in Caroline County, north of Richmond. Mercer lived north of the Rappahannock River in Stafford County, as did Mason before he moved to Loudoun County sometime after July 1769.[16] Jefferson became, and remained throughout his years at the bar, the lone westerner.

Each semiannual session of the General Court began on the tenth of April or October and continued six days a week for four weeks.[17] By contrast, county courts met briefly every month, weather permitting. Hence the circuit-riding county lawyer had to make several trips a month, generally fairly short in both distance and duration. The General Court lawyer who lived away from Williamsburg left home less frequently but stayed away longer.

Preparation for county court practice varied considerably in kind and degree. Joseph Jones of Spotsylvania had qualified as a barrister in England. Gabriel Jones of Augusta had served an apprenticeship with an English solicitor. Edmund Pendleton and Paul Carrington began their legal careers as apprentices to county clerks. More commonly, county court lawyers had received their training as apprentices or understudies to older lawyers. George Wythe learned from his uncle, Stephen Dewey of Prince George, and Peter Lyons from his uncle, James Power of King William. In Williamsburg, Wythe, Nicholas, Benjamin Waller, and John Tazewell all took understudies. Patrick Henry illustrates still another method of preparing for the county practice. He taught himself barely enough to scrape by his examiners and learned his craft on the job.[18]

Jefferson's contemporaries as General Court lawyers had achieved this eminence by one of two recognized avenues. Pendleton, Wythe, Nicholas, Bland, and Mercer had practiced in the county courts before graduating to the higher court.[19] Randolph, Blair, and Mason, having attended the London Inns of Court and become barristers, proceeded directly to the General Court.[20]

What were the requirements for becoming a county court lawyer or a General Court lawyer? The requirements for county court lawyers were specified by statute.[21] Barristers were automatically accepted because a lawyer entitled to practice in the superior courts of the mother country, as a barrister was, could hardly be denied a like privilege in the colonial courts. For those who had not qualified as barristers, the key requirement was passing an examination administered by General Court lawyers. Before taking the examination, a candidate had to produce a certificate of good character from an inferior court where he intended to practice and to pay a twenty shilling fee. If he passed the examination, he was granted a license by the examiners. All he had to do thereafter to be admitted to any inferior court was to take the locally required oath.

The Virginia statutes were silent regarding admission to the General Court. Undoubtedly there were requirements laid down by the court itself. But the court records do not survive, and we must look elsewhere to determine what was necessary for admission. Barristers, it may be assumed, were admitted as a matter of course. As to others, evidence indicates that the requirements were not severe.

The license of Peter Lyons to practice in the county courts is revealing.[22] Dated 5 February 1755, it was signed in Williamsburg by his examiners, Peyton Randolph, John Randolph, and Robert Carter Nicholas. On the back of the license is a record of admissions to individual courts, beginning with "the Hustings" (the Williamsburg hustings court) on 1 March 1756, followed in the next six months by several county courts. On 10 October 1757 he was admitted to the General Court, having been in practice for only a year and a half. At that time (1757–61) it was permissible to practice in the General Court while maintaining a practice in the inferior courts, and Lyons did so until dual practice was again proscribed in 1761.

The case of St. George Tucker is even more striking. On 4 April 1774 he was examined by Wythe and John Randolph and licensed to practice, and he was admitted in Dinwiddie

County a few days later.[23] The county courts were closed to civil litigation shortly thereafter, not to reopen for some years. It is unlikely, therefore, that he began a practice before the closing, and if he did, the practice aborted almost at once. Nevertheless he was admitted to the General Court on 4 April 1775, exactly one year after his admission to practice in the county courts. A certificate by Governor Dunmore dated 1 May 1775 states that "at a General Court held at the Capitol in this Colony on the fourth day of April last past Saint George Tucker Gent. was by me and the rest of the Judges of the said Court admitted to practice as an Attorney of the said Court."[24]

Tucker's admission took place when the pre-Revolutionary General Court was in its death throes. The General Court lawyers had boycotted the November 1774 session as the result of a plan adopted at the time of the first Virginia convention in August. The scheme, to prevent the trial of civil causes, had succeeded. On 25 March 1775 the second Virginia convention had decreed a continuing boycott by parties and witnesses as well as by lawyers.[25] The court itself had not given up the ghost. Despite the absence of lawyers, it had met in October 1774 to hear criminal cases and was scheduled to meet again on 10 April for the same purpose.[26] But war was imminent. The Virginia convention, after Patrick Henry's "give me liberty or give me death" speech, had authorized the raising of a military force.[27] Apparently worried lest the rush of events cancel the court session scheduled for 10 April and thus postpone indefinitely his admission to the General Court bar, Tucker must have persuaded the court to meet in special session a week before that date in order to admit him.

Considered together, the Lyons and Tucker cases suggest that nonbarristers became eligible for admission to the General Court one year after being licensed to practice in the inferior courts. The rationale for the one-year waiting period may have been to encourage new lawyers to get some experience in the inferior courts before coming to the General Court," but such experience was not required.

Alan McKinley Smith has argued that "only the most capable lawyers in Virginia were permitted to appear before the General Court,"[28] but he seems to have been mistaken. The experience of Lyons and Tucker, as well as Jefferson's, shows that neophytes could be admitted. Also, when Jefferson turned his practice over to Edmund Randolph in 1774, Randolph was barely twenty-one years old.[29] Subsequent events were to prove him capable, but his capacity could not have been known when he was admitted.

Relying on a 1736 letter of William Byrd II, Smith also believed that "new members were brought into the charmed circle only with the approval of both judges and attorneys."[30] Byrd's letter was written to Daniel Horsmanden, a New York lawyer whom Byrd was encouraging to come to Virginia to practice in the General Court. Byrd told him that Sir John Randolph (the father of Peyton and John, Jefferson's contemporaries) would give assistance and that Horsmanden could also rely on friends among the judges. The letter does not say explicitly that the approval of both judges and lawyers would have been required for Horsmanden's admission, but even if such approval was required in the case of a New York lawyer moving to Virginia in 1736, it does not follow that the same procedure would apply to local applicants in Jefferson's time. Assuming it did, it does not seem to have presented a serious obstacle to such qualified applicants as Lyons, Tucker, Jefferson, and Edmund Randolph despite their lack of experience.

If requirements for admission to the General Court were easily met, why did not more lawyers become General Court practitioners? Why did Peter Lyons, who had been admitted to both county courts and the General Court, elect to give up the General Court and to continue his county court practice when compelled to make a choice?

Although the scale of fees prescribed by statute for the General Court was higher than that for the county courts, a county court lawyer who practiced in several counties had more days of court work per year, and his cases, being simpler, were less protracted. Hence a successful county court lawyer could probably approximate, if not better, the General Court lawyer's income. We are told that Paul Carrington, a county court lawyer, earned almost £600 in 1771; and even assuming that the figure represents charges to clients and not receipts, it was considerably more than Jefferson charged in any year of his General Court practice.[31] Jerman Baker, another county court lawyer, boasted in 1771 that his "emoluments as an attorney are not inconsiderable," and Patrick Henry seems to have earned more before 1769, when he transferred to the General Court, than he did thereafter.[32] John Blair, Jr., left the practice in 1770 to become clerk of the governor's council at a salary of £150 per year, plus an uncertain sum from the General Assembly in years when it met for services as its ex officio clerk.[33] Jefferson's own experience, detailed in chapter 9, does not speak well for the rewards of being a General Court lawyer. His collected fees, before deducting expenses, during his eight years at the bar were only about £1,200.

The General Court docket was years in arrears. Some of Jefferson's cases begun in 1767 were still awaiting trial when he quit the practice in 1774.[34] Since a lawyer's fee was not earned until the case was over, a new entrant's earnings were low. Only when a lawyer had been in practice long enough to have a mix of old and new cases would his income reach a normal level. Until he had reached that stage, the neophyte faced a lean period.

In summary, the small number of General Court lawyers seems to have been due, not to a selection process that made it difficult to qualify, but to economic considerations that discouraged all but a few.

Yet somehow the cream rose to the top. The relative standing of General Court lawyers and county court lawyers just before the Revolution is evident from the fact that when the courts were reorganized after Independence with full-time salaried judges, Pendleton, Wythe, and Nicholas were unanimously elected by the legislature to the three top posts—the judgeships on the High Court of Chancery.[35] Blair became chief justice of the revamped General Court, later replaced Nicholas on the High Court of Chancery, and still later became the first Virginian on the United States Supreme Court.[36] Mason, whom St. George Tucker regarded as the most able member of the pre-Revolutionary bar, was among the five originally elected General Court judges but resigned before taking office.[37] The remaining four posts on the General Court went to county court lawyers—Joseph Jones, Paul Carrington, Bartholomew Dandridge, and John Tazewell.

The eminence of the General Court bar was itself a formidable barrier to new entrants. With standardized fees, who would want to hire a young upstart when, for the same fee, he could hire Pendleton or Wythe? The prospect would be discouraging unless the neophyte was able to count on a loyal clientele. Jefferson probably expected his western Virginia connections to provide him with such a clientele, and they did.

Also joining the General Court bar at about the same time as Jefferson was Richard Starke, who advertised in the *Virginia Gazette* of 15 January 1767 that, "having met with great encouragement from the Gentlemen in the trade of James river to undertake business in the General Court," he proposed to settle in Williamsburg and practice there.[38] Even with the additions of Jefferson and Starke, the General Court bar remained pitifully small for the tremendous caseload that perennially overwhelmed the court. Into this small but elite group Jefferson entered at the age of twenty-three, inexperienced and unknown, to emerge eight years later at the height of his powers.

But before his years as an active practitioner are examined, it will be helpful to take a look at the training Jefferson received as a law student in mid-eighteenth-century Virginia.

2

Thomas Jefferson, Law Student

The five-year period in Jefferson's life beginning April 1762, when he completed his studies at the College of William and Mary, is not well documented. What is certain is that he spent part of that time under the tutelage of George Wythe preparing to practice law. Wythe, only thirty-five years old in 1762, was an eminent General Court practitioner and a leader of the House of Burgesses who afterwards distinguished himself as signer of the Declaration of Independence, judge, and first occupant of the chair of law and police at William and Mary.

The standard account of the five years makes three assertions: first, that Jefferson's studies occupied the entire period except for summer vacations; second, that they occupied the entire day, every day, from dawn to bedtime; and third, that the curriculum can be reconstructed from notebooks he kept and advice he later gave to law students. This chapter questions all three points.

The first assertion, that Jefferson's studies continued throughout the entire period, was voiced as early as 1858 by Henry S. Randall and as recently as 1976 by Julian Boyd. This tradition was so firmly established that Wendell Garrett repeated it even while protesting that "five years of study was practically unheard of for young men at the law in the eighteenth century—two years was considered more than ample, and in many cases a year or less was deemed sufficient." John Adams, for example, studied law for two years while teaching full-time and boasted that his preparation exceeded that of any other law student of the time. Alexander Hamilton read some lawbooks in college before the Revolution but spent only six months afterward preparing for the bar. John Marshall studied "nearly three months."[1]

Apparently without realizing the significance to the tradition that Jefferson's prelaw course consumed five years, V. Dennis Golladay, in his 1973 doctoral dissertation, remarked that Robert Carter Nicholas examined Jefferson in 1765 for fitness to practice law. Appendix A examines in detail the validity of this remark and concludes that Jefferson did indeed take his bar examination late in 1765. One would expect the examination to mark the end of Jefferson's student days in Williamsburg. That assumption is corroborated by the evidence of his garden book, which shows that he spent the spring of 1766 at Shadwell. In May, he began a trip to Annapolis, Phildelphia, and New York that lasted from early May to late July. One purpose of the trip—probably the principal purpose—was to be inoculated against smallpox by Dr. William Shippen, Jr., in Philadelphia. If the procedure used by Dr. Shippen followed the one prescribed by his fellow townsman Dr. Adam Thompson, it required approximately a month. The trip back to Virginia was by water, and Jefferson stopped briefly in Williamsburg before setting off to visit various friends in King William County and Gloucester.[2]

In the fall of 1766, his position as a member of the Albemarle establishment was affirmed by his appointment as a justice of the county court. He was one of twenty appointed or reappointed to the Albemarle court on 6 November 1766 and held the post until June 1771 when he declined reappointment.[3] (Thus, though Jefferson never practiced in the county court system, he knew it well.) In making such appointments, the governor always accepted the names submitted to him by the incumbent justices, so that Jefferson in effect was selected by his Albemarle peers.[4] One may reasonably infer that he had spent the fall in Albemarle, renewing ties with his neighbors.

We can say with some certainty, then, that Wythe's tutelage of Jefferson ended late in 1765. But when did it begin? Did it begin in April 1762, as soon as he finished his studies at William and Mary? Marie Kimball thought so, and Jefferson himself seemed to say so in later years,[5] but doubts persist.

Jefferson wrote his friend John Page on Christmas Day 1762, on his way home from Williamsburg, that he was reading *Coke on Littleton,* the first of the four volumes of the encyclopedic *Institutes of the Laws of England* by Sir Edward Coke. He had begun the reading in Williamsburg, and he said he was sure to get through it before the winter was over. Very likely *Coke on Littleton* was Jefferson's first assignment as a law student; he implied as much in his letter of 10 February 1814 to Thomas Cooper.[6] After his student days were over, he advised other students of the law to begin with Coke.[7] Some of his contemporaries are known to have begun with Coke.[8] It is a cruelly difficult book to read, even for an adult with some familiarity with the law, and must have been a severe test for a novice not yet twenty. But even a novice would not require a year to read it. In other words, if he was still in the first stage of his legal schooling by Christmas 1762, as seems likely, that schooling must have begun considerably later than April.

Having left Williamsburg to go home at Christmas 1762, he did not return to the capital for nine months. He had planned to return earlier but delayed because of a report of smallpox in Williamsburg. By early October 1763 he was back in the capital, attending "constantly" the General Court session that began on 10 October.[9] He went to Williamsburg intending to stay, and he was still there two years later, preparing to take his bar examination.

Thus Jefferson spent some part—probably a small part—of 1762 in Williamsburg with Wythe as a beginning law student, most of 1763 reading lawbooks at home, and approximately two years beginning in October 1763 in Williamsburg with Wythe. He then passed the bar examination, returned to Albemarle, and, except for his trip north, spent 1766 at home.

This plausible set of facts and inferences is clouded, to say the least, by a letter that Jefferson wrote on 18 January 1790 to Dr. Thomas Walker, one of his father's executors. He said, "During a part of the time that I was a student in Williamsburg my expences were greater than they ought to have been. It was therefore agreed that they should be paid by the estate, but that I should repay so much as they exceeded what they ought to have been. Mr. Harvie [another of his father's executors] has left a statement of my expences during the period objected to; it comprehends those of the years 1760.1.2.3 being exactly the four years I was in Williamsburgh, two of them at the college, and the other two a student under Mr. Wythe." He asked Dr. Walker's opinion as to what the reasonable expenses should have been. The reply was, "The two years you were at the college, I know of no charge which ought to be against you. The two years you studied under Mr. Wythe, my opinion is that your expences ought not to have exceeded £125.per year."[10] They seem to be saying that Jefferson's studies under Wythe comprised the two years immediately following his two years at William and Mary. How can one explain the apparent discrepancies between their recollection and the contemporaneous evidence? What did they mean when they spoke of the "two years under Wythe"?

Three explanations are possible. The first begins with a reminder that Jefferson became twenty-one years old on 13 April 1764, four years after he entered William and Mary, and assumes that he was spending his own money after he became of age. On this assumption, the "two years under Wythe" began sometime in 1762, ended on 13 April 1764, and do not include the time after that because it did not concern the estate. One trouble with this explanation is that Jefferson was away from Williamsburg nearly half of those two years, and the correspondence speaks of two years "in Williamsburg" under Wythe. The second possible explanation, subject to the same infirmity as the first, is that Wythe's oversight of Jefferson's study terminated at the end of 1764 or early in 1765 and that Jefferson's study in Williamsburg after that time was unsupervised.

The third possible explanation, and the most plausible, is that Jefferson and Dr. Walker were thinking of the two years beginning with October 1763 but were confused about dates. This explanation assumes that they overlooked the time Jefferson spent with Wythe in Williamsburg in 1762, possibly because it was a very short time, or possibly because Wythe's guidance at that juncture was only nominal. In any case, it seems clear that the letter cannot be accepted at face value.

In evaluating the correspondence, we must remember that Jefferson's memory of distant events was fallible. For instance, he said in his autobiographical memoir that William Small, his college teacher, left William and Mary in 1762; the correct date was 1764.[11] Jefferson wrote Elbridge Gerry in 1812 that he had met him in New York in 1764; the encounter was in 1766.[12] In the preface to his volume of General Court cases, published after his death, he said the Revolution had closed the courts of justice in 1772; the year was 1774.

We want now to take a closer look at the two years Jefferson spent in Williamsburg beginning in October 1763. During this period the emphasis of his study shifted from the theoretical to the practical side of law practice. As Julius Goebel said of Alexander Hamilton's preparation for the bar, "Books alone could not supply the sort of technical command of New York practice of which a postulant for admission would stand in need. This was, of course, the point where a preceptor experienced in the 'practick part' of the law was close to being indispensable."[13]

When Jefferson wrote John Page in October 1763 he said he was constantly attending the General Court; its semiannual session began on 10 October and lasted for twenty-four working days.[14] It seems likely that he followed subsequent semiannual sessions of the General Court, as well as the "rule days" between sessions when procedural matters were disposed of by the clerk. He probably attended some sessions of the Williamsburg hustings and James City County courts, which met monthly in Williamsburg.

A good part of Jefferson's subsequent law practice consisted of caveats and petitions for lapsed lands, proceedings relating to land titles. Jefferson's first case was a caveat, his second was a petition. He must have become familiar with the pertinent procedures during Wythe's tutelage. That meant spending time in the land office where all patent records were kept. He undoubtedly attended the June sessions of the governor's council when caveat cases were heard and decided. He also, as he said, "paid attention to what was passing in the legislature."[15] It was there he heard Patrick Henry's unforgettable "treason" speech on 30 May 1765.

The lawbooks he bought from the *Virginia Gazette* in 1764 and 1765 were of a practical nature.[16] On 15 February 1764 he bought two works by Robert Richardson, *The Attorney's Practice in the Court of King's Bench* and *The Attorney's Practice in the Court of Common Pleas,* and Joseph Harrison's *The Practice of the Court of Chancery.* Each of these works was in two volumes, the second volume consisting of examples of pleading. A few days later he bought the *Attorney's Pocket Companion,* or "Guide to the Practicers of the Law. Being a translation of law proceedings in the Courts of King's Bench and Common-Pleas, containing a collection of forms, with Treatise on Ejectments. By a Gentleman of the Inner Temple." These purchases indicate a thorough study of pleading, which, as the editors of the *Legal Papers of*

John Adams have said, "was the heart of the traditional common-law jurisprudence under which Adams practiced."[17] Because a standard part of a lawyer's training consisted of copying legal instruments, exercises in the drafting of pleadings undoubtedly supplemented Jefferson's reading.[18]

He also studied the statute law of England and Virginia. On 3 October 1764 he bought William Rastell's *Collection in English of the Statutes Now in Force* (British statutes from Magna Carta to the reign of James I). That work alone must have absorbed several weeks of reading and analysis. On 30 April 1765 he bought *Virginia Laws since the Revisal* and on 10 October *Grounds and Rudiments of Law.* These purchases are not presented as a complete list of his legal reading during 1764 and 1765. Jefferson had access to Wythe's library and other lawbooks in Williamsburg, and he may have bought books from other sources. But the *Gazette* purchases indicate the kind of book he considered important enough to own when, presumably, he did not own many.

When Wythe later taught at William and Mary, his pedagogical method was to let his students read on their own and to emphasize the practical side of the law in the time he spent with them. Charles Cullen has said that "it is most likely that John Marshall spent his summer term with Wythe reading law and taking notes, attending lectures, arguing in moot court, participating in mock legislatures, and debating with the Phi Beta Kappa Society and other groups."[19] It seems likely that Jefferson's curriculum included similar sorts of training. Finally, the fact that Jefferson emerged from his years with Wythe equipped to practice in the General Court by himself, having had no prior experience in any court, indicates that he had mastered the mechanics of law practice as a student.

The two years in Williamsburg beginning October 1763 were not devoted exclusively to the study of law and law practice. The records of the *Virginia Gazette* show that interspersed among his purchases of lawbooks in 1764 and 1765 were purchases of Milton's *Works,* Hume's *History of England* (in six volumes), Robertson's *History of Scotland* (in two volumes), Stith's *History of Virginia,* Yorrick's *Sermons,* Sali's *Koran,* Dr. Bacon's *Philosophy,* and the *Thoughts of Cicero, Dictionary of the Sciences,* and *Poemata Italianorum* in two volumes. And this is not a complete list.

Jefferson, in a letter to "a young friend," Bernard Moore, prescribed for law students a study of the physical sciences, ethics, religion, and natural law before 8:00a.m., four hours of law study after breakfast, history in the afternoon, and literature in the evening.[20] Some Jeffersonian scholars have assumed that Jefferson himself followed this rigorous schedule as a student.[21] Perhaps he did at Shadwell, but it seems unlikely that he followed it in Williamsburg. There would have been no room in this regimen for activities of a practical kind, such as attending court or drawing pleadings, or for the social life and recreation we know he enjoyed in Williamsburg. He lived with fellow students, kept horses, played the violin, dined frequently at the Governor's Palace with Small, Wythe, and Governor Fauquier, and did some courting. That he was spending more money than he ought during those two years, as his correspondence with Dr. Walker indicates, shows that he was not working all the time.

An attempt has been made to reconcile Jefferson's supposed dawn-to-bedtime reading schedule with his known diversions by assuming that the play occurred in the early part of his Williamsburg residence and that the rigorous schedule represented a more mature phase.[22] A more plausible reconciliation is that the rigorous schedule of reading was followed at home in Albemarle County where recreational opportunities were limited and that he followed a quite different regimen in Williamsburg, involving plenty of reading to be sure, but much besides.

The surviving copy of the letter to Moore is one that Jefferson sent "near 50 years" later to John Minor in 1814, noting that he had modified the original list of recommended reading by substituting later and better publications in some instances. Assuming that the original and the 1814 versions were the same except for book titles, it is clear that even the original version reflected ideas Jefferson had developed after completing his studies under Wythe. For instance, the letter recommended that the English law reports be read in chronological order, but Jefferson's commonplace books show that he had not read them in that order. In short, Jefferson's own student reading cannot be reconstructed from the advice he gave to Moore.

Jefferson's commonplace books were notebooks in which he

entered summaries of reading materials. One, known as his legal commonplace book, was devoted to common law materials, and one comprised notes on equity.[23] On 10 February 1814 Jefferson wrote Thomas Cooper, "When I was a student of the law, now half a century ago, after getting through Coke [on] Littleton, whose matter cannot be abridged, I was in the habit of abridging and common-placing what I read meriting it."[24] That statement, and Jefferson's advice to law students to do likewise,[25] might lead one to conclude that Jefferson's commonplace books represent student work in their entirety. But clearly they do not.

Entries in the commonplace books are not dated, and many obviously were made after he had begun practice and even after he had left it. The problem is to determine which entries, if any, were made when he was a student. Even the elder Jefferson could not be sure. In his correspondence with Cooper, he identified item 873 in the legal commonplace book as one he entered as a student; but items 741–48 are clearly identified with the fee bill controversy of 1774, and all subsequent entries, of course, were made later.

Marie Kimball believed, on the basis of analyses of paper and handwriting, that the equity commonplace book was begun in 1765 and that items 1–174 of the legal commonplace book were entered in 1766. If she was right, the equity notebook was begun in his last year of study and the legal notebook after Wythe's tutelage was over. One notes with interest that John Adams's commonplace book was begun after his formal legal education had ended.[26]

Gilbert Chinard, who studied only the legal commonplace book, was dubious about dating the entries by analysis of handwriting and ink, but he concluded that articles 1-694 represent "the work of a young lawyer trying to get acquainted with the procedure of the Courts" and, somewhat inconsistently, that "the first hundred pages or so, containing some 550 entries, were compiled at a time when Jefferson, either as a student of law or a young lawyer, was primarily interested in questions of legal procedure."[27] Clearly one cannot say how much, if any, of Jefferson's commonplace books represent reading he did as a student. (Incidentally, none of the lawbooks purchased from the *Virginia Gazette* in 1764 and 1765 is mentioned in either the commonplace books or the

Bernard Moore letter. One tempted to use either source as evidence of Jefferson's course of study under Wythe must find that fact hard to explain.)

Jefferson's preparation for practice, then, began with the reading of *Coke on Littleton* in Williamsburg, probably under Wythe's guidance, in the fall of 1762, several months after he completed his studies at William and Mary. This and other reading continued at Shadwell during most of 1763. In October 1763 he returned to Williamsburg for two years of reading of both law and humanities, mixed with observation and training in the practical aspects of being a lawyer. Late in 1765 he left Williamsburg and Wythe behind, returning to Albemarle County where, both before and after his trip north, he pursued an intensive schedule of reading.

3

The Tribunals before Which
Jefferson Practiced

As a circuit-riding lawyer, John Adams of Massachusetts tried cases in several courts, not only in Boston but also as far south as Martha's Vineyard, as far west as Worcester, and as far north as what is now Maine.[1] In contrast, Jefferson tried practically all of his cases in Williamsburg and before the same group of men, sitting as the General Court or as the governor's council.

The governor's council of colonial Virginia consisted of twelve men from prominent families, appointed by the king on the recommendation of the governor. Once appointed, members were reappointed upon changes of king or governor and in effect served for life.[2] During the eight years of Jefferson's law practice, there was little turnover in the membership of the council. Seven members, Robert Carter Burwell, William Byrd III, Robert Carter III, Richard Corbin, Philip Ludwell Lee, Thomas Nelson, and John Tayloe II served throughout the period. William Nelson, George William Fairfax, and John Page served six or more of the eight years.[3]

Council members wore several hats. As the privy council, they met approximately twenty times a year on matters of concern to the executive. They were also the upper house of the General Assembly, whose concurrence was necessary to the passage of legislation. They, with the governor, constituted the General Court, although most had no legal training. Thomas Nelson had qualified as a barrister, and Carter and Lee had attended the Inns of Court, but in the eighteenth century such credentials did not guarantee any legal training. In fact, Carter's years in England were devoted to "the life of a London blade."[4] Members of the council also served as judges of the court of oyer and terminer (law French for "to hear and determine") that met for a day or two each June and December to try prisoners accused of felony.[5]

Collectively these responsibilities did not require the full time of the councillors. They were, after all, the colony's preeminent landowners, planters, and businessmen, and most of them lived at some distance from Williamsburg and traveled to the capital as necessary. Members' services as privy councillors and as legislators were unpaid. As General Court judges, they divided £1,200 per year in proportion to attendance, and those who served as judges of each oyer and terminer court divided £100.[6]

The colonial General Court, sometimes called the Supreme Court of Judicature,[7] was both a court of equity and a court of common law. In combining these functions it differed from the English model, but it preserved a symbolic differentiation by requiring the judges to take two oaths, one as common law judges and another as chancery judges. The court met twice a year on 10 April and 10 October. According to the governing statute, the first five days of the twenty-four-day sessions were supposed to be devoted to chancery trials and appeals, the sixth day to criminal cases. the seventh to petitions for lapsed lands, and the remaining seventeen to common law cases and appeals.[8] This structure was not rigidly adhered to. The court made it a point to dispose of all felony cases on its calendar, and this sometimes required more than the one allotted day.[9]

The court's criminal calendar consisted of two parts, felony cases and "pleas of the crown." Both involved indictments and prosecution in the name of the king, but the resemblance ended there. Felonies were major crimes prosecuted by the attorney general. Pleas of the crown involved relatively minor charges carrying minor penalties, with active prosecution conducted by a private individual and a lawyer hired by him. For example, in Jefferson's Norfolk anti-inoculation riot cases, proponents and opponents of inoculation against smallpox brought criminal charges and obtained indictments against each other. Those who had been responsible for the inoculations were charged with nuisance in exposing the citizens of Norfolk to smallpox. Leaders of the opposing faction were charged with inciting a mob to riot. Jefferson was hired to prosecute the rioters and to defend those charged with nuisance.[10] He had other cases of this kind but, so far as his records show, never defended an accused felon.

It was probably a rare thing for an accused felon to be represented by counsel in colonial Virginia. The present-day rule requiring the state to provide indigent felons with counsel did not exist then. In England an accused felon was not entitled to counsel even if he could afford one, with very limited exceptions. The Virginia statute entitling such defendants to counsel on petition was intended to change the English rule, not to require representation of indigent defendants.[11] Most accused felons were poor and hence undefended.

The pre-Revolutionary General Court kept no official reports of cases heard. Jefferson compiled a volume of reports, published shortly after his death under the title *Reports of Cases Determined in the General Court of Virginia from 1730 to 1740, and from 1768 to 1772.* These reports were known about and referred to long before their publication. In 1800, when Jefferson was a candidate for president, John Beckley published a short account of his life.[12] Referring to Jefferson's years as a practicing lawyer, Beckley said, "During this period . . . the industrious mind of Jefferson found time to digest the first volume of reports of adjudged cases in the supreme courts of Virginia, which were ever exhibited in that state, and to this day, are admitted authority in those courts, remaining a monument of his early labors, and useful talents." As the title of Jefferson's book indicates, the reports fall into two segments. The later ones (1768-72) were based on notes he had made himself; of eleven cases reported, he had participated in three.[13]

The Library of Congress collection of Jefferson manuscripts includes his notes on four more cases decided during his years at the bar, although he was not a participant in any of these.[14] None of the published cases was argued after October 1772 when, as he mistakenly asserted in the preface, "the Revolution dissolved our courts of justice." If these four cases had been available when Jefferson selected the cases for the book, he would not have made that mistake because three of the four were argued in 1773. They must have been mislaid. Parts of two of the four manuscripts (*Blair* v. *Blair* and *The King* v. *Dugard*) were written on pages that already had writing on them. The previous writing consisted of letters dated 30 September 1781 that Jefferson had addressed but never sent to acquaintances in Philadelphia, introducing William Short.[15] At least these two manuscripts were written after that date, and almost certainly within two years of that date, when Jefferson returned to public life.

How does one explain why these manuscripts were written eight years or more after the arguments occurred? They must be later versions of his original notes, edited during a lull in his public life after June 1781. Another of the unpublished manuscripts *(Wormeley* v. *Wormeley)* appears to be his unedited notes of that case, made at the time of argument. One may reasonably conclude that the "volume of reports" described by John Beckley in 1800 was a collection of Jefferson's edited notes of the eleven cases posthumously published, plus, perhaps, edited notes of other cases, lost or mislaid before publication.

The earlier reports in Jefferson's book (1730-40) were based on notes made by Sir John Randolph and other lawyers active during that period. Jefferson had obtained the notes from John Randolph, Sir John's son and Jefferson's colleague at the General Court bar. From the Randolph notes, Jefferson selected thirty-one cases for publication in his *Reports*.[16]

Jefferson's habit of taking notes on cases in which he did not participate is one he shared with John Adams.[17] Of course, both kept notes of their own cases, though the nature of the notes varied considerably. In Massachusetts, unlike Virginia, court records survive in large part, and a three-volume account of Adams's law practice, based on his notes, official records, and other sources, has been published under the title *Legal Papers of John Adams.*

In Jefferson's case, there is less to work with but enough to enable us to perceive the nature of General Court practice. The central fact that emerges about the colonial General Court of his time was that it was years behind in its work. In Massachusetts, John Adams could start a case in January and try it in April.[18] Not so in Virginia, where a typical chancery case at the trial level consumed more than eight years from commencement to trial and the typical common law case lasted almost as long. Appeals were not decided for two or three years from their inception.[19] Yet the court proceeded in a leisurely manner. Commonly, two lawyers appeared for each side, and apparently the court imposed no time limits on argument. In *Blair* v. *Blair,* where Dr. James Blair's estate was resisting the widow's claim for dower on the ground that the marriage had not been consummated, John Randolph argued for four hours on behalf of the widow. The time used by his associate, Patrick Henry, or by Edmund Pendleton and James Mercer, their opponents, does not appear.[20]

At each session of the court, the input of new chancery and common law cases was roughly equal to the number of cases disposed of. Hence the backlog remained relatively constant in those important categories. Felony cases were disposed of promptly because the accused were in jail. Pleas of the crown—minor criminal cases—were almost current. Petitions for lapsed lands, the principal remaining category of General Court business, typically were disposed of in two or three years from inception.[21]

The other tribunal before which Jefferson regularly practiced was the privy council. From its minutes we know that most meetings were not held on any fixed schedule. In a cold winter or hot summer month there might be only one meeting or no meeting at all. During "publick times" when the General Court was in session, a number were held. The business at such meetings included a wide variety of matters—Indian affairs, issuance of rights to take up land, and commissioning sheriffs and justices of the peace, to mention a few recurring examples.

The great bulk of Jefferson's practice before the council involved caveats, proceedings relating to the acquisition of land patents. Many of these cases were adversary proceedings, with contending parties and attorneys. In such cases, the council was, to all intents and purposes, a court. Caveats were considered at only one meeting each year, immediately following the June session of the court of oyer and terminer. Caveats were a major item in Jefferson's law practice; hence he always attended this meeting. One writer, noting that Jefferson was in Williamsburg at the time of the June oyer and terminer court, concluded that he practiced before that court,[22] but he did not.

During the last two years of his legal career, Jefferson's practice before the council broadened to include a number of cases of a quite different sort. In October 1772, when he was in Williamsburg for the General Court session, he appeared on behalf of Robert Doack in a dispute over the site of a proposed courthouse for the new county of Fincastle, but the council selected a competing site on land in which William Byrd III, a member of the council, had an interest.[23] That same month, Jefferson defended John Bowyer, a justice of the peace, against a charge of being partial to clients of his lawyer brother. The matter was put over to the June 1773 meeting when Bowyer was given a gentle reprimand and allowed to keep his post. Jefferson was well rewarded; Bowyer paid him £5 at the time of hiring and another £10 after the decision.[24] In October 1773 Jefferson's client John Coleman lost in a dispute over the post of sheriff of Brunswick County.[25] In June 1774 Jefferson successfully represented John Davies in an uncontested petition for land[26] and William Meade against a charge of misconduct as justice of the peace of Bedford County. As in the Bowyer case, Meade was reprimanded but allowed to keep his post.[27] Jefferson's appearances before the council in June 1774 were his last before any tribunal. In August he turned his practice over to Edmund Randolph.

Practice before the council differed in various respects from General Court practice. The rule that forbade county lawyers to practice before the General Court did not apply to the council, and county lawyers could and did practice there.[28] The statutory maximum fees for General Court work did not apply to council cases; and whereas Jefferson's fee for council cases was usually £2.10.0, the fee for most General Court work, he sometimes charged more. Since council cases were generally simpler and shorter-lived than General Court cases, the less prestigious council practice was more profitable than General Court work.

Like the General Court, the council decided cases immediately upon hearing them and seldom wrote opinions. Records of council meetings show which members of the council were present but not how they voted. Both bodies sat in the Capitol in Williamsburg, the General Court in the courtroom and the council in the council chamber.

A few of Jefferson's cases were tried before arbitrators, sometimes one, sometimes three. Considering how long it took to bring a General Court case to trial, one wonders why arbitration was not more widely used. But out of the many hundreds of cases he handled in his eight years of practice, only a handful are known to have gone to arbitration.

Arbitration was particularly well suited to complex issues that might baffle lay judges. A competent arbitrator could be selected, and the arguments could be made to him in writing, giving him the opportunity to analyze the case before rendering his opinion. An example was *Hughes' Case* (case book [CB] item 233), in which the lone arbitrator was Benjamin Waller, the clerk of the General Court and an able lawyer with a practice in the county courts. In *Bolling* v. *Bolling* (CB 489), the name of the arbitrator is unknown, but the opposing arguments of Jefferson and Wythe have survived. Judge Edward Dumbauld's book *Thomas Jefferson and the Law* contains an extensive analysis of the very complicated arguments of counsel. Dumbauld, an experienced federal judge, concluded: "The arguments of counsel in *Bolling* v. *Bolling* constitute a splendid specimen of the professional powers and proficiency of the Virginia bar in the years immediately preceding the American Revolution. Both Thomas Jefferson and his former preceptor George Wythe displayed enormous erudition and handled with skill and resourcefulness the pertinent legal materials relating to the novel, intricate, and difficult questions under consideration."[29] Jefferson's records do not tell us who won the argument, but since Jefferson charged £5 and Robert Bolling paid him twice that amount, it seems likely that Jefferson's client prevailed.[30]

An advantage of arbitration was that a local dispute could be resolved locally. *McLure* v. *McGill* and *McLure* v. *Smith* (CB 103, 104) were actions of slander brought on the same day, in which the plaintiff and both defendants were residents of Augusta County. Jefferson represented the defendants. The arbitration, agreed upon by the parties, was conducted at the Augusta County courthouse, and John Madison, Sr., the clerk of Augusta, was one of the arbitrators.

As though they did not have enough to do in their various official capacities, members of the governor's council were popular choices as arbitrators. A February 1764 letter by Robert Carter III mentions a pending chancery case concerning a marriage settlement. The parties had agreed to arbitrate, and the matter was to be referred "to any two of the council, with power to choose an umpire." Again, Carter wrote to Edward Hunt in London in September 1767 asking Hunt to serve as arbitrator in the place of Governor Fauquier, who had declined the assignment.[31] In the Norfolk riot cases arbitration was considered at one stage but did not materialize. William Nelson was the arbitrator favored by Dr. Campbell of the pro-inoculation faction.[32]

Unlike his mentor, George Wythe, and his Massachusetts contemporary John Adams, Jefferson never engaged in admiralty cases. His court work was confined to the two prolonged General Court sesions and the mid-June session of the governor's council. Although the council session took no more than three days, his June visit to Williamsburg usually lasted several weeks, probably so that he could spend time in the land office preparing his caveat cases and petitions for lapsed lands. He never appeared before the council except on one of these regular trips, because it would not have been worth his while to make a special trip from Albemarle for only a few cases.

The time between these Williamsburg visits afforded Jefferson some opportunity for nonlegal pursuits, but much of that time was spent in out-of-court work related to his practice—interviews, correspondence, keeping books and records, local travel, reading lawbooks, and preparing cases for trial. The practice of law was not a sideline; it was his principal occupation.

4

Jefferson Begins
the Practice

The first sixty-eight items in Jefferson's case book bear 1767 dates. That does not mean, of course, that he tried sixty-eight cases in 1767. In fact, he tried only one. The 1767 entries simply mean that clients brought him sixty-eight items of business during that year. What kinds of business were involved, and how long it took to dispose of them, is the subject of this chapter.

It was an auspicious beginning. It was much better, for instance, than the experience of John Adams, who, having been admitted to practice in November 1758, found himself with little to do in calendar year 1759.[1] One reason for Jefferson's better luck, if luck is the proper word, may be that he was the only General Court lawyer who lived in western Virginia and therefore was more accessible to westerners who had General Court business. Another reason is that, unlike Adams, who hung out his shingle in his hometown and waited for business, Jefferson went after it.

Consider the problem of a new lawyer, living in a rural area with poor roads, in the days before postal service worthy of the name. Jefferson realized that he had to present himself where people gathered and lingered. Happily, there were such places in Virginia—the county courts. Each county had a court that met periodically—usually monthly—for several days. The meeting was "an event for the whole countryside. Not only did litigants and their witnesses assemble on those occasions, but from miles around people in all walks of life came to collect and pay debts, to make contracts of various kinds, to trade horses, to sell Negroes, and to auction property. Peddlars came selling their wares; wandering bands of entertainers came to get such pickings as they could from these pricipal meetings of county people."[2]

Should the young lawyer make sporadic visits to several counties on court days, or should he concentrate on one or two and attend them regularly? Jefferson chose the latter alternative. He would probably have selected Albemarle as one of his counties in any event, but he had no choice, since he was one of the judges.

The other county court whose sessions Jefferson attended regularly was Augusta. Superficially it seems an odd choice because it lay across the formidable Blue Ridge. Jefferson could more easily have visited one or more neighboring counties on his side of the mountains, but Augusta had several points in its favor. First, it was a huge territory. In 1767 it included everything west of the Blue Ridge from the present Rockingham County on the north to the Carolina border on the south. Its western boundary—at least in theory—was the Mississippi River. It was growing rapidly in population, fed by the westward tide from eastern Virginia and by immigrants who were penetrating the Valley of Virginia from the north.

Second, it was frontier country. It was the scene of fierce fighting during the French and Indian War, and Indian raids continued after the war. As recently as 1764 a party of Indians attacked a home about sixty miles southwest of Staunton, the county seat, and killed the entire household.[3] Large tracts of undeveloped land were held by "adventurers"—a term that did not carry the pejorative connotation it does today—not for their own use but for speculation. Imperfect titles, grist for a lawyer, abounded.

Third, the Augusta court, like the Albemarle court, met only quarterly rather than monthly as most county courts did. Hence, regular attendance was not precluded by Jefferson's other commitments. The Albemarle sessions, held in Charlottesville, began on the second Thursday of March, May, August, and November. The Augusta court met in Staunton on the third Tuesday of those same months, so that, more often than not, the Augusta meeting followed the Albemarle meeting with only a Sunday and Monday between.[4] Dabney Carr, Jefferson's friend and brother-in-law, practiced in both counties, and it is likely that they made the trip over the mountains together. Their mutual friend William Fleming of Cumberland also practiced in Augusta, as did Patrick Henry.[5]

A county court met on the day designated by statute and sat until its current business had been completed. The surviving court records reveal that the Augusta sessions usually lasted more than a week. The Albemarle records do not survive, but their sessions must have lasted only two or three days, because Jefferson, an Albemarle justice, usually left Albemarle in time to arrive in Staunton for the opening of the Augusta court. He would customarily stay in Staunton for a few days and leave before the session was over. He attended all four Albemarle and all four Augusta courts in 1767. The August and November visits are documented by his account book. The March and May visits are evidenced by his case book records of business obtained from Albemarle and Augusta clients while the courts were in session.

His courtship of Augusta was rewarded. Of sixty-eight items listed in the case book for 1767, forty-one were cases in which one or more of his clients lived in Augusta, as against twelve in which one or more clients lived in Albemarle, and fifteen in which there was no client from either county. His first client was Gabriel Jones, the leading lawyer in Augusta County.[6] In February, Jones hired Jefferson to bring a caveat with respect to 100 acres of land in Augusta. It would be interesting to know where they met because the Augusta court was not in session. Perhaps Jefferson had called on Jones to tell him of his plans and to solicit his support. During the May session of the Augusta court, Jones hired Jefferson on behalf of other Augusta residents to defend two actions for slander pending in the General Court (CB 16, 17). Jones's endorsement of the young Jefferson was probably made known, and it must have helped to get him off to a good start.

Jefferson picked up two cases in Williamsburg in June while attending the council session[7] and four more while attending the General Court in October. One of the June cases was an action pending against George Wythe in the General Court, in which Wythe asked Jefferson to assume the defense (CB 20). "My friend," Jefferson wrote in his case book after Wythe's name. "Defend him totis viribus. Take no fee." The nature of the case does not appear, but it came to trial in 1771, with a verdict in Wythe's favor.[8] In October, Jefferson was employed by Col. Richard Corbin, a member of the governor's council and judge of the General Court, to assist John Randolph in representing former governor Dinwiddie in an action for debt (CB 43). Williamsburg became an increasingly productive source of new business for Jefferson as time went on.

Whereas any business at all was probably welcome to a beginning practitioner, some kinds were more welcome than others. The least desirable kind was the commencement of a new chancery suit or common law action, because such a case in the General Court normally would not come to trial for many years. The consequences of the gap between the beginning of a case and its completion were, first, that the fee might be withheld in whole or in part until the case had been completed and, second, that the experience of trying cases and the reputation of being a good trial lawyer might be a long time in coming.

It was better to be hired by one (usually a defendant) whose suit had been pending for some time. The case against George Wythe is an example. Jefferson was hired in June 1767; the case came to trial in 1771. That was a long time, but it was several years less than it would have been if Jefferson had been hired when the suit began.

Best of all was to be hired by a defendant on the eve of trial, as Jefferson was when retained in August 1767 to help Edmund Pendleton defend Francis Thorpe, accused of assaulting Susanna Williams (CB 37). Jefferson noted in his account book: "Depend principally on her character. She has declared she would not take 200 lib. for her chance. If we fail, we are to apply to Gov. for a remission." At the trial in October, Jefferson's only one in his first year at the bar, Thorpe was found guilty and fined ten shillings. Jefferson probably played a subordinate role, since his cocounsel, Pendleton, was so senior to him.

Because the lawyer's fee was the same whether or not a case dragged on for years, shorter cases were better. Appeals had a shorter life span and accordingly were more desirable than cases at the trial level. Caveats and petitions for lapsed lands were even less time-consuming, on average. Better still were criminal cases, if the criminal was able to pay a lawyer's fee, since the General Court did not allow criminal cases to linger on the docket.[9] Best of all was employment that did not require going to court, such as writing an opinion (CB 36, 61, 62) or drafting a pleading (CB 23). That type of business was limited, and getting it was more a matter of luck than choice.

Whether by luck or by choice, Jefferson's practice emphasized caveats and petitions for lapsed lands, which were proceedings dealing with the patenting of land. A caveat was a challenge to an application for a patent, on the ground that the challenger had a better claim to the patent or that the applicant had not followed the specified procedure within the specified time. A petition for lapsed lands challenged the right of a patent holder to keep his patent, on the ground that he had not made the specified improvements or paid the quitrent. A great deal of frontier land was held by persons who had never perfected their patent rights or who, having obtained patents, had not improved the property or paid quitrents. Consequently, one who brought a well-timed caveat or petition for lapsed lands was very likely to succeed, and many such proceedings were undefended.

The landholder who was vulnerable to such a challenge but who wanted to retain his property without the expense involved in complying with the law had one weapon of defense—the "friendly" (that is, collusive) caveat or petition. Since the first caveat or petition precluded all others, the landholder might get a friend to be the first to file one. As John Blair, president of the council, in his role as deputy auditor for the colony wrote to Governor Fauquier in May 1767:

> A Custom prevails that to save their Lands, without paying Quitrents, they get a Friend to Petition for them as lapsed: and these Petitions (which keep off all other Petitioners from entering) are by collusion kept many years on the Docket without paying. The Court has lately, on a Motion, resolved that if not decided in three Courts they shall be struct off the Docket, and so left open to any other Petitioner; But that by contrivance may be another Friend And at last take out perhaps a new Grant in a Friends Name and then all Arrears are lost. Some great Tracts are now held in this manner and many smaller to the great prejudice of His Majestys Revenue.[10]

Jefferson's second case (Gabriel Jones's caveat being the first) was a friendly petition. Jefferson's nominal client, the petitioner, was Nicholas Meriwether of Albemarle County. The real client was Francis Meriwether of Amherst County, who had a patent to 650 acres on Tuckahoe Creek in Bedford County. It was he who brought the case to Jefferson, with

Nicholas allowing his name to be used as petitioner. This case remained on the General Court docket until April 1774, but neither party minded the delay, which in fact was the point of the friendly petition, though not all of them dragged on as long as this one. Three months after Francis Meriwether hired Jefferson, the roles were reversed. This time (CB 19) Francis was the petitioner and Nicholas the client-defendant. Jefferson billed Francis for the first case but did not bill Nicholas, his friend and colleague on the Albemarle County court, for the second.

In October 1767 Jefferson arranged to have friendly caveats filed against himself "for my three tracts of land in Bedford" and chose Nicholas Meriwether to serve as the nominal petitioner. In May 1771, having meanwhile patented the Bedford property, he arranged for the filing of friendly petitions against himself with his mother, Jane Jefferson, as the nominal petitioner. They remained on the docket until October 1773, when they were dismissed.[11]

During the November 1767 session of the Augusta County court, Jefferson was hired by Patrick Henry and his father-in-law, John Shelton of Augusta, to institute six friendly petitions for lapsed lands (CB 55-60). The collusive petitioner was John Syme of Hanover, Henry's half-brother. The case book entry listed six tracts of land, ranging in size from 150 to 1,400 acres, located on the Clinch and Holston rivers in what is now the southwestern tip of Virginia. The patents, granted to Shelton between March 1748 and December 1750, were among the earliest in that area. At that time both England and France claimed the territory, but the French claim was extinguished by the treaty ending the French and Indian War. Indian claims, recognized as valid by the British government, survived the war and persisted when these petitions were brought.[12]

Jefferson had known Patrick Henry ever since he was seventeen years old. As a law student he had listened spellbound to Henry's "if this be treason" speech in the House of Burgesses in 1765.[13] In 1767 Henry was a successful county lawyer and had had a colonywide reputation since the Parson's Cause in December 1763. He was a member of the Augusta County bar and presumably attended regularly. During the March session of the Augusta court, Jefferson gave him an errand to do in

Williamsburg (CB 6). In short, by November 1767 they knew each other fairly well, and relations must have been friendly or Henry would not have brought the six cases to Jefferson.

Henry was probably the source of the business, rather than Shelton, who held the patents but had mortgaged all six tracts to Henry and was unable to pay the debt. In listing amounts due from clients in his 1768 accounts, Jefferson debited both Henry and Shelton; a year later, he listed only Shelton as owing the money, but it was Henry who paid it in 1771.[14] Jefferson case book entry concerning these petitions says, "Charge but half a fee in each of these." It is not clear whether the discount was given as a professional courtesy to a fellow lawyer or as a wholesale rate because of the amount of business involved. Half fees would have amounted to £7.10.0. Jefferson eventually collected £9.

The six petitions remained on the docket until April 1772 when they abated. Shelton had died, and his death resulted in a family dispute over three of the six tracts. In his will Shelton left his "back lands" to his two sons and to Alexander McLanahan, a son-in-law. Henry asserted that Shelton had deeded three of the parcels to him (940, 955, and 1,400 acres) and that the will applied only to the remaining three (150, 650, and 1,000 acres). In 1774 McLanahan sought Jefferson's advice (CB 926). Jefferson wrote an opinion, and his copy survives.[15] It states that Shelton mortgaged all six properties to Henry on 19 November 1767 (the day before the six petitions were entered) to secure a preexisting debt of £200. Principal and interest, due in six months, were not paid, and in August 1768 Shelton released to Henry his interest in the three tracts of 940, 955, and 1,400 acres. McLanahan and Shelton's sons argued that this instrument, though absolute in form, was given to Henry to permit him to sell the properties and recover the amount due, with any excess to go to Shelton. Since Henry had not sold them, the argument went, the estate retained an equity in them. Jefferson said that the question was what Henry and Shelton intended, one "merely of fact, involving in itself no mater of Law," and "may as well be pronounced on by the unlearned as learned." However, he went on to suggest how the evidence for the family might be presented.

Patrick Henry's biographers, Robert D. Meade and Richard

R. Beeman, discussed the transactions between Henry and his father-in-law with respect to these six properties as reflected in Henry's account books.[16] Apparently neither knew of the Jefferson documents, and their accounts need to be modified. Henry did not buy any of these properties from Shelton before November 1767, as Beeman thought. Rather, as Meade said, Shelton authorized Henry to sell three of the properties and to apply the proceeds against Shelton's £200 debt to him. On 19 November 1767, having been unable to effect a sale, Henry took a mortgage on all six properties. Meade said Jefferson was a witness to the mortgage. At the time, Shelton was subject to a judgment debt of £365 to British merchants, and Henry was afraid the lands would be sold to satisfy that claim. The next day Henry and Shelton hired Jefferson to institute the six friendly petitions for lapsed lands. In 1768, when the debt secured by the mortgage was not paid, Henry took three of the properties in satisfaction of his debt. Meade said that Henry bought the three properties to save his father-in-law from bankruptcy. Jefferson's notes show that Shelton received nothing of value beyond release of Henry's debt of £200 against him.

At one point, apparently before he took title to three of the tracts in 1768, Henry made a trip to the area to locate the Shelton lands but was able to find only one of the parcels. At this time the British government still recognized Indian rights to the land, but it was later acquired by treaty and Henry got a good title to all or nearly all of the land deeded to him by Shelton.

Both Meade and Beeman suggested that Henry was being at least unfilial and perhaps avaricious in these dealings with his father-in-law. On the contrary, it would seem that Henry exercised restraint in taking a deed to only three of the properties when he had a mortgage on all six. The land was potentially valuable but unmarketable in view of the Indian claims to the area.

Table 1 breaks down the sixty-eight cases that Jefferson booked in 1767 by type of case and disposition. It should be emphasized that the disposition indicated may have occurred in any year from 1767 through 1774. The fifteen common law cases still undecided by 1774 illustrate the patience required of a plaintiff starting such a case. If Jefferson had had a representative number of chancery cases, the showing would have been at least as bad. Relatively speaking, caveats and petitions were short-lived.

Jefferson probably did not expect his first year at the bar to be profitable, and it was not. He debited clients a total of £183, of which £176 represented fees charged and £7 represented amounts advanced by him to pay taxes and fees required of plaintiffs at the commencement of an action. He collected only £17, and after deducting amounts advanced for clients, his net receipts for calendar 1767 were only £10. If his costs, including the expenses of four trips to Augusta County and three trips to Williamsburg, are considered, he was considerably out of pocket. Even if he had expected an unprofitable first year, Jefferson must have been disappointed at these dismal figures. More financial disappointments lay ahead.

Table 1. Jefferson's 1767 cases

Disposition	Type of case					
	Chancery	Common Law*	Petition for lapsed lands	Caveat	Other†	Total
Aborted in initial stages‡		4	1			5
Abated by death of party		9	7	1		17
Withdrawn by plaintiff	1	3	3	1		8
Decided by tribunal or otherwise completed	1	1	7	6	5	20
Turned over to E. Randolph in Aug. 1774 as unfinished	1	15				16
Other§		1	1			2
Total	3	33	19	8	5	68

*Includes ten actions of slander, four actions of debt.
†Includes three opinions, one drafting pleading, one criminal case.
‡In one instance TJ was merely instructed to appear for defendant if he should be sued. In others, the defendant was not served with initial process. In others, the case book is silent after the initial entry.
§The common law case was referred to arbitration. The petition was dropped after repeated attempts to serve process on the defendant.

5

The Waterson-Madison Episode

In 1769 a few of Jefferson's Augusta County clients concocted a get-rich-quick scheme that came to an inglorious end three years later. There is no evidence that Jefferson was a coauthor of the scheme. What is clear is that he acted as counsel on the understanding that his fee would be contingent on its success. If it had succeeded, he would have collected a large fee. As it turned out, he did a great deal of work for a small reward.

The plan involved a large-scale use of caveats and petitions for lapsed lands, types of legal proceedings that constituted over half of Jefferson's business during the eight years of his practice.[1] A person who had obtained a patent for Virginia land was obliged to "seat and plant" the land within three years and to pay an annual quitrent of one shilling per fifty acres. Those who failed to seat and plant within three years or who were three years or more in default on quitrents could be brought before the General Court by informers to show cause why the land should not be forfeited. The first informer to establish the delinquency of the patent holder was rewarded with a certificate that entitled him to a patent to the land in question once the appropriate fees were paid. Such a proceeding was known as a petition for lapsed lands or, in Jefferson's usage, a petition.[2]

Because law enforcement machinery was minimal in colonial Virginia, it was common for statutes to promote compliance by permitting informers to sue violators. Some statutes provided for dividing the penalty between the crown and the informer;[3] others allowed the informer to keep it all. Such proceedings, generically described by the Latin phrase *qui tam,* go far back in English legal history. The petition for lapsed lands and the informer's caveat were examples of *qui tam* proceedings in which the informers kept the whole penalty. It was

the rule of *qui tam* proceedings that the first to be brought
precluded all others for the same violation.[4] The violator
often procured a friend to be the first to file; hence the terms
"friendly petition" and "friendly caveat."

The typical procedure for obtaining a patent for land in
Jefferson's time was this: if the property in question contained
more than 400 acres, a petition was submitted to the governor's council. (Note the difference between such a petition
and the petition for lapsed lands, which was addressed to the
General Court. Almost all of the "petitions" in Jefferson's
practice were of the latter sort.)[5] If the council granted the
petition, the applicant, upon paying five shillings per fifty
acres, received an order for land (also known as a warrant or
"right"). He took this to the official surveyor of the county
where the land was located. An entry was made in the records,
and, as soon as possible, the land was surveyed. If the size of
the property was 400 acres or less, the applicant could bypass
the council, pay for and obtain the warrant, and have the
survey made.[6]

The holder of a survey was supposed to deliver a plat of the
land to the colonial land office within three months, pay the
required fees, and obtain his patent[7]—in Jefferson's words,
"return the works." Land speculators were tempted to postpone such submission indefinitely for several reasons. A patent cost money. The secretary of the colony received 10s. 6d.
for making out the patent and recording it, and the governor
exacted a fee of one pistole (£1.1.6) for affixing his seal.[8]
Furthermore, when the patent was issued, the obligation to
pay annual quitrents arose, and the three-year period began
within which seating and planting had to take place. If the
patent was not obtained within the allotted time, however, the
land became subject to forfeiture. The first informer to enter
a caveat and prosecute it before the governor's council was
awarded rights to it.[9] Despite this risk, many tracts of land
were held by people who had had their lands surveyed but
who had failed to obtain patents.[10]

The informer's caveat was also used in related situations. A
man who had successfully prosecuted a petition for lapsed
lands and obtained a certificate from the General Court but
had not proceeded promptly to obtain a patent was subject to
caveat.[11] So was one who had successfully prosecuted a caveat

before the council but had not obtained a patent promptly thereafter.[12] The original purpose of a caveat was to allow conflicting claims to a property to be presented to the council before a patent was issued.[13] Jefferson had cases of this kind, but they were an insignificant minority. Most of his caveats were either the *qui tam* variety brought by informers or friendly caveats filed to fend off informers.

Petitions for lapsed lands presupposed that the land was patented. If no patent could be found, the petition was dismissed. Caveats, on the other hand, presupposed that the land had not been patented; if a patent turned up, the caveat was dismissed. Petitions for lapsed lands were heard and decided by the General Court on the seventh day of each term. The governor's council considered and acted on caveats at a meeting held annually in the middle of June and lasting for one, two, or three days. Notwithstanding these differences, the two forms of proceeding were obviously closely related. A neglected parcel of land was apt to be fair game for either petition or caveat, and Jefferson was sometimes instructed to investigate the possibility of entering one or the other against the owner of land, depending upon whether it turned out to be patented or unpatented.[14]

Many of Jefferson's clients, like John Shelton and Patrick Henry, brought him several cases at one time, caveats or petitions or both. Nevertheless, *qui tam* caveats and petitions were essentially a retail operation until John Madison, Jr., and various associates began to exploit them on a wholesale basis. Madison was the son of the Augusta County clerk, John, Sr., and the brother of James, afterwards president of the College of William and Mary and Episcopal bishop of Virginia.

The scheme had its first manifestation when Jefferson filed fourteen petitions at one time in the name of James Greenlee of Augusta against John Buchanan, a "land dealer in the west."[15] Jefferson noted in his account book on 23 March 1769: "Greenlee's name is used, but J. Madison junr. and James McDowell are partners." These petitions are not listed in the case book. Four of them survived to appear as Jefferson's cases on the General Court docket for April 1770 with the notation that they had abated by Buchanan's death.[16]

The Greenlee operation pales in comparison with the operations of a group that included, in addition to Madison, Wil-

liam Waterson, Hugh Donaghe, and Andrew Johnston, all of
Augusta. Jefferson's notes refer to them from time to time as
"the company" or "Waterson and company." Madison was the
leader and spokesman—"primum mobile," Jefferson called
him. Waterson was the "front man." Jefferson knew him,
somewhat unfavorably, and subsequent events were to justify
any reservations that Jefferson may have had about him.[17]

The group's purpose was to identify all the delinquent land
in Augusta County and to bring caveats or petitions against
the owners. On 29 July, Jefferson noted in his account book,
"Send 20/ which H. Donaghe left with me to Auditor's clerk to
send him a list of all the lands in Augusta for which q. rents
are 3 years behind, and to set down the particular years, by
whom and when paid." On 3 September 1769 Jefferson wrote
in Latin to his friend John Walker: "Are your father's grazing
lands in Augusta safe? That is, may they not be subject to
lapse through lack of cultivation or quitrents? I have no doubt
but that they are safe, but see to it while you can. A word to
the wise. A great loss will soon come to those who are
otherwise."[18]

The group's operations began on 19 April 1769, when Waterson brought five petitions and fifteen caveats to Jefferson.
In five of the fifteen caveats, the defendant was Col. William
Preston, another "land dealer in the west," who has been
called "the most important of all the pioneers of southwest
Virginia." He had twice been elected burgess from Augusta;
and, with the creation of Botetourt County from the southern
half of Augusta at the end of 1769, he was appointed to the
county court and elected a burgess from the new county.[19]
Although no summons had been served on him, somehow
Colonel Preston got wind of the Waterson caveats against him.
Jefferson's account book entry of 18 August describes what
happened next:

> 4 caveats were entered as per. mem. of April 19. Colo. Preston
> suspecting this borrows money of Colo. Syme and Fr. Smith his
> father in law, posts down to Wmsburgh, where he arrives May
> 18. He hires one of the boys to receive his works, and immedi-
> ately to make out his patents which were antedated (perhaps).
> After this he comes to Waterson's Atty. (myself) tells him he
> had entered caveats for lands which he had patd. The atty. on
> seeing this scratches out the caveats. It seems there happened

to be some blk. patents signed in the office. Colo. Preston con-
fessed all this to William Crow, and dropped some hints to
John Bowyer. Enquire into this and bring a bill in Canc. to
rectify. Preston told all this to J. Mills.

As indicated above, five caveats, not four, had been brought
against Preston. One survived the incident described. So far as
Jefferson's records show, no bill in chancery regarding the
other four was ever brought.

Having given Jefferson five petitions and fifteen caveats on
19 April, Waterson brought forty-four more caveats on 28
May. These three groups of cases appear in the case book as
Waterson v. Gilbert (CB 211-15), *Waterson v. Allen-Stevenson* (CB
223-32), and *Waterson* v. *Armstrong-Bullett* (CB 246-85).[20]
There were four stages through which each of these groups of
cases passed: submission of the list to Jefferson, screening of
the list by Jefferson's agent in Williamsburg,[21] submission of
those selected to the office of the secretary of the colony to
obtain priority over petitions or caveats filed subsequently,
and commencement of proceedings before the court or
council.[22] As a list of cases passed through these stages, the
number was apt to diminish. For the *Waterson* v. *Gilbert* group
of five petitions, the four stages occurred practically simulta-
neously. For the caveats, the process took longer, and the
fourth stage—commencement of proceedings—was postponed
until July, probably because the clients did not have the ready
money to pay for summonses. The last five summonses in
Waterson v. *Armstrong-Bullett* were not taken out until 28 January 1770.

The case book records no more company petitions or caveats in Waterson's name, but the greater part of the business
was yet to come. On 30 July 1769 Jefferson sent a list of 270
more Waterson cases to his Williamsburg agent, John May, for
screening. May replied on 2 September that he had entered
195 caveats in the secretary's office. Jefferson did not send for
summonses until 28 January; the list by then had been reduced to 190.[23] In addition, an account book entry of 2 September 1769 shows that 127 caveats and 12 petitions had been
filed with the secretary in the name of Andrew Johnston. All
of this business, except two petitions, was lumped as one item
in the case book, *Johnston's Case*, no. 367.[24] Later, when sum-

monses were taken out, all but three of the caveats were switched to Waterson's name.[25]

Clearly the case book is an inadequate record of the scope of this business. Even the record in the account books is incomplete as far as petitions are concerned. The April 1770 General Court docket lists seventy petitions in Waterson's name and fourteen in Johnston's name besides those already mentioned. A few, but not all, are mentioned in the account books. By April 1770 the company had over 450 caveats and petitions pending. The principal expenses had been taxes of 2s. 6d. per proceeding and fees of 5s. 9d. per summons. The company, like most people in those days, was strapped for cash. The money was paid to Jefferson in seven installments over two years.[26] When Jefferson on 28 January 1770 forwarded to Nathaniel Walthoe, clerk of the council, £71.3.1½ together with instructions to file 321 summonses for caveats, he agreed to pay any deficiency. Actually, the shortage amounted to some £15, for which he was personally responsible until the company later compensated him.

If he had completed and won as many as 400 of the cases, Jefferson's fees, at the usual rate of £2.10.0 per case, would have amounted to at least £1,000, about half of what he earned in his eight years at the bar.[27] But none of the cases was completed, and fees were contingent on success. However, "for my very great trouble in these matters," he was allowed to keep without payment a horse worth £20 he had bought on credit from Waterson, and Madison gave him another horse worth £35.[28]

The citizenry of Augusta and Botetourt counties were outraged by the actions of Jefferson's clients. In September 1769 Thomas Lewis, writing Colonel Preston, referred to "the business of caveating here" by a "combination" whose members had not been identified. He said:

> It is (& I fear with too much Justice) suspected we have a number in sd Combination, villains they certainly are from the highest to the lowest. . . . Seeing the people Defensless without adviser or friend, I attempted to form a Petition . . . & put into the hands of Some people to procure Signers, with advice to raise some small sums of money to bear the expense of Some one who might have the charity to be at the trouble to present to the Gov. & council. This Petition I Expect will be taken

Down by Ab[ne]r Smith & I shall accompany him if nothing
Extraordinary prevent. I think Expedition in this matter necessary & therefore proposed setting off next Sunday or Monday.

He urged Preston to join them if he could. He said he had a
strong hope that the council "will be moved with Compassion,
& do wt they can for the [relief] of the Distressed poor." He
concluded by saying: "Be there. If we can do good it will be a
pleasure to us, that can never be felt by any that are in this
cursed Combination." From a subsequent letter, it appears
that Preston did join Lewis in Williamsburg and added his
influence.[29]

Their pleas must have been effective. Shortly after the General Assembly convened on 21 May 1770, Edmund Pendleton
was ordered to prepare a bill "to compel certain persons to find
security in certain cases." Presented on 8 June, the bill was referred to a special committee consisting of John Blair, Jr., Pendleton, Jefferson, and Thomas Walker. In the resulting statute,
the legislature stated its finding that "divers litigious persons
have, of late, preferred petitions . . . for grants of lands, under
pretence that they were forfeited for non-payment of his maj-
esty's quitrents, or for want of seating and planting . . . ; others
have entered caveats . . . pretending that the rules of government have not been complied with, in the progress of making
and returning the surveys." The statute accordingly authorized
court and council to require a petitioner or caveator to post
security for costs on pain of dismissal.[30]

There can be little doubt that the statute was aimed at Jefferson's clients. It was a clever way to deal with a troublesome
threat. The concern was not truly that the plaintiffs would lose
a large number of cases and be unable to pay the winners'
costs; it was that the plaintiffs would win. Pretending that it
was the former, the legislature imposed a crushing burden on
the plaintiffs in the expectation that they would be unable to
meet it.

Realizing that their cases before the General Court and
council were doomed, the company made an effort to have
them referred to arbitration, but the arbitrators refused to
serve. Lewis wrote Preston on 28 August 1770:

An argreement has been made by Buchanan[?] Dr. Walker &
Waterson or rather his attor[ne]y, referring said loss of·caveats

to Mr. Trimble, Hartsell[?] McDowell & Jno. Poage. Some of
those gent[leme]n Seem to think that their taking on them to
Execute the purport of sd agreement would be attended with
Ill consequences and therefore Decline having any concern
therewith when you see sd agreement & reflect on sd consequences I am of opinion you will be of their Sentiments. If you
have not seen the agreement I wish you would send to Mr.
Trimble for a copy thereof.[31]

The new statute was promptly put to its intended use. Court
and council required the plaintiffs to provide security for opponents' costs, the security was not provided, and the cases
were dismissed. Jefferson's copy of the April 1771 docket of
the General Court has a note in his handwriting opposite *Waterson* v. *Gilbert,* the first of the company's cases on the docket:
"ruled to security."[32] The October 1771 docket similarly notes,
"all these dismd fr wnt of security."

When the council met in June 1771 to consider the caveat
cases on its docket, it ordered Waterson to provide, before the
end of the next April court, security for payment of costs to
each person against whom one of his caveats was pending if
he was unsuccessful. On the following day, another resolution
defined the costs allowable to a successful defendant; they
included witness fees and lawyers' fees. In June 1772 all of
Waterson's caveats were dismissed with costs, 125 specifically
for failure to give approved security and 180 for unstated
reasons. The council then took another unprecedented action.
It allowed the defendants in the Waterson cases three months
from the date of its order to comply with the conditions for
obtaining patents.[33]

Why did the colonial government crack down so hard on
these plaintiffs? The *qui tam* petition and caveat were designed
for the very purpose of enforcing governmental requirements
and enhancing revenue from quitrents. These plaintiffs were
doing exactly what the designers had in mind, except that they
overdid it. A modern analogy might be the enforcement of
speed laws. Enforcement within limits is desirable, but strict
and absolute enforcement is considered excessive. The colonial
government did not want to put the land speculators out of
business. Delinquency was kept to a tolerable level by the threat
of actions by isolated informers; but a massive assault, such as
Madison mounted, threatened the fabric of frontier society.

The authorities may also have asked themselves what Madison and his associates would do with all the land if they won their suits. Obviously, they could not seat and plant all the unimproved land or pay quitrents on all the land that was in default. The authorities may have concluded that the plaintiffs intended to turn a quick shilling by exacting tribute from the defendants for dropping the cases or to sell the land quickly to others no more apt to seat and plant or to pay quitrents than the incumbents. Neither course would benefit the royal revenue.

Madison had a hand in one other group of Jefferson's cases. On 19 April 1770 John (or Alexander?) Reid of Amherst County brought Jefferson five petitions and added another fifteen in October (all of these are one item in the case book, no. 459). The defendants were the heirs and executors of James Patton, including Colonel Preston. This time Jefferson had an agreement that he was to be paid full fees, that is, £50, win or lose. He actually collected £32.10.0, £5 of it from Madison.

Jefferson's records do not say whether Reid was required to post security for costs. A letter of 29 April 1771 to Preston from Pendleton, his lawyer, indicates that Pendleton considered asking for security. He said, "If I can fix Reids Circumstances I will get him ruled to Security for costs." If the requirement was imposed, Reid complied, because the cases went to trial on the merits at the April 1773 court and were all dismissed, with costs assessed against Reid. On 23 April 1773 Pendleton wrote Preston, "We have given Mr. Reid a total defeat."[34]

Those against whom Madison and his associates brought their proceedings bitterly resented their machinations; whether the resentment against his clients affected Jefferson's business is not clear. During the first three years of his practice, Augusta County produced more business for him than any other county, including Albemarle. During the last three years, he had almost twice as many cases from Albemarle as from Augusta, Botetourt, and Fincastle (an offshoot of Botetourt) combined. But the change may not be attributable to the Waterson affair. Jefferson himself was neglecting Augusta. During the early years he regularly attended the quarterly sessions of the Augusta County court, whereas in 1772 he went to Staunton only twice, in 1773 once, and in 1774 not at all.

Did his standing with the Willamsburg establishment suffer? Apparently not. After June 1770, when the legislature enacted the statute that killed the company's scheme, he continued to represent William Byrd,[35] and council members Burwell and Nelson brought new business to him.[36] When John Blair, Jr., quit his General Court practice to become clerk of the council in late 1770, Jefferson succeeded, with Blair's assistance, to a part of his practice.[37] Robert Carter Nicholas, who had had a highly successful practice in the General Court before becoming treasurer of the colony in 1766, asked Jefferson in October 1770 to take over what was left of his practice. Jefferson first accepted but later declined.[38] Pendleton, his opponent in the Waterson affair, retained him in one case.[39] Clearly his reputation in the capital had not suffered from the affair.

Did the Waterson-Madison episode contribute to his decision to give up the practice of law? Chapter 11 argues that he reached that decision in 1773, and that for some time before then his enthusiasm for the practice of law had been waning. It may well be that the Waterson-Madison fiasco played a part.

6

The Norfolk Anti-Inoculation
Riots

In Jefferson's time at the General Court bar, a lawyer accepted all or nearly all legal business offered to him, whether or not the representation in a particular case was at odds with his personal philosophy. Jefferson was no exception. Nevertheless, it must have gratified him to argue for a cause in which he believed. Inoculation against smallpox was such a cause. He had been inoculated in 1766[1] and subsequently reiterated his faith in the process. Hence he must have welcomed the opportunity to represent some of the victims of the Norfolk anti-inoculation riots of 1768 and 1769.[2]

The Jenner vaccination against smallpox was introduced in 1796. Before that, those who wished to protect themselves against the disease had to resort to inoculation. The process consisted of transmitting matter from a person who had a mild case of smallpox to the one being inoculated, in the hope of inducing a similarly mild case. Inoculated persons developed typical smallpox and had to be quarantined until the disease had run its course. Even though the treatment was fatal in a small percentage of cases, it was a reasonable gamble from the patient's standpoint, because the resulting immunity from smallpox was almost total.[3]

The neighborhood where the inoculation was to be performed viewed the procedure with a more jaundiced eye. Could infection be confined to the inoculation site? How far from a populated area should such a site be? How long should the inoculated person be kept in quarantine? In 1768 a small-scale epidemic of smallpox in which two people died near Yorktown was attributed to the premature release of inoculated patients from quarantine. This experience probably explains the bitter anti-inoculation bias subsequently manifested by William Nelson of Yorktown.[4]

In June 1768 and in May 1769 confrontations in Norfolk between pro-inoculation and anti-inoculation factions resulted in riots. Leading figures of the pro-inoculation side included Cornelius Calvert, within whose one-year term as mayor of Norfolk both outbreaks occurred; Dr. Archibald Campbell; and James Parker, a Norfolk merchant. Strongly opposed to inoculation were Cornelius Calvert's brothers Maximilian and Joseph. Maximilian was an alderman of the borough of Norfolk and a justice of the peace of Norfolk County. He succeeded his brother as mayor. Joseph was sergeant of the hustings court of the borough. The three Calverts were sons of Cornelius Calvert, a sea captain, ten of whose eleven sons grew to maturity and became masters of vessels. The anti-inoculation faction also included other prominent men of Norfolk: George Abyvon, Paul Loyall, and Dr. James Taylor, all former mayors of the city; Samuel Boush, Jr., former burgess and clerk of the county court; and Thomas Newton, Jr., a justice of the peace at the time of both riots and burgess at the time of the second riot.[5]

Jefferson's notes regarding the subsequent indictment of doctors Campbell and John Dalgleish characterize it as an "indictment for introducing inoculation in Norfolk."[6] The implication is that the 1768 inoculations were the first ever performed in Norfolk County, although there had been at least one prior instance, when Dr. Dalgleish inoculated his apprentice, Robert Bell, in June 1767.[7] Cornelius Calvert's account of the 1769 riot says inoculation had been practiced in the colony for fifteen or twenty years in different counties, specifically mentioning York.[8] He did not mention Norfolk, as he surely would have done if local inoculation history had warranted such mention.

The 1768 riot grew out of the desire of Dr. Campbell and some of his Norfolk friends to have their wives and children inoculated by Dr. Dalgleish. They selected a site for the purpose, but the anti-inoculation faction objected to it, so Dr. Campbell changed the proposed site to his plantation, three miles out of town. The opponents objected to Dr. Campbell's invitation to others to be inoculated at the same time and place, and he agreed to limit the group to those already enlisted. This concession mollified a few, including Samuel Boush, but most of the anti-inoculation faction wanted the project abandoned entirely. When word got around that it had been carried out on 25 June, the antis demanded that those who had been inoculated be moved to the Norfolk pesthouse. Under severe pressure, Dr. Campbell agreed, stipulating only that the pesthouse first be put in tolerable order. Work was begun; but unwilling to wait, Joseph Calvert organized a mob that attacked Dr. Campbell's house on 27 June and drove the patients to the pesthouse in foul weather. Among those inoculated who were mistreated were the wife and son of James Parker and Mrs. William Aitcheson, Mrs. Parker's sister and the wife of Parker's business partner.

Two days after the riot, Dr. Campbell's house was burned. The colonial government offered rewards for the arrest and conviction of those responsible, to no avail.[9] Dr. Campbell's friends suspected Samuel Boush.[10] An unsigned account of the riot in Rind's *Virginia Gazette* of 25 August said that when Dr. Campbell agreed with two of the opposing faction to limit the number of those to be inoculated, one of the two said he was glad because otherwise Dr. Campbell's house would have been destroyed that night. The account continued, "These two gentlemen owned afterwards that they were to have paid a proportion of the value of the house, if it had been pulled down." Samuel Boush identified himself as one of the two in a letter published in the same paper a week later. As a pro-inoculationist put it in commenting on Boush's letter: "Whether Mr. Boush's avowal of a levelling principle, declared by his willingness to contribute towards indemnifying Doctor Campbell, had any influence on those infatuated people, is hard to know; but it certainly had much the appearance of an indirect sanction, and we think Mr. Boush had reason to blame his impudence in uttering such sentiments publicly, especially as he seems to have known so well the temper of the mob."[11]

On 20 December 1769 Dr. Campbell asked Jefferson's opinion whether this evidence would justify a suit against Boush.[12] Jefferson's opinion does not appear among his records, but he probably concluded that the evidence was insufficient. In any event, no suit was brought against Boush or anyone else for burning Dr. Campbell's house.

Various civil suits and criminal proceedings were brought, however, as a result of the mob action of 25 June. On 9 September 1768 Jefferson received a letter from Alexander Donald retaining him "on behalf of the sufferers by the riot in Norfolk." In October when the General Court was in session, Jefferson instituted three civil actions. Dr. Campbell was the plaintiff in one, and he and his wife were coplaintiffs in another (CB 156). Parker was the plaintiff in the third (CB 157). The defendants in the Parker case were Maximilian Calvert, Joseph Calvert, Thomas Newton, Jr., and John Lewelling. Jefferson's records list the defendants in the other two cases simply as "Calvert et al.," but they probably were the same four. These cases were placed on the very long list of General Court common law cases awaiting trial, and they were still there when Jefferson turned his business over to Edmund Randolph in August 1774. The long wait was not abnormal.

At the same time, other men whose wives and children had been similarly abused after their inoculation brought suit. Cornelius Calvert brought two suits, with John Blair, Jr., and Edmund Pendleton as his lawyers. One was against Maximilian Calvert and John Calvert (did he mean Joseph?),[13] the other against Thomas Newton, Jr., and Isaac Talbot. These suits came to Jefferson when Blair quit the practice in 1770; and like the Campbell and Parker cases, they were turned over to Randolph when Jefferson himself quit the practice in 1774 (CB 490, 574). William Aitcheson sued Newton and others; Lewis Hansford sued Calvert and others. All we know about these cases is that they were grouped on the General Court docket with the cases of Jefferson's clients. Presumably their progress, or lack of it, was the same.

Criminal charges were also brought and moved faster. At the April 1769 General Court each faction sought and obtained an indictment against the other. *The King* v. *Calvert et al.* was an indictment for a riot; *The King* v. *Dalgleish et al.* was an indictment for a nuisance. Shortly thereafter Parker called on Governor Botetourt and reported to Charles Steuart, his London friend and business associate:

> I avoided the mob subject. He brought it on himself, by observing if the rioters had anything to advance in mitigation of their crimes they would have a fair opportunity on the trial of the indictment brought against the doctor, and at the same time it would appear whether or not we had taken due care to prevent danger. I said whatever way it was ended I should consider as

right; that I hoped in time the people of Norfolk would be concerned that we were all bound by the same laws, and that the people they were pleased to call foreigners had as good a claim to protection and justice as if their ancestors had first settled this colony. Says he, "I would not live a day in any country where the law was partially executed. I do believe there is not one of the judges as well as myself but what will hear this matter fully and judge it with impartiality, according to its merits; and I shall be always glad to hear that the gentlemen of Norfolk who have been injured do not depart from that moderation with which they have hitherto conducted themselves."[14]

So matters stood when the second riot occurred in May 1769. Fearing that some of his slaves had been exposed to smallpox while working on one of his ships in Norfolk harbor, Cornelius Calvert had Dr. Dalgleish inoculate them at the pesthouse. Word spread, and the next day Maximilian Calvert as borough justice ordered the sergeant to produce Dr. Dalgleish "to answer to such matters as shall be objected against him" by named persons. He was required to post bond for good behavior until the 15 June meeting of the county court. At the foot of the order is a notation by Joseph Calvert as sergeant of the borough that Dr. Dalgleish had been arrested and jailed.[15]

That night a mob appeared, first at Cornelius Calvert's house, then at Dr. Campbell's, and finally at James Parker's. Some damage was done at the first two. Parker's was left unharmed only because, having been forewarned, he was prepared to defend it with guns.[16]

More suits, civil and criminal, followed. Cornelius Calvert sued Henry Singleton and others; this case came to Jefferson at the same time as the other Calvert cases (CB 491). Although his records do not show that it too came from John Blair, it seems likely that it did. Here again the case lingered on the docket until Jefferson left the practice in 1774.

An attempt to proceed criminally against the rioters at the local level fizzled. Parker wrote Steuart on 22 June 1769: "We had several of the rioters taken up. However, they were only bound in small sums and found security amongst the mob magistrates." An attempt in the General Court was more successful. On 20 October, Parker wrote Steuart: "I have just returned from Williamsburg, where I was with Cornelius Calvert indicting some more of the mob for the last offences of which I wrote you. The bills were all found, viz., against three for breaking into my enclosure and threatening to burn my home, and for breaking C. Calvert's windows."[17]

As it happened, the 1769 incident was the first to come before the General Court. The charge on which Dr. Dalgleish had been jailed was brought to the General Court by habeas corpus. The matter was heard on the eighth day of the October 1769 session. As was customary in the case of relatively minor crimes, the prosecution, though nominally in the name of the king, was conducted by the complainants, and their counsel, in this case Thomson Mason. The defense was represented by Blair and Pendleton. Parker wrote Steuart:

> Mr. Mason . . . wanted to make appear that the mayor . . . and the doctor maliciously intended to spread the infection all around to make a fortune for the doctor. He quoted some causes wherein damages were recovered from one who had put poison amongst his oats whereby some of neighbors' fowls were destroyed, and some other cases fully as foreign. . . . [He] concluded that . . . their honors would have evidence sufficient to induce them not only to continue the recognizance, but to bond C. Calvert over also. . . . His Lordship [Governor Botetourt] asked, if the pesthouse was commonly occupied for that purpose, and if at that time Cornelius Calvert was mayor of the town. G. Abyvon answered in the affirmative to both. "Then," says he, "the doctor has done his duty. Do you know," says he, "any place so proper for confining that disorder as a house built for the purpose, under the inspection of the mayor and the care of a judicious physician?"

At the urging of Col. George William Fairfax, a member of the court, various anti-inoculation witnesses were allowed to testify, and then,

> The court came to judgment. John Page was of opinion that Dr. Dalgleish and C. Calvert intended to spread the infection, that the recognizance should continue, and C. Calvert be bound over. Bob Burwell, continue the recognizance. R. Carter, Col. Corbin, Col. Fairfax, Tayloe, Byrd, W. Nelson and president [Blair] and governor [Botetourt], discharge the recognizance. Col. Pressley Thornton came in too late to give an opinion. The governor then recommended to the doctor not to inoculate any more except in cases of necessity till this matter which made so much noise was determined.

After the hearing was over, Parker continued, William Nelson, "extending his right arm, his face as red as fire," said, "If I had the power I would hang up every man that would inoculate even in his own house." Governor Botetourt replied, "Now, my friend, you have given your opinion, and very freely too; I shall give you mine as freely. . . . The man who first discovered inoculation stands unparalleled in merit. It is the greatest addition ever was made to physical knowledge, and has disarmed the most destructive foe to mankind of all its terrors; and in a little time the whole world will be convinced of this truth. Now, sir, this is my opinion."[18]

Jefferson became involved in the criminal cases for the first time in April 1770, when the charges and countercharges arising from the 1768 riot were about to be tried before the General Court. Jefferson had recently suffered the loss of his Shadwell home by fire and on 21 February 1770 wrote his friend John Page, Jr., that all of his papers, public and private, had been lost in the flames. He said, "I had made some progress in preparing for the succeeding general court, and having, as was my custom, thrown my thoughts into the form of notes, I troubled my head no more with them. These are gone, and 'like the baseless fabric of a vision, Leave not a trace behind.' The records also and other papers, which furnished me with states of the several cases, having shared the same fate, I have no foundation whereon to set out anew. I have in vain attempted to recollect some of them. . . . What am I to do then in April?"[19]

The notes that Jefferson had made when retained by Campbell and Parker in 1768 and when consulted by Campbell about the burning of his house in December 1769 were probably lost in the Shadwell fire. Nevertheless, he accepted a last-minute invitation to participate in the criminal cases. His account book shows that he was retained on Monday, 16 April, to defend Campbell and Parker, with the case expected to be tried "about Wednesday."[20] The explanation for the late hiring does not appear, but it was by no means the only time that Jefferson was hired on the eve of trial. Blair, who had represented Dr. Dalgleish the preceding October, presumably was still acting for him. Probably Blair and Pendleton were Cornelius Calvert's counsel in the criminal cases, as they were in the pending civil cases. Since all the defendants were in much the same position, and Blair and Pendleton were no doubt fully prepared, the defense probably did not suffer from Jefferson's late hiring. On 1 May, Jefferson was employed by Dr. Campbell to assist in the prosecution of the rioters (CB 410).

Parker wrote Steuart on 8 May: "We have been all detained at the Capitol three weeks about our indictments. . . . You would have been greatly surprised had you seen the torrent of opposition that appeared against us, and the visible partiality in favor of the rioters."[21] On 19 May he wrote again:

> Our affair with the mob came on the 6th day of the court. 11 days was taken up in examining evidences [witnesses] and two in the pleadings. Both of the Nelsons, John Page and R. Burwell showed their inclination to favor the mob from the beginning, and their weight has I think given the affair an unfavorable [turn] for us. The treasurer [Robert Carter Nicholas] was drawn from his retirement[22] to plead their cause and Thomson Mason figured highly in praise of mobs.
>
> "What, gentlemen of the jury, was the good people in England in the reign of King James but a mob, and thirty or forty sturdy beggars had more influence in the lobby of the House of Commons towards preventing the excise acts than all the power of Sir Robert Walpole. . . . What, my friends, were the good people of Virginia in the days of the Stamp Act but a mob? Mobs are justifiable, useful, necessary and commendable."
>
> The jury on the nuisance [charge] against us stayed up ten days and brought down a special verdict, in which every circumstance that made against us was found, and only one or two favorable circumstances. However, it is fortunate for us that nothing is found against us contrary to law. The Court say they have nothing to judge upon. Messrs. Pendleton, Blair and Jefferson say it must drop. . . .
>
> On the other hand, though they have [not?] found specially against the rioters, yet they have found almost all the facts and these facts are illegal so that they will be found guilty. The jury cleared the two Hutchings, T. Veal and Loyal. . . . They [the anti-inoculation faction] had a strong coffee house advocate in the Speaker [Peyton Randolph]. The matter is to be finished in October.[23]

When the cases came on again in October 1770, Lord Botetourt, the friend of inoculation, was dead, and John Blair, Sr., had resigned from the council and court. William Nelson, who had indicated his animosity, was acting governor and presided over the court. Having become clerk of the governor's council, John Blair, Jr., was no longer counsel for Cornelius Calvert and Dr. Dalgleish.[24] Jefferson was now leading counsel for the pro-inoculation side.

In the case in which Jefferson's clients were charged with nuisance, they were found guilty by the judges on the basis of the special verdicts handed down in April. Parker wrote Steuart:

> Mr. Jefferson did us all the justice he possibly could or we expected. . . . In vain were the cases of Lord Hardwicke and Lord Mansfield quoted, though absolutely case in point. There was a fixed resolution in the judge [Nelson] to oppress us. However improper, he had declared openly upon the bench long before the examination of one evidence, his own opinion, and on other occasions talked of bringing the affair to a drawn battle. I think there are some on that bench would not have voted as they did had his Lordship been there.[25]

Jefferson's clients applied to the court for permission to appeal to England. According to Parker, Jefferson thought the appeal might be granted, but "the court took three days to consider of it, and then refused it as being contrary to the royal instructions because the fine was under £100 sterling. . . . I then applied to the court that I might be fined £100, that I might be entitled to that justice which I expected from the King and his council but was refused."[26]

Neither Jefferson's records nor Parker's letters tell what the judgment was in the case against the 1768 rioters. But at the same term of court that found Parker and his friends guilty of committing a nuisance, the 1769 rioters were convicted. Singleton was fined £25 and three others £10 each. Costs of prosecution were assessed against them, and the Norfolk County court was ordered to require them to post peace bonds with sureties.[27]

The reaction of the Norfolk County court was insolent and insubordinate. When the General Court order was presented to them in November 1770, the county justices objected that no cause had been shown "whereby they are deprived of judging between Man and Man" and announced that they conceived the order to be "contrary to Law and our happy Constitution, and therefore humbly hope that the Honorable Court will reconsider the said Order."

The General Court responded at its April 1771 session by ordering the sheriff of Norfolk County to take the four defendants into custody and hold them until they furnished the bail and sureties required by its order. Apparently the sheriff did not do so, and the October 1771 court ordered the sheriff to make his return "on this day fortnight." The order was then carried out. The sureties posted included Maximilian Calvert, Joseph Calvert, Thomas Newton, Jr., Samuel Boush, and doctors John Ramsay and Taylor—in a word, the Norfolk establishment.

Nor did the recalcitrance of the Norfolk County court end there. Sometime before the April 1773 term of the General Court, the Norfolk court discharged the defendants, permitting them "to swear out as insolvents." Jefferson was hired on 17 April by William Aitcheson, himself a justice of the county court, to obtain a General Court order superseding the county court order (*The King* v. *Ward*, CB 812) and on 7 May by Cornelius Calvert for the same purpose (*The King* v. *Singleton*, CB 838). He obtained the desired order in October 1773.

In the spring of 1773 Jefferson was also hired in another case (*The King* v. *Portlock*, CB 858) that had some unspecified relation to the preceding cases. Portlock's first name does not appear. John Portlock was a justice of the county court, and Samuel Portlock was a deputy sheriff. The sheriff seems to be the more likely defendant. Jefferson's case book entry of 9 August 1773 reads, "I was employed to move against him which I did and obtained judgment last April. I somehow omitted to enter it in Memorandum Book, so have forgotten who employed me, but I expect it was either Mr. Aitcheson when he employed me April 17 in the King v. Ward, or Cornelius Calvert when he employed me May 7 in the King v. Singleton."

The financial results for Jefferson of all the cases considered here were unusually good. The details are instructive. When he was first retained by Campbell and Parker in 1768 to bring civil suits, he charged each of them £2.10.0, his standard fee for common law actions. Nothing was paid by either at that time. Parker paid £2.11.6 in April 1769. When Campbell consulted Jefferson in December 1769 about the possibility of suing Boush for the destruction of his house, Jefferson charged him £1 for his opinion. Campbell paid him £2, of which Jefferson regarded 1s. 6d. as a gratuity for the opinion, crediting 18s. 6d. to Campbell's civil suit. The balance of Campbell's £2.10.0 fee was never paid. In preparing to turn his legal business over to Edmund Randolph in 1774, Jefferson realized that he had brought two civil suits for Campbell and had charged him for only one. The list of amounts due furnished to Randolph indicated that Campbell owed him £4.1.6.

For his services in the two criminal cases arising out of the 1768 riot, Jefferson charged "Campbell et al." £2.10.0 for each case when he was retained. He was paid £10 at that time and another £10 when the case was over. Jefferson regarded the £15 difference between payments and charge as a gratuity. Such gratuities were few and far between in his legal career.[28]

Cornelius Calvert paid nothing to Jefferson for his services in the three civil actions arising out of the riots. At the time of hiring, he did pay Jefferson's charge of £2.10.0 for services in *The King* v. *Singleton,* as did Aitcheson for services in *The King* v. *Ward.* Since Jefferson's task was the same in each case—to appeal the same county court order—he was well paid for this relatively simple job. Jefferson could not remember whether his client in *The King* v. *Portlock* was Calvert or Aitcheson. On his books he indicated that either one or the other owed him £2.10.0. Not surprisingly, neither paid. Jefferson's charges in all of these cases came to £28.10.0, and he was paid a total of £29.11.6, a result markedly at odds with his general experience.

While the inoculation controversy was in the courts, it was also before the Virginia General Assembly. At the November 1769 session, the Committee on Propositions and Grievances presented two resolutions to the House of Burgesses. The first found reasonable "the Petition of the Inhabitants of the Borough of *Norfolk* and other Parts of this Colony" that the practice of inoculation be regulated. The second rejected petitions of "divers Inhabitants of this Colony" that the practice be prohibited. An act was accordingly passed on 27 June 1770 that in effect made inoculation a matter of local option, permitting anyone who wanted it to apply to the local magistrates, who might either deny the application or grant it "under such restrictions and regulations as they shall judge necessary." The effect was to stop the practice almost entirely in Virginia.[29]

Parker was surprised that the act was not disallowed by the

king in council. He wrote Steuart on 15 July 1773 that two subsequent acts had been repealed; and he speculated that the inoculation act "never was sent home, or if it did go and was repealed, the fate of it probably arrived in Old Billie's [William Nelson's regime as acting governor] and he suppressed it to encourage the mob. Pray if you can learn anything of it let me know."[30]

In 1777 a legislative committee of which Jefferson was a member (as were Pendleton and Nicholas) proposed a more liberal scheme, which was enacted. It allowed inoculation anywhere if a majority of the neighbors within two miles consented and if a proper quarantine was maintained. According to Julian Boyd, "To what extent TJ contributed to this Bill cannot be determined, yet it unmistakably bears the impress of his mind and influence." Under this law Jefferson had his children inoculated at Ampthill in Chesterfield County in 1782. Yet even under this law, shortly after the turn of the century, Dr. John Gilmer of Albemarle was placed under bond for good behavior for three months when one of his inoculated patients died.[31]

7

A Williamsburg Scandal
Notes on Divorce

English law in Jefferson's time made it impossible to get a divorce without an act of Parliament. Divorce *a vinculo matrimonii* (literally, "from the chain of marriage") could be obtained from an ecclesiastical court only for one of the canonically recognized impediments, such as consanguinity. But in today's terms, that was annulment, not divorce. For certain causes arising after marriage, such as adultery, one could obtain from the same court what was then called a divorce *a mensa et thoro* ("from bed and board"). In today's terms, that was a legal separation; neither party could remarry. An absolute divorce could be obtained from Parliament for adultery, but the petitioner must first have obtained a decree of separation from an ecclesiastical court and a verdict at law for criminal conversation. The obstacles were so great and the procedure so expensive that it was available only to a wealthy few.[1]

Although an absolute divorce was available on less stringent terms in some of the northern colonies, it was unknown in Virginia and the other southern colonies until after the Revolution.[2] In the face of these difficulties, Jefferson contemplated in 1772 the possibility of obtaining a legislative divorce for Dr. James Blair of Williamsburg. His notes on the subject appear in full at the end of this chapter.

Dr. Blair was the son of John Blair, Sr., who, as president of the governor's council, had twice served as acting governor of Virginia. Dr. Blair's brother, John Blair, Jr., formerly Jefferson's colleague at the General Court bar, was at the time clerk of the governor's council. Born in 1741, Dr. Blair studied medicine at the University of Edinburgh. Arthur Lee of Virginia was a student there at about the same time and knew Blair.[3] A year before his marriage in 1771, Dr. Blair suffered

a serious illness while he and Lee were in London. The nature
of the illness is not clear, and it may or may not be relevant to
his subsequent marital difficulties. On 1 January 1770 Lee
wrote John Blair, Sr., that he was writing at his son's request,
"as he is himself incapable." He explained: "He was seiz'd six
or seven days ago with a violent nervous disorder that effects
his brain and every part of his body. I know not what the
Physicians call it, but he now lays very ill." He wrote again on
24 January that Dr. Blair's indisposition "was nearly con-
quered," but that his doctors "considered it indispensably necessary that he should go to Bath to perfect his recovery." Blair
went to Bath but reported to Lee in July that the waters had
not had the salutary effect hoped for and that he was plan-
ning to return to Virginia. Lee replied, "You seem to be
rather low . . . you must exert yourself & banish all gloomy
ideas."[4]

On 21 May 1771 Dr. Blair married Kitty Eustace of New
York.[5] The bride was the daughter of Dr. John Eustace, a
physician who, after practicing in New York, moved to North
Carolina in 1765 and died there in 1769. Her age does not
appear, but the fact that her mother was "fortyish" and her
brother John was not quite eleven suggests that she was probably at least ten years younger than Dr. Blair. Her mother,
Margaret, was one of six children of Lauchlan Campbell of
the Scottish island of Islay. Kitty's uncle Donald Campbell and
her brother John claimed kinship with the duke of Argyll and
with John Campbell, earl of Loudoun. John Murray, earl of
Dunmore, governor of New York in 1770-71 and then of
Virginia until the Revolution, was a friend of the family and a
kinsman of unspecified degree. Kitty's brother John traveled
from New York to Virginia with Lord Dunmore in 1771, and
Dunmore paid his tuition for three years at the College of
William and Mary.[6]

Kitty and her mother visited Virginia in 1769 and 1770.
Charles Steuart of London, a friend of the Eustaces, had
paved the way for them. One of the people he had written to
introduce them was his business associate James Parker of
Norfolk. On 20 October 1769 Parker wrote Steuart: "Mrs.
Eustace is here. In the Words of Zachry Boyd, she has the gift
of the Gab. Miss Kitty is Clever but I think Rather Forwd. I
see the Randy as plain as if I had been by yr side, & the

description Comes so fully to my idea that I was highly diverted with it."[7]

In August 1770 Mrs. Parker wrote Steuart that "Mrs. Eustace and her pretty daughter" were among those sending him their compliments, that they proposed spending the summer and autumn in Norfolk, and that "they are really two very agreeable ladies." Her husband was less complimentary when he wrote Steuart in May 1771: "Kitty Eustace, the chip which you forwarded to this country, is to be married immediately after the General Court to Doctor Blair. There's a club of all our women out at Kemp's Landing fixing the riggin'. I think the doctor will marry more than one, not that I entertain a thought of Kitty's being concerned in any contraband trade, but the mother and her must go together. She's a clever managing sort of a lady and has played her cards exceeding well."[8]

The marriage broke up at once. Kitty left Dr. Blair's home and "removed to another house, but not 100 paces off," where Mrs. Eustace took lodgers. Kitty brought a suit against Dr. Blair, variously described subsequently as a suit for specific performance of a premarital agreement, as a suit for separate maintenance, and as a suit for alimony. The matter was referred to arbitration. Mrs. Blair's claim was denied, perhaps in the hope, as John Randolph said later, that a reconciliation would be forced.[9]

A reconciliation was almost a necessity from the Eustaces' point of view. Their circumstances were clearly modest. Denied separate maintenance and with divorce legally unavailable, Kitty faced a bleak future unless she could repair her marriage. An attempt to repair it was made after the April 1772 General Court. Parker reported to Steuart on 25 May that Dr. Blair, his wife, his mother-in-law, and his sister were among the guests at a dinner given by the governor. Parker continued:

A most damnable fuss has been at Williamsburg with Dr. Blair and his rib. Nothing was talked of but separation. Matters were painted blacker than they really were, and she is acquitted of everything but not allowing him to have a fair chance ever since they have been married. By the prudent counsel of Dr. [Archibald] Campbell [of Norfolk] they are seemingly reconciled and she was to let him make a push the night we left the Court. Common report says she is not capacious enough, but he has different instruments, and amongst them lie it.[10]

On 12 June Parker wrote again: "There's nothing yet done at Williamsburg in Kitty's case. We thought the matter was entirely settled at the last arbitration, but it seems she jumped out of bed and would not do anything. I shall advise the next time I see him to lay a young whore in the bed beside her that she may see what he requires of her. There never was such a piece of work. Her thing is talked of all over the country."

Letters preserved by St. George Tucker pick up the story here. Tucker, a recent immigrant from Bermuda, was only twenty years old in 1772 and a student at William and Mary. He was a nephew by marriage of Dr. Campbell and was lodging at Mrs. Eustace's house.[11] He thus found himself in the midst of Kitty's marital problem. The earliest relevant document among Tucker's papers is Kitty's letter of 18 July 1772 to Dr. Blair's sister Anne. Kitty addressed her as "My dearest Nanny, the sister of my Heart." The letter includes Kitty's admission that she had not married for love. She said:

> The little pains your Brother took to be ascertained of my Affection before Marriage, is too well known to you all and as I knew it was perfectly agreeable to the best of parents, & that I loved & valued your family one and all of them, at the same time no particular Objection to your Brother—nor no partiality in Favor of any other person in my mind—I had no reason to doubt that Gratitude, and Esteem for the Affection he had for me would enable me to discharge the most rigid Duties of a good wife—when that accursed Letter which fell into my Hands the Evening after blasted every sanguine wish of your Friend.[12]

"The accursed letter," which Kitty's letter does not further describe, was an anonymous note to Mrs. Eustace saying: "I have believed & Experience will confirm it that Doctor Blair is incompetent." When Kitty said that it fell into her hands "the Evening after," she must have meant the evening after the attempted reconciliation in April. Mrs. Eustace, subsequent correspondence tells us, had shown the letter to Tucker, and he had advised her that she should consider it the work of a meddler, intended to prevent the reconciliation then under way.[13]

Kitty continued: "Forgive me when I tell you there were too many Circums[tance]s in y[ou]r Br[other]s Manner of Conduct, that seem'd a confirm[atio]n of the Charge ag[ains]t him wh. chased from my Heart that Esteem I shou'd otherwise have felt for him." Doubtless aware that the public blamed her for the separation, Kitty told Anne, "I have as much Sensibility as your Brother, and . . . I have suffered as much & deserved it as little. I have received Indignities I would not if I might inflict from cruel & hard hearted Strangers. But notwithstanding, I have as many weekly speaking Testimonies of worthy Hearts bleeding for my Distress as he can boast, and nothing shall tempt me to take upon myself a Guilt my Heart does not accuse me of." Up to this point, she declared, she had not disclosed the reasons for her conduct, "which if they cannot wholly exculpate me, will at least be some Excuse."

Nevertheless, with the help of time, Kitty had brought herself to the resolution to resume her marriage. She told Anne (who had recently returned from a trip to Baltimore):

As his Conduct to me has been uniformly tender since Marriage I resolved from the Time you left Williamsburg to cherish every grateful Thought on that Theme, 'till my Heart was softened towards him, from which Event only I could have the Power of giving or receiving Happiness. This, and this only has been my Reason for deferring a final Reunion. . . . The Time is now arrived in which I can assure you with Truth, that your Brother nor any of his Family shall have no just Cause to complain of me for the future and nothing I more ardently wish than an affectionate Embrace from one & all of them which will be most sincerely return'd by me.

The reunion was delayed by Dr. Blair's absence from Williamsburg and by his illness (a recurrence of his 1770 ailment?). During this period, Kitty said to her mother, "If a reunion does not take place it is not my fault." Mrs. Eustace understood Kitty to mean that the reunion was contingent on his recovery and reported this comment to Dr. Campbell, who relayed it to Dr. Blair. After his recovery, when those three were together, Dr. Blair gave Dr. Campbell one hand and Mrs. Eustace the other. She interpreted this gesture to mean that all was well.[14]

Fate intervened, however. Dr. Blair not only learned of the anonymous letter but heard that Mrs. Eustace had shown it to others. He demanded to know with whom she had discussed it. She replied: "I never made a Confidant but of one Lady [Anne Blair?] & Dr. Campbell, who you yourself first informed long before I was from you acquainted with your Sentiments. Mr. Tucker who had his first intelligence f[ro]m the World I have often talked to on the odious Subject; after them both let Dr. Campbell too produce my Letters." Dr. Blair wrote a stiff letter to St. George Tucker, quoting Mrs. Eustace and saying, "I presume that I am to ask you among others what passed in the frequent Conversations you have had with Mrs. Eustace relative to the odious Subject; and that you may be at no Loss to understand what that is, I will tell you that the odious subject here referred to is neither more nor less than a Question concerning my Virility."[15]

Tucker's evasive reply of 20 September did not mention the "odious subject," probably because he knew that Dr. Blair was about to receive a copy of the "accursed letter." Kitty had asked Tucker to make a copy for Dr. Blair or to have a copy made by someone else. He tried to get William Gwatkin, his mentor at William and Mary, to make the copy, but Gwatkin declined.[16] Tucker refused to make the copy himself, on the ground that the one who made the copy might be suspected of being implicated in the writing of the original. Apparently Tucker and Kitty then agreed on a way around that difficulty. He wrote Dr. Blair on 24 September, saying that Mrs. Eustace had requested his permission to tell Dr. Blair that he was one of the persons to whom she had shown the anonymous letter. He said he thought he could quote the letter practically verbatim, and proceeded to do so.

Thus ended all hope of reconciliation. On 18 November Parker wrote Steuart: "Matters are now come to an open rupture at Williamsburg. A suit is commenced by Mrs. B. for a separate maintenance." Apparently Dr. Blair had heard a rumor of misconduct between Governor Dunmore and Kitty and had written an accusatory letter to Dunmore. Dunmore called John Blair, Jr., before him, denied the charge, and said that unless Dr. Blair retracted it, his brother should resign as clerk of the governor's council. Dr. Blair backed down. "So the matter stands," continued Parker. "The old lady persists her daughter is still a maid, and that the Dr. never has and indeed cannot do as a man should do. For my own part, I was once of the side that blamed Kitty. I have now altered my opinion."

On 25 November Jefferson noted in his account book:
"Catherine Blair wife of James Blair M. D. (Wmsbgh) v. the
sd. James Blair. A bill in Chancery for a specific performance
of the condn. of a bond which was to give her half the estate
of def. Empld. by def. if it should be brot on again." It was
probably at this time that Jefferson was asked to look into the
possibility of a divorce.

Dr. Blair died 26 December 1772 at the Albemarle home of
his uncle Dr. George Gilmer. His will made no provision for
Kitty. In that circumstance a widow was entitled under Virginia law to dower, that is, a life interest in a portion of her
husband's property.[17] In February 1773 Parker wrote Steuart:
"Doctor Blair has very opportunely taken his departure for
the other world, by which 'tis to be hoped Kitty's case will be
helped. She'll get his dowry at all events." He wrote again in
May: "Madam Eustace with her maiden widow daughter is still
at Williamsburg. They refuse to give her dower. There is a
suit for it in James City Court. I do not see upon what principles they withhold it from her. I think 'twould be best to give
them something and let them decamp."[18]

The James City County court denied Kitty's claim for
dower, and she appealed to the General Court. She was represented there by Randolph and Henry, Dr. Blair's estate by
Pendleton and Mercer. The case was argued and decided on 3
November 1773. Jefferson, who had been retained by the estate before the case reached the General Court, did not participate in the oral argument. We do not know why. However,
he probably assisted in the preparation of Pendelton's argument.[19] In any event, he was in court when the case came
up and wrote a detailed account. The Randolph and Pendleton presentations are reported fully, while the Henry and
Mercer arguments are summarized in a few lines each. Jefferson said of Henry that "he avoided, as was his custom, entering the lists of the law, running wild in the field of fact."[20]

In an introductory review of the facts, Jefferson's report
asserts that the marriage had not been consummated and continues: "The evidence was voluminous and indecent. That of
the defendant tended to prove on the complainant original
hatred, ill-temper, disobedience, refusal of conjugal rights, departure not without some hint of adultery, that of the complainant to fix on Dr. Blair impotence and hidden causes of

disgust, and it was difficult to say on which side the evidence preponderated. The suspicions of adultery were with Lord Dunmore, who, presiding at the court at the hearing of the cause, might be the reason why those suspicions were not urged." Pendleton argued for the defense that dower was a perquisite of marriage, and since there had been no consummation (a fact admitted by both sides), there had been no marriage.

On the day after the argument, Mrs. Eustace wrote to her friend Thomas Burke:

> Yesterday . . . my dear Kitt's law suit was determined in her favor with every person of the court but one the professed slave of Miss [*sic*] Blair with Lord Dunmore at their head. . . . The great Pendleton abashed, confused, in a state remarked by all of almost total stupefaction, and what he said so little to the purpose that he lost credit as well as cause. Not so my worthy friend Henry. He, they say, shined in the cause of justice backed by the law.
>
> The Attorney General insisted on opening the cause. . . . He did so in so masterly a manner that everyone says he outdid his usual outdoings and pled to it four hours, then seconded by Mr. Henry. . . . All is settled respecting lands, negroes, money and the rest of the personal estate.

Kitty herself wrote Burke a year later. She signed herself "C. Blair" and wrote beneath the signature, "How long I shall be distinguished by this name I can't positively say."[21]

Kitty continued to live in Williamsburg until she married Maj. Seth John Cuthbert of Georgia in February 1777.[22] She was back in Williamsburg in June for an entertainment, however, where she "made the best Appearance as a Dancer."[23] Whether then or later, her second marriage seems to have run into trouble. Cuthbert married again, apparently during Kitty's lifetime. His second wife was Mary Clay Cuthbert, by whom he had two sons, one born in 1785 and one in 1788. He died in Savannah in September 1788. A notice in the *Georgia Gazette* the following April said his widow, Mary Cuthbert, and Joseph Clay, Jr., had applied for letters of administration. Kitty seems to have died about the same time. A notice in the *Georgia Gazette* for 13 November 1788 said Margaret Eustace of Chatham County, Georgia, presumably Kitty's mother, had made application for letters of administration on the estate of

"Catherine Cuthbert (formerly Catherine Blair)." Unless Kitty had been dead for four years or more, which seems unlikely, it would seem that Cuthbert's sons were born during her lifetime. An 1802 digest of all Georgia laws passed from 1755 to 1800 lists eight legislative divorces but none for Cuthbert or Kitty.[24]

With this background in place, we turn to Jefferson's notes on divorce. As is so often true of Jefferson manuscripts, they bear no date. They must have been prepared between 25 November 1772, when Dr. Blair retained Jefferson to represent him if Mrs. Blair renewed her claim for separate maintenance, and 26 December of that year when Dr. Blair died. Jefferson had returned to Albemarle from Williamsburg after the October General Court and was there during most of November and December. It seems clear that the notes on divorce were written at Monticello and that the research was done in Jefferson's own library.[25]

Jefferson must have known that the chance of obtaining a legislative divorce for Dr. Blair was slight. There was no Virginia precedent for a divorce, even on the ground of adultery,[26] and proving adultery was out of the question. The problem, therefore, was to persuade the General Assembly to follow Parliament's practice in granting a divorce by special act, but to grant it on grounds that Parliament had never recognized.[27]

In the notes can be perceived the outline of the case Jefferson would have made to the assembly. As in his great argument three-and-a-half years later for dissolution of another kind of union, the presentation would have been based primarily on natural law, which Baron Samuel von Pufendorf defined as "that most general and universal Rule of human Actions, to which every Man is obliged to conform, as he is a reasonable Creature."[28]

Pufendorf's treatise, *The Law of Nature and Nations,* is the work most frequently mentioned in Jefferson's notes. First published in Latin in 1692, it was a prodigious collection of learning on a broad range of subjects, including marriage and divorce, the topic of book 6, chapter 1. The French translation of 1707 by Jean Barbeyrac, a Huguenot jurist in exile, was crammed with additional notes by the translator, and subsequent editions of the 1703 English translation by Basil Kennet incorporated the Barbeyrac annotations. Both the French translation and the 1749 edition of the English version were in Jefferson's library in 1815.[29]

Jefferson cited Pufendorf more than twenty times, but his reliance on that authority was even greater than this number indicates. Pufendorf must be credited with some notes for which no citations are given, and even with some for which other references are cited without mention of Pufendorf. It is very unlikely that Jefferson, in the limited time available, read all the books he cited,[30] though it seems clear that he read, in addition to Pufendorf, at least Locke, Hume, and Montesquieu. Even though Locke is cited in one or more Barbeyrac footnotes to Pufendorf, Jefferson's references to Locke demonstrate an independent reading; and Hume and Montesquieu wrote after Pufendorf and Barbeyrac had completed their work.

Did Jefferson get his references to Milton from Pufendorf, or did he read Milton himself? Pufendorf gave considerable space to the Miltonian arguments for divorce, though he disparaged them. Some of the notes attributed to Milton seem to paraphrase Pufendorf's summary rather than Milton's text, but others indicate direct access to Milton, even though one may doubt that Jefferson had time to read and absorb Milton's essays on divorce in their wordy entirety. Jefferson's 1815 library included Milton's prose works.[31]

What were Jefferson's sources for the notes under the heading "Scriptural"? He cited Pufendorf twice; and he could have found in Milton the argument that "fornication," in Christ's prohibition against divorce except for fornication, was a word of much broader scope than "adultery"; but neither Pufendorf nor Milton used the Greek New Testament word that the King James version translated as "fornication."[32] Jefferson did. Milton is said to have gotten his argument from John Selden's *Uxor Ebraica* (1646), a work never published in English. Selden apparently used the Greek word. Did Jefferson read Selden's book, which was written in Latin said to be "tortuous enough to keep the unscholarly reader at a safe distance"? Jefferson's 1815 library contained a copy of Selden's complete works in Latin.[33] Or was Jefferson's knowledge of Greek sufficient to enable him to embroider the Miltonian argument himself? The same questions arise concerning his use of the Greek and Latin equivalents of the Old Testament word that the King James version translates as "uncleanness."

Nor does Jefferson tell us where he got the material on the Prussian law of divorce. His source may have been a two-volume work, published in English in 1761, on the Frederician Code, the body of laws attributed to Frederick the Great. Jefferson's 1815 library included these volumes.[34]

None of Jefferson's sources supported his case in its entirety. Pufendorf was noncommittal; after setting forth Milton's arguments at length, he observed, "But these Matters we leave undetermin'd, as not tending directly to our main purpose."[35] Milton was a dubious ally; he argued for a return to the Mosaic law that permitted a husband to discard a wife practically at will, without even having to go to court. Hume, while willing to consider the subject apart from biblical authority, concluded that monogamy without the possibility of divorce was the best of alternatives. Locke, who held that marriage was dissoluble under the law of nature, was not very helpful where the real world was concerned.[36] Montesquieu clearly favored divorce where both parties consented but was somewhat vague about divorce over the wife's objections, which he called "repudiation." Jefferson had to manufacture his own argument from the grist supplied by these sources.

Blair v. Blair. On a bill of Divorce to be
proposed to the General assembly[37]

Arguments:Pro[38]
Cruel to continue by violence an union made at first by mutual love, but now dissolved by hatred. Hu. ess. To chain a man to misery till death.

Liberty of divorce prevents and cures domestic quarrels. ib.
Preserves liberty of affection. ib. (which is natural right).

End of marriage is Propagation & Happiness. Where can be neither, should be dissolved. Should add Education.

Since procreation, education, & inheritance taken care of, no necessity from nature of thing to continue the society longer, but it may be made at the time of contracting dissoluble by consent, at a certain time, or on certain conditions as other compacts. Locke. 265.[39]

Moral obligation on Man to propagate. Puff. B. 6. c. 1, 2, 6, 7.

Nature has excited the appetite, God has forbidden a meretricial gratification—he therefore enjoins a new marriage.

Private desires of an heir &c.

Constant residence & admission of copulation is implied in the covenant.[40]

Scripture commands to put away all obstacles to piety. Milton.[41]

Permitted to cure disorders of body, why not this greatest of the mind[?] Milton.[42]

Nature of covenants

    Where both parties consent, must be dissoluble from nature of things. Qu. if children have not negative?

    So where one party breaks it essentially. Puff. 6.1.20, 21. And he makes base desertion an essential breach.

    So also obstinate unkindness in the affair of the bed. ib. 21. So adultery. ib.

    Sterility is not.[43]

    Enormous violation of inferior duties, as of Comfort, Assistance, Protection &c is sufficient cause, proves it by right of father to discard undutiful son.[44]

    Physical disability, as Castration, good cause of dissolution. ib. 25.

    Moral inability, as praecontract, consanguinity, affinity.

While continue man & wife, law of England will make her children, his.[45]

No partnership can oblige continuance in contradiction to it's end and design.[46]

Marriage is a Moral union, but that can not be where the minds are directly opposite, admitting no possibility of union. The bond is broken. Milton.

Arguments:Con

What is to become of children—divided? To stepmother or stepfather? Their education would be neglected.[47]

We are formed to submit readily to Necessity, and soon lose inclination which we know is impossible to be gratified. ib.

Frivolous quarrels will be avoided, or forgotten, when a necessity of making up again, whereas would be inflamed to hatred, if prospect of easy separation. ib.

Danger of uniting two interests so closely, if they may be ever separated. "Pilfring temper of a wife." ib.[48]

When divorces most frequent among Romans, marriages were most rare. ib.

Man may get wife at any age—woman cannot when the charms of youth are gone.[49]

Mixture of fortunes. How to be divided?

When 2 have become joint traders for life, neither can take

his stock out without consent of other. Woolt. Sect. 8.3. (But what if both consent[?])[50]

Impolitic to allow divorce on consent of parties.

Danger of adulteries by the parties having private correspondence after their 2d marriage to another, which their former intimacy would readily produce.[51]

Scriptural

I. Cor. 7.15. "If the unbelieving depart, let him depart.["] And here St. Paul, after saying Unbelief is no cause of divorce, sais Departure is. See Puff. 6.1.21, note ([*illegible*]). The word "bound" v. 15. is explained v. 39.

Deut. 24.1-5. allows divorce "if the wife find no favor in his eyes["]?

Jerem. 3.1-8. implies that Adultery is cause.

Matt. 5.31.32. Whoso putting away his wife, saving for fornication &c.   19.3-12. "Except it be for fornication" &c.

Mark 10.2-12. Whosoever putteth away his wife committeth adultery. This is answered by shewing the word πορνειη[52] signifies among the Helenistic Jews every vicious & dishonest action. Puff. 6.1.24. note (3.). (Answer to ασχημον πραγμα in Deut. 24.) Again the question to St. Paul, I. Cor. 7, and his answer shews adultery not the only cause of divorce.[53]

Obj. Moses allowed it for hardness of hearts.

Ans. Is it consistent with power of god to allow what he does not approve[?] Again are the Jews alone hard of heart?[54]

Miscellaneous Observations

In begetting children parties bound by nature to provide till they can provide for themselves. This done, no being can reproach him with injury in dissolving marriage, unless the other party, and that must depend on nature of his particular contract. Hume's ess.

Restores to women their natural right of equality. Cruel to confine Divorce or Repudiation to husband who has so many ways of rendering his domestic affairs agreeable, by Command or desertion, whereas wife confined & subject.[55]

Divorce is where both parties consent, Repudiation where only one. Montesq. S. L., L. 16. C. 15.[56]

Nature of matrimonial compact is such a right in one another's bodies as is necessary to Procreation, a mutual support and assistance, & such a communion of interests as is necessary to provide for children till can provide for themselves. Locke. 262.[57]

The several convenants for propagation, Comfort, assistance, protection &c so closely interwoven that when one is broke they naturally fall asunder. Puff. 6.1.22. Therefore he sais should be no such thing as a divorce a mensa et thoro, because of injury done to the innocent party.

Marriage never declared indissoluble till by the Popes, who made marriage a sacrament, and so took cognizance of it to themselves. Puff. 6.1.23. & note (2.).

Miscellaneous Practices of several Nations.

In Tonquin the Sailors marry for the season, and wives faithful & oeconomical. Hu. ess.[58]

So do the Dutch in Japan. Puff. 6.1.20.

Antient Britons, (i.e., Celts) would join in societies of 10. or 12. and hold their wives & children in common. ib. Caesar. Bell. Gall. L. 5. c. 14.[59]

In Athens on extraordinary loss of Citizens, each man was allowed 2. wives to repair loss. ib., Puff. B. 6. c.1, 16.

Among brutes. Where food furnished with ease to the offspring, the present embrace terminates the marriage, as in domestic fowls, & viviparous animals who feed on grass and nourish the young from the teat—but where food more difficult, the union continues till the young able to get it, as in fowls in general, and in beasts of prey whose young feed on prey. Hu. ess, & Locke gov. 263.[60]

Tho' there was liberty of Divorce to the Romans, it was never used till by Carvilius Ruga, 520 years after city, who repudiated his wife for sterility. Valer. Max. B. 2. c. 1.—Dion. Hal. L. 2.[61]

Romulus's law permitted Repudiation in 3. cases—it was permitted in all other cases, the man giving ½ his substance to the woman, the other ½ to Ceres, to which terms Carvilious submitted. This was the law till the 12. tables, which extended the causes & power of repudiation, being taken from Greece. Montesq. L. 16. c. 16.

Laws of the Maldives permitted the repudiated wife to be taken again—those of the Mexicans forbad it on pain of death. Montesq. L. 16. c. 15.[62]

Custom of the Amazons to copulate at certain times, & then return home dissolving the alliance. Justin.[63]

Among the Jews, Consummation as well as consent requisite to compleat marriage. Seld. L. 4. C. 4. Puff. B. 6. c. 1, 14.

Among the same, as well as other people, polygamy allowed.

Among the Turks is a kind of marriage called Kabin, where parties agree on the fixt time of separation, securing to the woman a sum of money on dismission. Puff. 6.1.20. note (5.).

Among Jews, obstinate refusal of embraces was remedied by an action of law, which compelled them. Selden, de Ux. Hebraica, L. 3. C. 6. 7. Montaigne's ess. L. 3, c. 5. Puff. 6.1.21. Hence perhaps our suit for Restitution conjugal rights.

Jews forbidden to take a wife again after putting her away. Deut. 24.4. Intended to prevent frequent divorce by cutting off all future hopes of reunion. Qu. from Jerem. 3.12. if m[igh]t not be taken back before a new marriage.

Canon & Civil law forbid a marriage between the repudiated party and the Adulterer or Adulteress, and so also the Jewish law. Puff. 6.1.27. & notes.

Causes of Divorce among several nations.[64]

Adultery, preparing poison, falsifying keys, by Romulus, but this only in favor of men, not women.[65]

Consent mutual among Romans. Puff. 6.1.20. note (3.). So also Assassination, forgery of wills, sacrilege, thieving, harboring robbers, woman going to feast with strangers without consent of husband, her lying abroad without good reason, going to plays, husband beating wife. L. of Theod. Lib. 5. Tit. 17. Lib. 8. Puff. 6.1.22. note (2.).[66]

Jews. Force, Fear, Mistake of person or other essential object, want of virginity, if hid, cause of Divorce. Puff. 6.1.5.

Deut. 24. allows the husband to write a bill of divorcement "if she find no favor in his eyes because he hath found some uncleanness in her." ασχημον πραγμα. ασχημον is forma carens, i. e. irregular, indecent.

Barrenness cause among Jews. Philo Judaeus. Puff. 6.1.23. and Jer. 3:1-8. implies as much.[67]

If a man falsely reported his wife proved not a virgin, she might depart, among the Jews. Puff. 6.1.23.

Among Jews two sects, Sammeans, & Hillelians: former held Divorce lawful only for Baseness & Dishonesty, latter for any dislike. Puff. 6.1.23. Seld. Ux. Heb. L. 3. c. 22.[68]

Among Christians, by Milton an intolerable disposition, or contrariety of mind is sufficient cause. Puff. 6.1.24.[69]

Prussia[:] these are causes of divorce

Want of consent

as if party had not use of reason, which includes man drunk.

compulsion by parents.

not seriously done.

Error as to person

Error as to condition, as if party were not free.

Non-age.

Want of consent by parents &c.

Praecontract.

Consanguinity.

"Not *fit* for marriage" & the other ignorant of it.

Not of the three religions tolerated.

Mutual consent before a judge.

Death natural or civil or either.

Enmity supervening

    1. from cruelty or ill language.

    2. from discovery of bad character.

Adultery.

Disease, as Lues veneris, Epilepsy, Leprosy, or other contagious malady where other party had no knolege of it.

Loss of reason for 2. years, subsequent or precedent to marriage if not known at time.

Ceasing to be fit for marriage after espousals.

Loss of hand, arm or foot, so that cannot get subsistence, and other dependence.

Pretending wealthy where person is in truth in Debt, or that he is noble, or of same religion.

England before 4. Jac. 1[70]

A Mensa et Thoro

Adultery. Moore 683.[71]

Cruelty. Cro. Jac. 364.[72]

Perpetual disease. 3. Bl. 94.[73]

Consequence

Alimony or Estovers if actually separated but not if they cohabit or if she elope, in which case loses dower if Commits adultery. Or be maintained by the husband.

A Vinculo matrimonii

Consanguinity or Affinity.

Marriage cum Judais Pecorantibus et Sodomitis. This also felony and to be burnt alive. 3 Inst 89[74] But qu. if cause of Divorce?

Frigidity before marriage, after 3. years trial and consummation.

Praecontract.

Consequences, loss of Dower, & Illegitimacy of children.

By act of parliament for Adultery. 1 Bl. 441.

8

Professional Ethics and
Conflict of Interest

Written codes of ethics for lawyers are a twentieth-century development fostered by the American Bar Association. Local rules tend to follow the ABA standards, though they vary in detail.[1] There is a sufficient consensus to permit some generalizations as to what sort of conduct today's standards permit.

Though comparable guidance was not available to the colonial lawyer, conflict of interest was recognized as a danger to be avoided. For example, Peyton Randolph, when attorney general of Virginia, withdrew as prosecutor when his wife's first cousin, John Chiswell, was indicted for murder.[2] Of course, the notion of conflict of interest had not developed to anything like its present-day sophistication. It must be remembered that the legal profession in colonial Virginia had only recently achieved the status of an honorable calling.

In the seventeenth century, American lawyers were held in low esteem. The Massachusetts Bay Colony forbade practicing law for monetary reward, and Virginia vacillated between prohibition and regulation.[3] Prohibition prevailed from 1682 to 1715 but apparently was not strictly enforced. In 1715 the governor's council took steps to reestablish regulation, finding that "divers persons take upon themselves to practice as Attorneys in the Courts of this Colony without being qualified with a sufficient knowledge in the Laws nor having that Integrity which is requisit for such an imployment."[4]

In 1732 the Virginia legislature reassumed jurisdiction of the profession. Finding that "the number of unskillful attorneys, practicing at the county courts, is become a great grievance to the country, in respect to their neglect and mismanagement of their client's causes, and other foul practices," it required all aspiring county court practitioners to be examined for competence. The 1732 statute was repealed in 1742, but a very similar statute, with an almost identical preamble, was enacted in 1745 and remained in effect throughout the rest of the colonial period.[5]

About the time that the Virginia council and legislature were decrying the quality of county court lawyers, a different breed of lawyer was making its appearance in the General Court. Sir John Randolph and Edward Barradall were trained in England and admitted to the English bar. So were Jefferson's contemporaries, Sir John's sons, Peyton and John Randolph, Thomson Mason (brother of George), and John Blair, Jr.[6] His American-trained colleagues Robert Carter Nicholas, Edmund Pendleton, and George Wythe were no less able.

The obvious quality of these men brought about a remarkable change in the public's perception of lawyers. As Richard B. Morris said of American lawyers generally, "The kind of training that college-bred lawyers were bringing to the bar, along with their impressive social credentials, contributed to the elevation of the entire profession as the eighteenth century advanced, and explains the emergence of lawyers as important figures in politics."[7] But the colonial bar as a respectable profession was still in its infancy, and not surprisingly, lawyers' behavior sometimes fell short of modern standards.

Today's standards, for example, require that a claim or defense be put forward in good faith. Present-day authority would disapprove of the petitions for lapsed lands in *Donaghe* v. *Leeper* (CB 310, 311), brought by Jefferson "(tho' no cause) in order to bring the def. into the country and give pl. an opportunity to arrest him."[8] It would criticize his appearance for the defendant in *Waterson* v. *Allen* (CB 800) "to keep it off as long as we can in hopes that the pl. may run away." It would frown on Jefferson's announced intention in *Hyneman & Co.* v. *Fleming* (CB 396) to "appear for def and protract the matter. He acknowledges the debt" or in *Bland* v. *Fleming* (CB 203) to "appear for defs merely for delay."[9]

In those days a party to a lawsuit was not allowed to testify. If a person was expected to be a hostile witness, the plaintiff's lawyer might make him a defendant in order to make his testimony inadmissible. Jefferson's opponent did so in *The King* v. *Thorpe* (CB 37), as did Jefferson in a group of cases (CB 65-68) where his clients were suing constables of Buckingham County for wrongful arrest. The servant of one of the constables, Jefferson noted, "must be made a def. to take off his evidence."[10] Because today a party may be a witness, that particular tactic is obsolete; but comparable behavior surely would be censurable now.

Another action by Jefferson that would be condemned by modern legal ethics was warning his friend John Walker of the scheme by Jefferson's clients to bring proceedings against all land in Augusta County with imperfect titles.[11] Jefferson thus gave his friend an opportunity to protect himself against Jefferson's clients. Confidentiality of client information is at the heart of modern legal ethics. That Jefferson wrote the warning in Latin and in language that was cryptic even in translation suggests that he was uncomfortable about what he was doing and indicates that confidentiality was understood even then to be part of the lawyer's compact with his client.

Most of the discrepancies between Jefferson's behavior and modern ethical standards involved conflicting duties to two individuals—two prospective clients, a client and a former client, or two present clients. One of two opponents in a controversy consults a lawyer; then the other seeks to hire him. Can he take his choice? Jefferson would decline employment by the second party if he considered himself already committed to the first, either formally or informally. Thus in *Jameison* v. *Hubard* he was employed by Hubard, but "since I have some doubt whether Jameison may not expect me to do his business, the defendant promises to let me off if Jameison chuses it."[12] But if he felt he had made no commitment, he considered himself free to accept the second applicant.[13] Under modern standards he was probably wrong. A modern Virginia ruling says that a lawyer may not accept the second party without the consent of the first. A Massachusetts decision says he may or may not, depending on how deeply into the matter the first consultation went.[14]

Consider now the duty of a lawyer when he is approached by a new client seeking representation against a former client. The modern formulation is that the lawyer may not accept employment against the former client if there is a "substantial relationship" between the new representation and the old, unless the former client gives his fully informed consent.[15] Virginia applications of this principle hold, for instance, that a lawyer who has represented both husband and wife in drawing a property settlement cannot thereafter represent either one in a contested divorce proceeding.[16] On the other hand, if a lawyer has earlier drawn a will for one client, he can later defend a new client against a suit by the old one having no relation to the will.[17] The test is whether the earlier representation was apt to develop disclosure by the first client usable in the subsequent case.[18]

Jefferson was aware of a duty to former clients. In *Evans* v. *Kincaid* (CB 392), he brought a caveat on behalf of Thomas Evans against David Kincaid relating to 150 acres on Mechum's River. Evans prevailed. Two years later, he was asked to bring three caveats against Kincaid, this time on behalf of William Wood. Evans told Jefferson that one of the tracts was the one involved in the earlier case. "So," Jefferson noted in his case book, "proceed no further in this one."[19] On the other hand, he accepted a case from Ambrose Rucker although he had previously represented Rucker's opponent, Lucas, in a case involving the same land (CB 493), explaining, "Note this is consistent with my engagement to Lucas, tho' for the same land. Burford claims the land v Rucker, but Lucas claims over both, so by establishing Rucker's title, I set up no new adversary."[20]

Harrison v. *White* (CB 361) raises an interesting question regarding client loyalty. If one examined only the notes in Jefferson's case book, one would conclude that, having been hired in November 1769 to bring a caveat for Harrison, Jefferson abandoned Harrison in March 1770 and agreed to represent White. Such a switch of clients would clearly violate modern ethical standards. Jefferson's letter of 19 April 1769 to White shows, however, that Jefferson was acting for White seven months before Harrison sought his services.[21] Apparently Jefferson absentmindedly accepted Harrison as his client, forgetting about White's connection with the case, and corrected the mistake when it came to his attention. But was it proper to resume his representation of White, having represented Harrison in the same matter, however briefly? If Harrison's consultation with him had proceeded beyond the stage of small talk, it would seem that Jefferson would be barred under modern principles from representing either party.

Another instance where Jefferson's conduct seems to have

fallen short of modern standards of duty to a former client was *McLanahan's Case* (CB 926). McClanahan (or McLanahan) sought his opinion regarding a claim against Patrick Henry, alleging that Henry had improperly acquired title to land from John Shelton (father-in-law to both Henry and McClanahan). Jefferson wrote an opinion encouraging McClanahan to pursue his claim in the Augusta County court.[22] He had earlier represented Shelton and Henry in relation to title to the same land (CB 55-60).

A lawyer's duty to present clients is different from, and greater than, his duty to former clients. Modern ethical standards take a jaundiced view of any action adverse to a present client, even where there is no substantial relationship between the new representation and the old. It is in this area that Jefferson's behavior most often fell short of modern standards.

If Jefferson was representing a client in one case, he would decline employment by another person in a subsequent case if he considered it inconsistent with the earlier representation. In *Wilkinson* v. *Fitzpatrick* (CB 313) he brought a caveat on behalf of John Wilkinson against Joseph Fitzpatrick. While that case was pending, he was asked by John Fitzpatrick to bring a friendly caveat against Joseph Fitzpatrick involving the same land. He declined, saying, "Note I am emploied by Wilkerson in former caveat agt. this land, so cannot do anything here but as a friend. Recd. 11/ so return 2/9 after paying tax and fee for summ[ons]." In 1768 he brought a petition for lapsed lands on behalf of Daniel Smith against Robert Patteson (CB 78). Later his friend John Madison, Jr., asked him to enter a petition for the same land. He declined, "as I am emploied for Smith."[23] Jefferson's awareness of potential conflict of interest was further demonstrated in litigation involving William Nelson. Jefferson brought a caveat on Nelson's behalf for a tract of 11,267 acres (CB 419). A few days later he brought for Patrick Coutts a petition for lapsed lands that involved 9,267 acres of the same land (CB 432). Jefferson noted in his case book, "Mr. Nelson thinks himself not concerned in the 9,267, the rest being sufficient to secure him."

If the subject matter of the second case was unrelated to the subject matter of the first, however, Jefferson had no compunctions against suing one of his clients on behalf of a second client or defending a second client against a suit by the first client. Modern standards of client loyalty would forbid either.[24]

A less obvious conflict of interest is presented when a client has a pending case against a person and his lawyer thereafter accepts that person as a client in an unrelated matter in which the first client is not directly involved. Since Jefferson saw no objection to the more flagrant conflict of interest discussed in the preceding paragraph, he saw no objection here.

On 18 June 1768, for instance, George Wythe turned his caveat cases—eight in all—over to Jefferson. They included two in which John Buchanan, a prominent land speculator of Augusta County, was the client (CB 128, 129). Two days later Jefferson agreed to represent Buchanan "in all his caveat business" (CB 130). The fly in the ointment was that Jefferson already had two cases pending against Buchanan. He represented the defendants in *Buchanan* v. *Bowan* (CB 25), a caveat, and *Buchanan* v. *Rutherford* (CB 26), a petition for lapsed lands. The meager record affords no evidence that Jefferson's defense in those cases was affected by the Buchanan retainer. Buchanan won the petition, and the caveat was abated by his death. Nevertheless, modern ethical principles would frown on Jefferson's acceptance of Buchanan as a client while representing Bowan and Rutherford, albeit in unrelated matters, without their informed consent.

The prejudice to the first client is accentuated if the second client is a particularly important person.[25] There were three instances in Jefferson's practice in which he accepted General Court judges as clients when he already represented one or more of the judge's opponents in another matter. The judges were William Byrd III, Robert Carter III, and William Nelson.

William Herbert brought Jefferson three cases against Byrd in May 1768 and paid part of the fees. Two of the cases, *W. Herbert* v. *Ferrell* (CB 135) and *D. Herbert* v. *Ferrell* (CB 136), were for unpaid wages. The defendants were the administrators of John Chiswell, of whom Byrd was one. The third suit was against Byrd as surviving partner (the other three partners, Governor Fauquier, Speaker Robinson, and Chiswell, all having died) for money advanced and merchandise sold to the partnership. These cases were still pending when Jefferson turned over his practice to Edmund Randolph in August 1774. One month after accepting this business from the Herberts, Jefferson noted in his case book that "the Hon. Wm. Byrd retains me generally" (CB 122). As was his custom, Jefferson charged nothing for the retainer. Thereafter he represented Byrd in several matters for which bills were submited but, with one exception, not paid.

Charles Carter of Corotoman retained Jefferson in June 1770 to bring suit against Robert Carter in order to establish title to certain land. On 26 October 1770 Jefferson met with Robert Carter, who, according to Jefferson's 1770 account book, retained him "in his business." Jefferson's case book (CB 464) simply says, "Take no case against him." Jefferson charged Robert Carter nothing for this commitment, and Carter never brought him a case. Five days after his commitment to Robert Carter, Jefferson received a fee of £5 from Charles Carter. Apparently he saw no reason why he should not proceed with the case that had begun before the "retainer." The case was among those turned over to Edmund Randolph when Jefferson quit the practice in 1774.

In April 1768 William Nelson, Richard Corbin, and Benjamin Waller sued Francis Willis, Jr., a close friend of Jefferson's, for debt (CB 84). Jefferson represented Willis without charge, as he did in subsequent debt actions against his friend (CB 455, 456). In all likelihood no valid defense existed, since Jefferson noted in his account book, "Use every dilatory." In April 1774 the actions were dismissed. Probably some settlement had been effected. According to Emory Evans, debt cases taken to court at that time were generally settled for 50 percent of the debt.[26] In the meantime, Jefferson accepted business from William Nelson. In June 1770 he took the caveat case already mentioned. In August 1770 he accepted a commission to collect money from Nelson's debtors in Amherst County. He was to "attend at" Amherst Courthouse on the following January 7 to "give day to April on good assurance of paimt then" or to sue in General Court otherwise.[27] Jefferson did go to Amherst Courthouse the following January, although his 1771 account book does not mention his business for Nelson. No suits were brought for him thereafter in the General Court.

If the story of the Willis-Nelson representation ended there, it would be simply a repetition of the Byrd and Carter examples. What follows is more serious. On 17 October 1772 Jefferson noted in his account book that he had received £10 from Nelson "for attending his business in Willis' affairs." We are not given particulars. No doubt Jefferson thought he had served Nelson's interest without any lessening of zeal for his friend. Nevertheless, under modern standards, representing Nelson, and particularly accepting the payment from him, was improper unless Willis agreed to it.

In summary, Jefferson's concept of the duty to his present clients was very similar to the modern concept of duty to former clients. With few exceptions, he would not accept a new representation opposing another client if there was a substantial relationship between the new representation and the older one, but if the matters were unrelated, he felt free to accept the new one.

How shall we judge the ethical behavior of eighteenth-century lawyers as exemplified by Jefferson? Not by today's standards, of course. We must try to put ourselves in a setting in which the populace was litigious and the General Court bar very small—always less than ten lawyers. The modern rule requiring a lawyer to reject a potential client whose interest is not completely compatible with those of present clients presupposes that the potential client can easily find another equally capable lawyer with no incompatible interest. In other words, the modern rule is made possible by the high lawyer-to-client ratio that prevails today but did not exist in Jefferson's time.

The modern rule also rests on the assumption that conflicts are readily ascertainable, a reasonable assumption in these days of adequate records and filing systems. Jefferson's recollection of commitments depended on loosely organized handwritten notes, only some of which could be taken with him when he was away from home, as he most often was when consulted by a potential client. The result was that commitments were sometimes forgotten or temporarily overlooked.

What can be said about the ethics of eighteenth-century judges? In Virginia, judging was a part-time occupation and, except for some lawyers who sat on county courts, colonial judges were laymen. They all took two oaths, one as common law judges and one as chancery judges, and the essence of both was that they would judge with impartiality.[28]

Written codes of ethics for American judges are even more recent than written codes of ethics for lawyers. Canons of Judicial Ethics were first adopted by the American Bar Association in 1924, inspired by the moonlighting of federal judge Kenesaw Mountain Landis as salaried commissioner of baseball while retaining his judgeship. William Howard Taft was chairman of the drafting committee. Revised canons were adopted in 1972, based on the work of a committee headed by Roger Traynor, chief justice of the California Supreme Court. The 1972 canons were adopted by the Judicial Conference of the United States and by various states including Virginia, and the section of the canons regarding disqualification of judges was incorporated into the federal statute on that subject.[29]

Can a judge be impartial when his son is counsel for one of the contending parties? Patrick Henry's father presided over the Hanover County court that heard Henry argue the Parson's Cause.[30] John Blair, Sr., sat on the General Court that heard John Blair, Jr., argue the Norfolk anti-inoculation riot cases.[31] The Taft committee proposed to forbid a judge to hear the argument of a near relative, but the proposal was not incorporated in the 1924 canons because the chief judge of the Supreme Judicial Court of Massachusetts, among others, objected to it.[32] However, the 1972 canons finally adopted the principle that Taft had proposed half a century before.

A judge who has more than a trivial interest in the outcome of a case should disqualify himself. That principle was recognized in Virginia before Jefferson was born. Governor Spotswood wrote in 1714 that seven out of the twelve members of the General Court were so closely related to the Burwell family that they would go off the bench whenever a Burwell matter came before the court.[33] William Byrd III was not so sensitive. He sat on the governor's council that decided between two competing sites for the courthouse of Fincastle County. The council minutes disclose that he owned one of the sites, and his was selected.[34]

Nor was Governor Dunmore a model in this respect. He sat on the General Court when Mrs. James Blair sued Blair's estate for dower. Evidence for the defense hinted at Mrs. Blair's adultery, but as Jefferson wryly commented in his report of the case, "The suspicions of adultery were with Lord Dunmore, who, presiding at the court at the hearing of the cause,

might be the reason why those suspicions were not urged."
Whether he was guilty of adultery or not, Governor Dunmore
was hardly impartial. He was a kinsman of Mrs. Blair, and
Mrs. Blair's younger brother, John Skey Eustace, was his
protégé. When Dunmore moved from New York to Virginia,
John Skey Eustace traveled with the Dunmore family. At the
time of Mrs. Blair's suit, Dunmore was paying her brother's
expenses as a student at the College of William and Mary.[35]

Should a judge disqualify himself if he has publicly taken a
strong position on a question before his court? William Nelson
presided over the court that tried Dr. Archibald Campbell for
having family and friends inoculated against smallpox in his
home, although he had publicly stated that "if I had the power
I would hang up every man that would inoculate even in his
own house."[36]

Modern standards of judicial ethics would require Nelson to
disqualify himself. Canon 3C(1) says that a judge should not
sit in cases in which his "impartiality might reasonably be questioned . . . including instances where he has a personal bias or
prejudice concerning a party." Was Nelson biased against Dr.
Campbell, or was his anger directed at the practice of inoculation? If it was the former, the canon would clearly apply. If
the latter, the question is more complicated. Cases say that the
canon does not require a judge to step down simply because
he has expressed an opinion on the subject matter.[37] When the
expression is as violent as Nelson's, however, it seems clear
that his "impartiality might reasonably be questioned."

Ever higher standards of ethics for lawyers and judges reflect ever-increasing public sensitivity to the dangers posed by
conflicts of interest. The legal profession of today, faced with
more and more detailed written rules and volumes of official
interpretations of those rules, may look back with nostalgia to
Jefferson's time when the only guide to conduct was the individual's conscience. But if the choice has to be between too
much guidance and too little, we can learn from Jefferson's
experience: too much is better.

9

Financial Aspects of Jefferson's Practice

On 20 May 1773 Jefferson joined his General Court brethren John Randolph, Edmund Pendleton, James Mercer, Patrick Henry, and Gustavus Scott[1] in placing this exasperated notice in Purdie and Dixon's *Virginia Gazette:*

> The fees allowed by law, if regularly paid, would barely compensate our incessant labors, reimburse our expenses, and the losses incurred by neglect of our private affairs; yet even these rewards, confessedly moderate, are withheld from us, in a great proportion, by the unworthy part of our clients. . . . After the 10th day of October next we will not give an opinion on any case stated to us but on payment of the whole fee, nor prosecute or defend any suit or motion unless the tax, and one half the fee, be previously advanced, except those cases only where we choose to act *gratis.*

To this notice Thomson Mason appended an equally testy message: "The subscriber by no means disapproves of the above resolution, but as he has long determined to quit his practice as an attorney, and practice only as a counsel in such causes as are ready for trial, he has declined signing the above, as he shall not engage in any cause for the future but such in which he shall previously receive an adequate satisfaction for his trouble, which they may be assured will not be less than the legal fees." George Wythe was the only member of the General Court bar who was not a subscriber.

The problem that Jefferson and his colleagues faced was that a case might take years to complete—how long depended on the type of case and how far advanced it was when the lawyer was retained. On the one hand, the fee was not wholly earned until the work had been completed. On the other hand, it was unfair to the lawyer to defer all compensation for an indefinite period. A compromise clearly made sense. Requiring a down payment of half the fee at the time of employment offered some protection against the irresponsible client while giving the lawyer an incentive to complete the work.

Although it had been Jefferson's practice to debit the client with the full fee when he was retained, he apparently had had no policy before the notice of April 1773 about requiring a down payment. On rare occasions, he collected the full fee at the time he was retained. More often he was paid something on account, and most often he received nothing at that time. In fact, very often he advanced out of his own pocket the taxes and clerical fees that the client was supposed to pay to get the case started. According to the *Gazette* announcement, he would do so no more after 10 October 1773.

The *Gazette* notice spoke of "the unworthy part of our clients" who withheld payment. One of the prime offenders among Jefferson's nonpaying clients was his cousin George Jefferson, who retained him in two cases in 1769, one in 1770, two in 1771, two in 1772, and two in 1773 and never paid a shilling. Carter Henry Harrison, himself a lawyer, paid nothing for nine cases from 1768 to 1773. At the end of 1774 John Reid of Amherst still owed a balance of £17.10.0 on the twenty petitions for lapsed lands he brought to Jefferson in October 1770. Among those who had paid nothing against small amounts owed were Richard Bland, former governor Dinwiddie, and various merchant firms that were suing laggard debtors.

Jefferson should have anticipated that his experience in collecting from clients would be poor. He surely knew about John Mercer, who had advertised in Rind's *Virginia Gazette* of 19 February 1767: "The great number of debts due to me for the last seven years of my practice, and the backwardness of my clients (in attendance of whose business, I unhappily neglected my own) to make me satisfaction, would of itself, if I had had no other reason, have obliged me to quit my practice." Mercer said he was unable to pay his own debts and would be obliged to sue those who did not pay him by the end of the next General Court session. He went on to say that such legal work as he could do at home would be done only if paid for in advance.

Similarly Thomson Mason advertised in Purdie and Dixon's *Gazette* of 24 May 1770 that he would not undertake any work unless paid in advance by cash or interest-bearing bond. He continued, "With regard to those who, at the time they pretended to be my friends, could cooly sit still and see me reduced to the necessity of selling my slaves to a very great disadvantage, and yet withhold the small sums due me, which, if paid, would have removed that necessity, I leave it to their own hearts to determine whether they deserve any further indulgence." He concluded by saying that suit would be brought on any debts not promptly paid.

With this background, verified by his own experience, it is surprising that Jefferson indulged his clients so long. Even after 10 October when the more severe credit policy promulgated by the May *Gazette* notice went into effect, he did not consistently require the specified down payment.[2]

The notice in the *Gazette* referred to the "confessedly moderate" fees allowed by law. The law in question was the "Act for regulating the Practice of Attorneys," which provided in part: "Lawyers practising in the general court may demand or receive for an opinion or advice . . . one pound one shilling and sixpence, and in any suit at common law, other than the actions herein after mentioned, fifty shillings; in all chancery suits or real mixed or personal actions, where the title or bounds of land may come in question, five pounds."[3] Charging more "for any of the above services, before he has performed the said services, or finished the said suits" made the offender subject to a penalty of £50 for every offense.

The fees permitted were indeed moderate. The basic fee of fifty shillings for a common law suit was the same as had been fixed by law in 1718. Marie Kimball rightly said: "No man could make a fortune on that basis. Indeed, in view of the prevailing habit of a leisurely settlement of debts, it was difficult even to make a fair living."[4]

The statutory fee limits did not apply to all work a lawyer did. They did not apply, for instance, to miscellaneous out-of-court work, such as drawing a deed or will. Jefferson did not have much work of this kind, however, and his charges for such work were never more than fifty shillings.[5] Nor did the fee limits apply to caveats and other matters before the governor's council; whereas Jefferson's normal charge in these instances was fifty shillings, he did occasionally charge more.[6] Nor did the limits apply to ecclesiastical cases in the General

Court, such as *Carlyle* v. *Dade* (CB 204) and *Goodwin* v. *Lunan* (CB 510), since they were neither "suits at common law" nor chancery suits. For the same reason the fee limits did not apply to petitions for lapsed lands. Nevertheless, Jefferson's standard charge in these cases was fifty shillings. Finally, it is very doubtful whether the criminal cases known as pleas of the crown were "suits," though they were common law proceedings, but Jefferson debited his clients fifty shillings per case.

If there were several clients in a case to which the statutory limits applied, could their lawyer charge one fee for each client? If so, could he charge the total to one client, if that client were willing? Read literally the statute seems to limit the lawyer to a single fee, but Jefferson charged multiple fees in some cases, though not all, and in some cases he charged them all to one client.[7] The statute forbade a lawyer to charge a client for an opinion if a suit were brought or defended by the attorney who had given the opinion. Jefferson violated this prohibition in *Muir* v. *Dade* (CB 362), probably through oversight. Thereafter he observed the rule (CB 857, 881).

In many cases Jefferson accepted payments that exceeded his charges. He called such payments "gratuities." Were they legal? The statutory prohibition was against asking or receiving more than the legal fees before performing the services or finishing the suit. By inference, a lawyer could charge more than the statutory fee after the case was over. The following section of the statute prohibited the lawyer from suing for more than the statutory fee, but the intention seems to have been to allow a lawyer to take what the client was willing to pay after the services were performed. Grateful clients for whom Jefferson had won jury verdicts might want to pay something extra. So they did in *Tazewell* v. *Savage* (CB 111)[8] and *Carlyle* v. *Alexanders* (CB 404).[9] These were perfectly legal payments. So were the extra amounts Jefferson received for his opinions in *Campbell's Case* (CB 266), *Harper's Case* (CB 398), and *Jameison's Case* (CB 550).

In *Bolling* v. *Bolling,* Jefferson complied with the spirit if not the letter of the law. The gratuity was paid before the case ended but after Jefferson's services were completed as a practical matter. Jefferson and Wythe were opponents in a case before an arbitrator. They had made elaborate arguments in writing, set forth at length by Edward Dumbauld in his book *Thomas Jefferson and the Law.*[10] Jefferson's account book entry for 2 December 1770 says, "Finished it this day." Jefferson debited his client with the statutory fee of £5 at that time, but he collected £9.17.0 on 13 September 1771. What remained to be done in the case is not clear, but it was still on the chancery docket of the General Court in October 1772, perhaps awaiting confirmation of the arbitrator's decision.

In two instances Jefferson took gratuities in clear violation of the law. In *Hite* v. *Fairfax* (CB 152), Jefferson was assisting Wythe in defending Lord Fairfax, the proprietor of Virginia's Northern Neck, in a very complicated chancery suit regarding land rights of settlers on proprietary land. Jefferson debited Fairfax £5 on 13 October 1768. In April 1769 he received £10 and, in April 1771, £20 more. The case had not been concluded when the payments were made. Since the payments came through Wythe, it may be assumed that he received comparable payments.

Another such case is *Muir* v. *Dade* (CB 362). Muir, Jefferson's client, sued the Reverend Townshend Dade, the rector of Fairfax Parish, for libel. The action was at common law; the ecclesiastical jurisdiction of the General Court was not involved. Therefore, the most Jefferson could legally receive before the case was finished was £2.10.0 plus advances. Yet he received three payments aggregating £10.10.0, though the case was still unfinished when he turned it over to Edmund Randolph in 1774. John Randolph was associated with Jefferson in the representation of Muir and presumably received similar payments.

Was it legal to agree with a client, before the services were completed, that a fee exceeding the legal amount would be paid at the conclusion of the case? The statute forbade not only receiving more than the legal fee before the services had been performed but also "exacting" or "demanding" more. The question is troublesome, but Jefferson made such agreements (CB 405, 743).

He made contingent fee arrangements under which success would have paid off handsomely. The first such instance occurred in 1770 when Roger Thompson instructed Jefferson to institute a proceeding regarding certain land (CB 46). Jefferson was to receive 30 pistoles (slightly more than £32) if he won, nothing if he lost.[11] Unfortunately, Jefferson's records offer no further information about the matter. He took two other cases (CB 120, 589) in which he was to receive no fee if he lost and a large fee if he won—£30 and £20, respectively. He lost both. He took another batch of three cases (CB 357-59) in which he was to receive no fee if he lost and only the normal fee if he won. He lost all three.

The most unusual contingent fee arrangement was in *Carter v. Carter* (CB 522). Edward Carter, grandson of Robert ("King") Carter, owned 10,000 acres of entailed land in the Southwest Mountains of Albemarle County. He had Jefferson institute a friendly petition for lapsed lands. On the day Jefferson was retained, 22 March 1771, he noted in his account book, "This is an order to dock the entail of the lands, for which defendant is to give me as much of his nearest mountain as can be seen from mine, and 100 yards beyond the line of sight. Agreed before Capt. Wm. Burton." In his fee book Jefferson debited only his standard fee of £2.10.0 (plus 2s. 6d. advanced for tax). The normal way to dock an entail was by special statute. The use of a petition for lapsed lands for this purpose was probably novel, and it was unsuccessful. The petition was dismissed in April 1773, and Jefferson collected neither fee nor mountain.

When he strayed from the statutory scale, it was generally by charging less, not more, than the law allowed. In many cases, he made no charge at all. On four different occasions he defended his friend Francis Willis, Jr., in debt cases without charge.[12] Others receiving like favors included George Wythe and Francis Eppes, his wife's brother-in-law.[13] In several cases he acted gratis for persons alleging that they were being wrongfully held in slavery, and he charged nothing for representing other clients who, he was told, were poor.[14]

Jefferson charged nothing for general retainers, although they involved watching the docket repeatedly to see whether suits had been brought against the client. He would also watch the docket without charge for one who feared that a particular action might be brought against him and wanted Jefferson to represent him if it were. He charged nothing for cases taken over from George Wythe or John Blair, Jr., if Wythe or Blair had been paid.[15] He often charged nothing in one case if he had been paid in a previous case with some relation to the second.[16] In a caveat proceeding he charged no fee if he found that the land was patented.[17] Several times he charged less than a full fee without recording why.[18]

Jefferson's leniency toward his clients, plus the inability or unwillingness of clients to pay their bills, proved to be his undoing. His eight years of practice in the General Court were not financially rewarding. Henry S. Randall was wide of the mark when he said that "his average annual profits, for his whole term of practice, reached three thousand dollars,"[19] as was James Parton, who said that Jefferson doubled his estate in his years of practice.[20] Nathan Schachner was right when he observed that what Jefferson collected from clients was "certainly not enough to keep him in gentlemanly style without other sources of income."[21]

To see how he fared, we may turn to his fee book, a neat compilation in which he listed debits on the left-hand side, credits on the right. The debits represented legal fees plus advances for costs. The fees were generally standard amounts determined by the type of proceeding. With these in mind, one can readily separate a debit in a nonstandard amount into its fee and advance components. For instance, a debit of £2.12.6, a very common figure, indicates a fee of £2.10.0 (fifty shillings) and an advance by Jefferson to pay the tax of 2s. 6d. required to begin a lawsuit. A debit of £2.18.3 indicates a fee of £2.10.0, one advance of 2s. 6d. for the tax, and another of 5s. 9d. to pay the fee charged for a summons or subpoena. A debit of £3.4.0 indicates a fee of £2.10.0 plus one tax and two summons or subpoenas.

The first debit in the fee book is £3.4.0 debited to Gabriel Jones and dated 12 February 1767, when Jones brought the case to Jefferson. The lawyer's fee of £2.10.0 probably was debited on that date, but the case book shows that the advances of 14 shillings were made later, the last 5s. 9d. being advanced on 18 June 1768. This sort of evidence, with other data such as items out of chronological order and omission of items that should have been included, indicates that the fee book was not a record kept contemporaneously with the recorded events.[22] It seems to have been compiled, or copied from an earlier version, no earlier than 1770 and brought up to date periodically thereafter.

Jefferson computed profits by fiscal years ending 31 May.

He treated the period from the start of his practice to 31 May 1768 as the first fiscal year. Table 2 illustrates how he computed profits, using Jefferson's figures for his third fiscal year, 1 June 1769 to 31 May 1770. The arrangement of the figures is more orderly than Jefferson's in order to make the computation easier to follow, but the method is the same. Every shilling owed by clients was counted as profit, without any allowance for bad debts.

At the end of each of his first five fiscal years, he computed his profits for that year and total profits for the period of his practice. After the end of the calendar year 1772, he added a similar calculation for the last seven months of that year. Table 3 shows his figures. He did not make such computations for the calendar years 1773 and 1774. Table 4 shows what the results would have been if he had.

Table 2. Jefferson's profits from his law practice, 1 June 1769 to 31 May 1770

Charges to clients	
1. Fees booked during the year	£354.10.0
2. Advances (taxes and fees)	14. 7. 3
3. Total	368.17. 3
Payments by clients	
4. Paid on account	145. 9. 2½
5. Gratuities	16. 1. 0
6. Total	161.10. 2½
7. Increase in client debt (line 3 minus line 4)	223. 8. 0½
8. Net receipts (line 6 minus line 2)	147. 2.11½
9. Profits (line 7 plus line 8)	370.11. 0

Table 3. Jefferson's profits from his law practice, 1768–72

	Net receipts	Legal fees due*	Total profits
To May 31, 1768	£ 43. 4. 0¾	£250. 0. 5	£293. 4. 5¾
" 1769	71. 6. 0	233. 2. 5	304. 8. 5
" 1770	147. 2.11½	223. 8. 0½	370.11. 0
" 1771	213. 6.11	307.18.11½	521. 5.10½
" 1772	154.10. 8	126. 1. 4	280.12. 0
To Dec. 31, 1772	167.19.10½	181. 5. 4½	349. 5. 3
Total	797.10. 5¾	1,324.16.6½	2,119. 7. 0¼

*I.e., charges during the period less payments on account. In table 2 this figure is labeled "Increase in client debt."

Table 4. Jefferson's profits from his law practice, 1773–74

	Net receipts	Legal fees due	Total profits
1773	£222. 0. 9	£73.17. 6	£295.18. 3
1774	89. 3. 0	(40. 1. 3)*	49. 1. 9

*Receipts exceeded debits by the amount shown.

Table 5. Jefferson's profits from his law practice, 1768–74

Charges to clients	
1. Fees booked less fees remitted	£2,400
2. Advances	100
3. Total	2,500
Payments by clients	
4. Paid on account	1,100
5. Gratuities	100
6. Total	1,200
7. Owed by clients (line 3 minus line 4)	1,400
8. Net receipts (line 6 minus line 2)	1,100
9. Profits (line 7 plus line 8)	2,500

Table 5 shows for the eight-year period of his practice a computation similar to that made above for his third fiscal year, rounding off all numbers to the nearest £100.

When he turned over his unfinished business to Edmund Randolph in August 1774, Jefferson transferred to him the clients' balances on that business, roughly £500. If we were to accept the testimony of the fee book alone, we would conclude that net receipts of £1,100 and £900 of client debt remained as his reward for his eight years at the bar.

The fee book figures give a fairly accurate picture, but certain adjustments need to be made to complete it. For instance, the fee book records no payment by Thomas Mann Randolph, who hired Jefferson thirteen times in eight years and incurred thereby legal charges approximating £55 (Jefferson put the figure at £62.4.6 in the 1774 account book, but his figure seems high). An entry in his personal accounts (25 Feb. 1774) shows that when they settled up Jefferson was a net debtor, so his receipts should be adjusted upward accordingly. Another £23 of receipts during his practice that were not recorded in the fee book are identified in Appendix D. After December

1774, when the last entry in the fee book was made, his account books show that he collected approximately £25 of legal debts in 1775 and another £2 early in 1776. If there were any collections after war broke out, they could not have amounted to much. Even with these adjustments, his net receipts approximated only £1,200 for the eight years, from which he had to pay expenses.

If we were to eliminate the first two years as atypical, in that he was just getting started, and the last year because he was in the process of retirement, his adjusted net receipts would average about £200 a year, before deducting travel and other expenses.

So far we have been considering the net receipts as though they were cash in hand. Actually they included many items other than cash. Beginning in 1769, Jefferson apparently realized that some clients could not pay cash and that he had better take payment in other forms. Sometimes he accepted the obligation of a third party as payment.[23] Whether these substitute debts were paid in full we do not know. In other instances, he assigned a client's debt to one of his creditors or arranged with the client to pay the creditor[24] and credited the client. This sort of finance could get complicated. John Winn owed Jefferson a legal fee in a case that Patrick Henry had brought for his friend to Jefferson (CB 533), Jefferson owed money to Richard Sorrell, who owed Richard Davenport; Sorrell told Jefferson to pay Davenport. Davenport in turn owed Patrick Henry and told Jefferson to pay Henry. Jefferson arranged to have Henry apply Winn's fee against his own debt to Henry.

He also accepted property in lieu of cash. In May 1770 he accepted books in payment of Lewis Burwell's debt of £3.15.0. In February 1771 he credited Daniel Maupin 18s. for nine geese, and the following month he accepted an acre of land and six bushels of wheat in satisfaction of Robert Sharpe's debt of £2.18.3. In August 1771 he canceled Samuel Huckstept's debt of £5 "by part of price of a horse" and credited James Black £1 "by 2 fawns." In September 1772 he credited John Ford with 8s. 9d. "by 7 days hire of a horse," and a year later he allowed James Tremble a credit of £2.1.8 "by surveying my lands at Natural Bridge." In January 1774 he credited John Hylton with £3 "by 2 gross of bottles."

To sum up Jefferson's financial experience as a practicing lawyer, we can say that he operated under severe legal restrictions on fees that he generally observed, even when they did not strictly apply; that his departures from the statutory scale were, with few exceptions, on the lenient side; and that if his debtors had been forthcoming, he would have earned a modest living. But his debtors disappointed him, and if any earnings remained after he had paid his expenses, they were a meager reward for his labor.

10

The Court Closing of 1774
Jefferson's Opinion

On 12 April 1774 a Virginia statute that fixed the fees of various officials for specified services expired. The General Assembly was scheduled to meet early in May and was expected to reaffirm the existing fee schedule or to enact a new one. In the meantime the officials in question, including court clerks and sheriffs, continued to perform their duties. The semiannual session of the General Court was in progress when the fee bill expired. The court decided that it had the power to fix the fees of its officials and ordered that they should continue to be compensated at the rates established by the recently expired schedule.

Was the court's order valid? Jefferson thought not. In his view, only the legislature could fix the fees of government servants. Edmund Pendleton, on the other hand, thought the court was right and wrote an opinion to that effect.[1] Jefferson's views are embodied in paragraphs 741-48 of his legal commonplace book, a notebook he maintained for many years beginning about 1766. Thereafter someone, perhaps Pendleton, made a copy of Jefferson's notes. The copy differs in some respects from the original.[2] It is easy to tell which version is the original and which the copy, because the copier inadvertently omitted some passages that are present in the original and the omissions robbed the passages of sense. It is the defective copy, however, that has attracted the attention of historians, apparently unaware of the original, and the copy has become known as Jefferson's "opinion."

Calling either version an opinion is misleading. The copy, like the original, is a reasoned expression of Jefferson's views—an opinion in one sense of the word. But *opinion,* if the writer is a lawyer, connotes a formal expression prepared for presentation to someone, usually a client. Jefferson's "opinion" is not that kind of expression. Enough of Jefferson's legal opinions survive to demonstrate what everyone would expect—that he could be clear and concise. This document is quite the opposite. It rambles. Large sections are paraphrases of Coke and other legal scholars in the archaic English of their time, and there is frequent resort to Latin or law French. In short, the words are not those of Jefferson the advocate. Like the rest of the commonplace book, they are the words of Jefferson the reader and note-maker. The full text of the commonplace book version appears, with some errors, in Gilbert Chinard's edition of *The Commonplace Book of Thomas Jefferson*. An abbreviated transcription of the defective copy, which has never been published, appears in Appendix C.

In his biography of Pendleton, David Mays stated that the copy is written in Pendleton's hand. He discussed the Pendleton and Jefferson opinions and inexplicably found Jefferson "in hearty agreement" with Pendleton.[3] George Curtis corrected that mistake but at the same time made a serious one of his own. In an essay on "The Role of the Courts in the Making of the Revolution in Virginia," he assumed that the General Court, opening its April 1774 session and finding itself faced with the imminent expiration of the fee bill, requested the opinions of Pendleton and Jefferson. Then, referring to an 8 May letter from Richard Henry Lee to Samuel Adams, he stated, "Lee did not inform his Massachusetts coconspirator that he and Thomas Jefferson had already initiated a move to obstruct royal government by dislocating the operations of the Virginia court system."[4] He based this statement on his assumption that Jefferson had already delivered his opinion.

Neither the Pendleton opinion, Jefferson's commonplace notes, nor his so-called opinion bears a date,[5] but Curtis's assumption about their timing is demonstrably wrong. The chief purpose of this chapter is to examine the record and to put Jefferson's notes in their proper time frame. Doing so negates the charge that they evidenced a plot with Lee, under way as early as April, to close the Virginia courts as a means of accelerating the Revolution. Having freed them of that incubus, we can look afresh at what Jefferson had to say.

Much has been written about the fee bill crisis of 1774, but some important aspects have never been covered and are relevant to the purposes of this chapter. Fee bills, or legislative authorizations for fees that certain officials were to receive for their services, were enacted every few years by the General Assembly. Sometimes the fee bill spelled out a complete schedule of fees; sometimes it merely extended the life of the existing schedule. The officials concerned were the secretary of the colony, county court clerks, sheriffs, coroners, constables, and surveyors. None of these positions carried a salary; all were compensated solely by fees collected for services rendered as specified in the current fee bill. The fee schedule in effect in early 1774 enumerated, for the various officials, over two hundred fees, most of them payable in small amounts of tobacco.[6]

Although discussions of the fee bill crisis of 1774 emphasize the fees associated with courts and litigation, the fee schedule included many items having nothing to do with litigation. Fees chargeable by the secretary of the colony, for example, included fees for issuing land patents, issuing letters of administration of decedents' estates, probating wills, and recording deeds. Of eighty-one items, over a third were of this variety. Likewise, of the fifty-five fees listed as payable to clerks of county courts, over half were items extraneous to litigation. Sheriffs collected fees not only for their services in civil litigation but also for services in criminal cases and caring for runaways. Coroners were paid for inquests, constables for whipping servants and slaves, and surveyors for surveys. In short, the services covered by the fee bill were necessary not only to keep the courts running but also to sustain a multitude of essential functions of government.

By 1745 the General Assembly had established the practice of giving each fee bill a terminal date. The 1745 act, for instance, provided that it should "continue and be in force, from the end of this session of Assembly for and during the term of three years and no longer." Adjournment was on 12 April. The fee schedule of 1745 was extended eleven times, the last extension expiring on 12 April 1774. Before 1774, renewal was always effected before the existing authorization expired.

The governor prorogued the General Assembly of March 1773 first to June, then to August, again to November, and finally to 5 May 1774.[7] In setting the May date, Governor Dunmore either forgot the fee bill was due to expire on 12

April 1774, or he assumed that it would be renewed retroactively when the legislature met.

Such an assumption would not have been unreasonable. Fee bills were not the only legislation adopted for specific periods. The House of Burgesses, at the start of each session, requested a committee—usually the Courts of Justice Committee—to determine what laws had expired since the last session or were about to expire and to recommend whether to revive or renew them. As Edmund Pendleton said, "The assembly were to meet on the 5th. May when it was not doubted but that they would take up the matter and either revive the former regulations or establish new ones."[8] County courts meeting after 12 April did business as usual; table 6 shows what went on in ten of those courts whose order books survive. John May, clerk of the Botetourt County court, informed the House of Burgesses on 6 June 1775 that his court had awarded judgments and issued executions thereon in April and May 1774, not knowing that the fee bill had expired; but it seems unlikely that such ignorance prevailed in all of the

Table 6. County court meetings, April–June 1774

County	April	May	June
Caroline	14 Normal	12 Normal	9 No litigation
Lunenberg	14 "	12 "	9 "
Essex	18 "	16 "	20 "
Pr. Edward	18 "	16 "	20 Closed
Chesterfield	18 —*	16 "	20 "
Augusta	19 Normal	(Court met only quarterly)	
Lancaster	21 "	19 Normal	16 ?
Halifax	21 "	19 ?	16 Closed
Cumberland	25 "	26 Normal	7 No litigation
Surry	26 "	24 Closed	28 "

Note: Most if not all county courts remained open for some purposes throughout the war. Instruments were acknowledged, estates were administered, and there was even some activity in the area of litigation, e.g., judgments by consent. Even in normal times, the degree, and sometimes the type, of activity varied from month to month and from county to county; so that it is not always easy to pigeonhole a court's activity as normal. One or more jury trials during the session evidenced normal activity; the contrary is not necessarily true—hence a few question marks. "Closed" means no activity at all.

*The Chesterfield court did not meet for litigation purposes in 1774 until May, when it had a normal session; so the failure to meet in April was not attributable to the absence of a fee bill.

county courts that met after 12 April 1774.[9] It may be assumed that coroners continued to conduct inquests, constables
to whip servants and slaves, surveyors to make surveys, and
sheriffs to care for runaway servants, receiving in each case
the fee that had prevailed for the past thirty years, all in the
confident expectation that the fee bill would be renewed in
due course.

Similarly, when the General Court began its semiannual session on 11 April (the tenth being a Sunday), there does not
seem to have been any concern, on the part of either court or
lawyers, about how the absence of a fee bill would affect its
operations. Criminal trials were held on 16, 18, 19, and 20
April.[10] Jefferson's records for the week he attended (18-23
April)[11] indicate normal activity on the civil side.[12]

The absence of a fee bill became an issue on or about 4 May
when a debtor against whom a judgment had been obtained
was thought to be about to remove his property from Virginia.
The creditor applied for an immediate execution, although
ordinarily executions on judgments were not issued until the
end of the session (7 May). Executions were procedures to
compel payment of judgments for damages and costs; costs
were computed by the clerk ("taxed," in legal terminology) at
the end of the session and added to the damages specified in
the judgments themselves. In the normal course, therefore,
the question would not have been raised before the session
was over. As it was, it came up a few days earlier. The clerk of
the General Court, Benjamin Waller, himself an able lawyer,
asked the court for directions concerning those fees that had
been paid to officials by the winning party after 12 April—
were they to be included in the bill of costs charged to the
losing party? The court ruled that they were to be included at
the rate established by the expired bill. This ruling was embodied in the order of 4 May decreeing that "the fees settled
by the said acts be charged and allowed for all services performed or to be performed in this court or the Secretary's
office since the expiration of the said acts until the General
Assembly shall re-enact or alter such fees, and that the same
be taxed to the judgments and decrees of this court and in-
serted in the executions sued out thereon accordingly."[13] This
was the order that gave rise to the Pendleton opinion and the
Jefferson notes.

Normally the largest part of a winning party's costs was his attorney's fee. It was not one of the fees enumerated in the fee bill and was not affected by its expiration. Nor were the fees paid witnesses for their attendance in court, sometimes a substantial item.[14] Even fees paid to court officials would not be affected if the winning party had paid them before the fee bill expired on 12 April. The question that Waller raised was a narrow one, relating only to scheduled fees paid after 12 April.

The court's order was intended to fill what everyone believed to be a temporary gap. If the fee bill had been revived as expected, the order of 4 May, having served a useful purpose, would never have been challenged. When the fee bill failed of revival, however, the order assumed a new aspect because, as it was phrased, it continued in effect indefinitely. What had been an insignificant technical problem became a serious constitutional question, affecting all the courts of the colony, and it was this question that Pendleton and Jefferson addressed.[15]

The General Assembly convened on 5 May. The next day the Committee for the Courts of Justice, with Richard Henry Lee as chairman, was assigned, as usual, the task of examining what laws had expired since the last session or were about to expire and making recommendations as to which "are fit to be revived and continued." On 10 May Lee's committee reported, recommending the revival of some laws that had expired but not the fee bill. No explanation was given on the record, and we can only guess what the committee had in mind. It may have been inspired by disputes with the council, going back to 1772, over the militia bill and a provision of the fee bill regarding cash equivalents for fees payable in tobacco.[16] Holding up the fee bill would put considerable pressure on one of the council's members, the secretary of the colony, whose fees were a major component of that bill. On the other hand, if the purpose was to close the courts to induce British creditors to bring pressure on their government to be more conciliatory—a tactic which had worked once before, at the time of the Stamp Act[17]—failing to renew the fee bill was an inept means to that end. The General Court had held that it had the power to set the fees required for its operation, so it would not be affected. And even if the county courts were to defy the General Court on the point (and it was by no means clear at that stage that they would), debts over £10 could still be brought to the General Court. On the other hand, the absence of a fee bill would affect many essential operations of government outside the courts and deprive many patriotic civil servants of their livelihoods. In any event, there is no reason to suppose that Jefferson was in any degree involved in the Lee committee recommendation. He was not a member and was not present in Williamsburg until 9 May.

The House of Burgesses overruled Lee's committee and directed it to bring in a bill of revival. A bill was presented on 11 May, and it was referred (together with five other important bills that the Committee on Courts of Justice had recommended be renewed or revived) to the Committee on Propositions and Grievances, chaired by Richard Bland. This was a large group that included all shades of political opinion. Among its members were Richard Henry Lee and several of his committee, and five General Court lawyers—Henry, Jefferson, Mercer, Pendleton, and John Randolph. The committee had taken no action on the fee bill when, on 26 May, the governor angrily dissolved the General Assembly because of the House's defiant reaction to news of the Boston Port bill.[18]

Charles Cullen has said, citing no evidence, that the burgesses rejected the fee bill,[19] but he seems to have been mistaken. The fact that the Committee on Propositions and Grievances had held the bill for a little over two weeks without reporting it back to the House does not signify its disapproval, given its heavy schedule. Several items of unfinished business remained on the committee's agenda when the governor's axe fell, including all five of the bills that the Lee committee had recommended for renewal or revival. One of these was the law "for the better regulating and disciplining the militia," which, like the fee bill, had expired and had to be revived. The failure to revive the militia bill certainly was not deliberate. George Washington deplored it as leaving the colony "without the means of Defences except under the old Militia Invasion Laws which are by no means adequate."[20] The House was counting on another month to complete its business, and the governor's abrupt action took it by surprise.[21]

Treasurer Robert Carter Nicholas, who was also a burgess and a member of the Committee on Propositions and Grievances, said, "That the fee bill has expired is a circumstance we lament and ought not to be blamed for."[22] Edmund Randolph, clerk of the Committee on Courts of Justice, speaking of the fee bill, said in his *History of Virginia*, "from the dissolution of the General Assembly, the usual opportunity of prolonging it beyond the stated termination of its existence had passed away."[23] Their evidence is that it was the governor, not the Committee on Propositions and Grievances, that killed the fee bill.

A rump session of burgesses was held at Raleigh Tavern on the morning of 27 May. The subject was measures to be taken in further protest against the Boston Port bill, including a proposal to halt all trade with Britain. Describing this meeting, James Parker wrote Charles Steuart: "There was some violent debate here about the association [to implement the trade embargo]. George Mason, Pat. Henry, R. H. Lee, The Treasurer [Nicholas], as I am told, were for paying no Debts to Britain, no exportation or importation & no Courts here. Paul Carrington was for paying his debts & Exportation, in this he was joined by Carter Braxton, Mr. E. Pendleton, Thos. Nelson jun & the Speaker."[24] A call was issued for a convention in August to which all counties would send delegates.

The key to the debate about whether the courts should be closed was the legal question whether the courts had the power to fix the fees of their officers, as the General Court had held they did. If not, it seems to have been agreed, they would have to close. The question of closing the courts, like the question of shutting off imports and exports, was to be considered by the August convention. Many county courts jumped the gun, however. As table 6 shows, some failed to hold their scheduled meetings in May and June, and others met but failed to act on pending civil litigation. On 29 June, Richard Henry Lee urged William Lee to expedite a pending case, "that no time may be lost . . . after the Courts are opened (for they are now Shut up)."[25]

There were three points of view regarding the county courts. One, championed by Pendleton, was that the courts should remain open and could legally do so despite the lack of a fee bill. Another view, voiced by Thomson Mason, was that the courts must come to a complete standstill because of the lack of a fee bill. Mason, writing as "British American" in

Rind's *Virginia Gazette* of 16 June, said: "The expiration of the fee bill, by the sudden dissolution of the assembly, must shut up the courts of justice. No sheriff is obliged to serve any process, since under a positive act of assembly he can no longer receive any reward." The third point of view was that the county courts should remain open for some purposes and be closed for others.

What most proponents of closing the courts wanted was a selective ban, limited to the collection of debts or, at most, to civil litigation generally. They wanted criminals to continue to be prosecuted, estates to be administered, and instruments to be sworn to and recorded. When county conventions were held preliminary to the colonywide meeting scheduled for August, eight counties addressed the question. Essex, Fauquier, Prince William, and Stafford advocated a suspension of all civil litigation; Fairfax, Gloucester, Richmond, and Westmoreland counties advocated suspension of debt cases. The Richmond and Westmoreland resolutions are attributed to Richard Henry Lee. The Albemarle resolutions, credited to Jefferson, were silent on the question of court closing.[26]

Although the August convention, according to unofficial reports, determined that "none of the county courts will proceed to do business until there be a session of general assembly," on the ground that, in the absence of a fee bill, officers' fees "cannot be legally taxed,"[27] the closing that ensued was the partial closing advocated by Richard Henry Lee and others. The county courts refused to prosecute civil litigation but continued to handle criminal cases and remained open for other business.[28]

Although it was possible to use the absence of a fee bill as a reason for closing the courts completely, it was logically difficult to use it as the reason for shutting down some functions and continuing others, since all functions required services compensated by fees. But logic was not the order of the day. As William Allason wrote to Walter Peter in July, "In this part of the Country, our Courts have given out doing business. Some of our Justices say they won't even grant attachments, however necessary they may appear, if the debt is due to Gent in G. Britain. Some Clerks also refuse to grant writs for the same reason tho' they would have it appear that their refusal proceeds only from the Expiration of the Fee Bill."[29]

With this background in place, we turn to Pendleton's opinion and Jefferson's notes. When were they written and for whom? Pendleton's opinion could not have been written before May because it recites the circumstances that gave rise to the problem (the judgment debtor about to abscond), and they occurred in May. The tenses he used confirm this view. He said, "The assembly were to meet on the 5th May." He recited the expiration of the fee bill and the expectation of legislative renewal and continued, "But as the General Court was sitting and many judgments would pass and executions be required before the assembly could make that provision . . . the clerk applied to the court for their direction and they gave it." So the Pendleton opinion was written after the General Court finished its session on 7 May, and presumably after dissolution of the General Assembly on 26 May, because only then did the absence of a fee bill present a serious constitutional question.

The Pendleton opinion had been preceded by a debate. It alludes to two arguments that had been made in opposition to his views. One was that "taxed" fees were taxes that only the legislature could levy—a ridiculous semantic argument. Another was that fees could be justified as customary (and therefore valid even if not authorized by legislation) only if the custom were immemorial. The first argument does not appear in Jefferson's analysis or notes; someone else must have made it. Jefferson's notes incorporated the second argument, but the same argument had been advanced by others during the debate, as evidenced by Pendleton's observation that "gentlemen object that we are not antient enough to establish any point upon custom."

Clearly the debate that preceded Pendleton's opinion was the debate at the Raleigh Tavern on 27 May. At that time Pendleton made his argument for keeping the courts open and followed his oral argument with his written opinion. Jefferson probably requested and obtained a copy of Pendleton's opinion; a copy is included with his papers in the Library of Congress collection.

Jefferson reacted to the Pendleton opinion in two ways. He first wrote a brief analysis[30] and later produced his definitive notes. The brief analysis may have been made before he left Williamsburg on 31 May, but the notes in his commonplace book are too detailed to have been written in a hurry. They must have entailed days of poring over lawbooks in his library at home, and he did not go home until mid-June. His 1774 account book shows that he was at Shirley on 1 June, at Westover on 3 June, in York on 5 June, in Gloucester on the eighth, and back in Williamsburg on the ninth, where he remained until after the council session of 14-16 June, when sixty-nine of his caveats and two other cases were decided or otherwise acted on.[31]

He must have completed the notes within the next month or so. How he intended to use them is not clear. If he had intended then to show them to anyone, he surely would have produced a shorter and more lucid version. Perhaps he thought of them as the basis for an oral presentation at the August convention if the 27 May debate should be renewed. But he suffered an attack of dysentery on his way to the convention and had to go back home.[32] He must have decided to forward his commonplace book to Pendleton, in hopes of persuading him of his error. How else can we explain the fact that the copy, the "Jefferson opinion," is in Pendleton's handwriting?

In any event, Pendleton decided not to offer further opposition to the court closing. On 28 July he wrote to Ralph Wormeley, Jr., from Williamsburg reaffirming his earlier opinion, but he added an undated postscript, "Since I wrote the above a great Majority of those present here have declared they differ with me in Opinion and think the Courts of Justice should not proceed in docket business—Except Attachments and motions against Sherifs and Collectors, tho' they have not changed my Opinion, perhaps it is become, my duty Not to publish it further than has been done, and therefore you'l do me the favor Not to Shew it."[33]

The above suggestion as to how the copy of Jefferson's notes happens to be in Pendleton's handwriting may or may not be the true one. But it is clear beyond any doubt that Pendleton's opinion was written no earlier than the end of May 1774 and Jefferson's notes were made sometime after the middle of June.

So much for the circumstances under which Jefferson's notes were written. We now look briefly at the substance of the notes, and here we put aside the version in Pendleton's handwriting, since we do not know who is responsible for the variations between that version and Jefferson's notes.

Jefferson's commonplace book notes depart from his earlier analytical outline. The notes do not mention Pendleton's point that a fee could be established by a jury verdict, although the outline considers it in some detail. His notes indicate that he had discovered some authority supporting Pendleton's point in situations where only one fee was involved. He probably decided that he could safely ignore the point, since establishing a whole fee schedule by jury verdict was plainly out of the question.

Jefferson's definitive argument was that under English law going back many centuries, fees of officials could be established only by the legislature or by ancient custom. A fee did not qualify as customary unless its origins were obscured by the mists of time; a fee based on written authority, no matter how old, did not meet the standard. He disputed the contentions of respected commentators that courts of law were not subject to the foregoing principles. Anticipating an argument that a winning party who had paid fees was entitled to recover them as costs from the losing party, whether they were authorized by law or not, he argued that recoverable costs were restricted to lawful items.

Jefferson does not say so explicitly, but implicitly he is agreeing with Thomson Mason: the logic of the situation required a complete shutting down of the courts, however inconvenient. Richard Henry Lee, on the other hand, favored partial closing. Jefferson treated the question as a matter of law, Lee as one of revolutionary tactics. We can dismiss the notion that they were acting in concert.

The Pendleton and Jefferson documents tell us a good deal about the relative styles and personalities of the two men. Pendleton's opinion included only two complete citations of cases (naming the reporters) and referred to only one other case "mentioned by Serjeant Hawk" (William Hawkin's *Pleas of the Crown*). Jefferson's notes bristle with citations and quotations in Latin and law French. Adverting to the history of fee bills, Pendleton said, "Our legislature for many good reasons thought proper to fix the quantum of the officers fees, how early and under what original regulations I am not Antiquarian enough to discover."[34] Jefferson, who was a collector of old statutes,[35] cites fourteen fee bills going back to 1661. Pendleton was obsessed with the practicalities of the situation; Jefferson appears to be indifferent to them. Pendleton's opinion was brief and to the point; Jefferson ambles through the byways of his theme.

Jefferson is the more convincing. Pendleton could have argued more strongly than he did that courts had inherent power to set the fees of their officers in the absence of legislative direction, basing the argument on authorities that Jefferson cited and criticized. Pendleton weakened his case by introducing a second point, that the fees were sanctioned by custom, an argument that Jefferson demolished. To be fair to Pendleton, one should consider that his opinion was probably written in Williamsburg under severe time pressure, whereas Jefferson's notes were probably written in his library at Monticello, with time to do a thorough job.

Jefferson emerges as a master of common law materials, aggressively sure of himself, willing to challenge such eminent authorities as William Hawkins and Matthew Bacon. He also stakes out a position in favor of legislative supremacy, a position he maintained throughout his career and that later brought him into conflict with John Marshall.

11

Jefferson Quits the Practice

In August 1774, at the age of thirty-one, Jefferson turned his unfinished General Court cases over to Edmund Randolph. Never again did he appear in court as a lawyer. Randolph sent a printed circular letter dated 27 August 1774 to Jefferson's clients saying: "Mr. Jefferson having declined his Practice in the General Court, and consigned the Business, which he left there unfinished, into my Hands, I find, from his Memorandums that he was retained by you. I shall therefore continue to attend to those Matters wherein you have employed him, and exert myself for your interest, unless you countermand it by Letter."[1]

Jefferson's case book treats 11 August as the date of the transfer. Edmund Randolph had celebrated his twenty-first birthday the day before. Presumably he had been admitted to the General Court bar, but his admission must have been recent and his caseload negligible. Although his ability as a lawyer had not been demonstrated, he had been trained by his father, John Randolph, the attorney general and a splendid lawyer.[2] Jefferson was a good friend as well as a kinsman of John Randolph and undoubtedly knew the family well. Jefferson's trust was justified by Edmund's subsequent career. Just two years after assuming Jefferson's practice, young Randolph became the first attorney general of the new commonwealth of Virginia, and went on to become governor at thirty-three and the first attorney general of the United States at forty.

Notwithstanding Edmund Randolph's promise, Jefferson probably would have preferred to put his business into the hands of a more experienced member of the bar. There is evidence that he intended in April 1774 to turn his legal business over to John Randolph, Edmund's father. The elder Randolph, though attorney general, had a private practice. The evidence of Jefferson's intention is found in a cryptic memorandum in his handwriting that reads:

> Such of my causes as are ready for trial. Of the rest I will make out a full state when I come to the Assembly.
>
> I must beg the favor of Mr. Attorney to support the Injunction of Randolph v. Hanbury. He will see my notes among the papers, and all the vouchers sorted.[3]

The memorandum is undated, but it was written between 1 December 1773 and 5 May 1774. Jefferson was retained in *Randolph* v. *Hanbury* on 1 December 1773, and the "assembly" was the session of the General Assembly which opened on 5 May 1774, the only such session between the spring of 1773 and May 1775. "Mr. Attorney" was the sobriquet of the attorney general, so he must have been the addressee of the memorandum and the recipient of the enclosed cases and vouchers.[4]

If Jefferson and John Randolph had agreed that the latter would take over Jefferson's unfinished cases, as seems to be the case, what happened between April and August to upset that plan? Perhaps the older Randolph later found himself unable to handle Jefferson's considerable caseload and persuaded Jefferson that his son was qualified to do the work.

Two hundred and fifty-three cases were delivered to the younger Randolph, each of them identified in Jefferson's case book by an asterisk in the first column and by a notation such as "1774, Aug. 11. E. R. to finish." A few of these cases had been virtually completed, but most of them were awaiting trial or hearing on appeal. Sixteen of them had been in Jefferson's hands since 1767, twenty-four since 1768, and twenty-seven since 1769 — eloquent evidence of the sluggishness of the litigation process in the General Court.

One type of case—caveats—was conspicuously absent from the package of cases turned over. Unlike petitions for lapsed lands, which they closely resembled in some respects, caveats were heard by the governor's council, not by the General Court. Not only did Jefferson retain caveats already in hand, but he also continued to accept new caveat cases throughout 1774 while he was shunning new business of other kinds. Apparently he intended to continue this portion of his practice. The caveat was a relatively simple procedure that demanded minimum effort, had a relatively short life, and paid relatively well. Hearings on caveat cases were held only once a year, in June, and lasted two or three days, as against the twenty-four days of a General Court session.

The financial arrangement between Jefferson and young Randolph was the usual one for such transactions; Jefferson assigned to him the unpaid fees appurtenant to the assigned cases, amounting to £519.[5] Jefferson calculated that the unpaid fees amounted to two-thirds of the charges initially made for the assigned cases. On the basis of Jefferson's experience, Randolph would do well to collect half of the £519 remaining due as his reward for carrying the assigned cases to completion. It was not an attractive proposition for an established lawyer, but it had the merit, from Randolph's standpoint, of providing him with a ready-made clientele.

The 11 August transfer to Edmund Randolph was the culmination of months of work—sorting out the cases on which work remained to be done, putting together the pertinent papers and Jefferson's notes regarding them, and calculating clients' balances. All of this took considerable time. Jefferson's memorandum to John Randolph shows that preparations were already well advanced by the spring of 1774. He must have made the decision to give up his practice sometime in 1773.

Other evidence corroborates that conclusion. His case book shows only twenty-nine new items of business for 1774, a very small number compared with previous years, but even that does not tell the whole story. Only two (CB 911, 936) were cases that had to be turned over to Randolph because Jefferson could not complete them. Two (CB 913, 937) were nothing but bookkeeping entries, cases from earlier years that he had neglected to record. In one (CB 925) he was hired on 16 April to make a motion at the court then in session; no continuing commitment was involved. Of the remaining twenty-four items in the case book with 1774 dates, five were opinions and nineteen were caveats,[6] types of business he planned to continue after retirement from the General Court bar. In fact, the last two items in the case book were cases accepted after the transfer to Randolph, one (CB 938) a caveat accepted in October and the other (CB 939) an opinion, requested and given in November. Although the case book ends there, we know from his 1775 account book that he continued to accept caveat cases in the early months of 1775 and from various records that he continued to give legal opinions from time to time for several years after retirement.

Hence, it is clear that sometime in 1773 he reached his decision to accept no more General Court business and that he intended the April session of the court to be his last. We can understand now why Jefferson, contrary to his usual practice, attended only one week of the four-week session of the General Court in April 1774. On 11 April, the day the session opened, he was "making a stone wall at Monticello."[7] He was busily engaged with court work the following week[8] but then departed for home and work in his vegetable garden.

On 9 May, Jefferson returned to Williamsburg for the General Assembly. He was late again; the session began on 5 May. This session of the legislature was the rebellious one that Governor Dunmore dissolved on 26 May after it had vigorously expressed sympathy with Massachusetts over the closing of Boston's port. Jefferson stayed in Williamsburg for the rump session of burgesses that immediately followed dissolution and lingered nearby until after the mid-June session of the governor's council.[9]

The council met annually in the middle of June to hear caveat cases, and Jefferson always attended because caveats were an important part of his business. Of 159 caveats considered at the 1774 meeting, 69 were Jefferson's.[10] His account book lists some forty of his cases that were finally disposed of at that time.[11] The June session was Jefferson's swan song as an advocate. His intention to continue a caveat practice was frustrated by the Revolution. Before June 1775 the governor's council had breathed its last, and caveat litigation, like other kinds, remained in limbo for years.

After the June council session, Jefferson returned home to prepare for the first Virginia convention scheduled to meet in Williamsburg on 1 August. During the next five weeks he drafted the Albemarle resolutions and *A Summary View of the Rights of British America* for presentation to the convention. During the same period he completed preparations for the transfer of his cases to Edmund Randolph. Stricken with dysentery, Jefferson missed the convention and did not get to Williamsburg again in 1774.[12] The papers for Randolph must have been sent there by messenger.

The August convention determined that the county courts should continue to be closed to civil litigation.[13] As a means of pressuring British merchants to use their influence for the colonists that decision left something to be desired because most important cases were heard in the General Court. Some means had to be found to close the General Court to civil litigation. Here again the history of the Stamp Act afforded a precedent. It was decided that the General Court lawyers would boycott the October session, and the scheme was carried out as planned.[14] Jefferson played no part in that decision. He was not present and he was not involved; his career as a General Court lawyer was over.

No one foresaw at that time that relations with Britain would deteriorate rapidly and that the pre-Revolutionary General Court would never hear another civil case. It was confidently expected that the closure was temporary.[15] Edmund Randolph must have thought so, or he would not have accepted Jefferson's business or sent out his circular of 27 August to Jefferson's former clients. Jefferson gave up his General Court practice—the predominant part of his total legal business—not because of the Revolution, but for other reasons. The decision was made and was in the process of being carried out before there was any agitation to close the courts and was effected before the imminence of revolution was apparent.

Jefferson's decision to quit the practice was foreshadowed in 1772 and 1773 by his neglect of the mechanics of lawyering. He did not even compute the profits from his practice for 1773 or 1774. Through 1772, the entry for each case in his case book was separated from the ones before and after by a neat line; after 1772, this practice was abandoned, and the case entries tend to become shorter and less informative. He had attended the quarterly sessions of the Augusta County court regularly before 1772, but he attended only twice in 1772, once in 1773, and not at all in 1774.

Economic considerations played an important role in his withdrawal from a legal career. In May 1773, within a few days after he had lashed out in the *Virginia Gazette* at "the unworthy part" of his clients who did not pay their bills,[16] his father-in-law died, leaving him, he thought, a wealthy man.[17] He was unhappy with the long absences from home required by attendance at court. Home meant a wife and child, a farm and garden, and the building of Monticello.

Construction of Monticello had begun in 1769, but when he brought his bride there in January 1772, the main house had yet to be built. In 1772 major changes were made in the plans for the mansion and for landscaping the grounds. He arranged that fall to have one hundred thousand bricks delivered in 1773 and 1774, and construction had reached a critical stage.[18] The law impeded his gardening as well. "No occupation is so delightful to me as the culture of the earth, and no culture comparable to that of the garden," he wrote to Charles Willson Peale in 1811.[19] Judging by the number of entries in his garden book, his gardening activity picked up markedly in 1772. In short, his zest for the practice of law was declining at the same time that his lifelong passions for building and horticulture were beginning to assert themselves.

One is tempted to say that he had lost not only his zest for the profession but also his respect for it. Dumas Malone has said that he never ceased being critical of it.[20] In 1810 Jefferson wrote Judge David Campbell, whose son was trying to decide whether to be a doctor or a lawyer,

> Law is quite overdone. It is fallen to the ground, and a man must have great powers to raise himself in it to either honor or profit. The mob of the profession get as little money and less respect, than they would by digging the earth. . . . The physician is happy in the attachment of the families in which he practices. . . . If, to the consciousness of having saved some lives, he can add that of having at no time, from want of caution, destroyed the boon he was called on to save, he will enjoy, in age, the happy reflection of not having lived in vain; while the lawyer has only to recollect how many, by his dexterity, have been cheated of their right and reduced to beggary.[21]

Yet one hesitates to accept this cynicism as characteristic. Throughout his life after leaving the practice Jefferson was a counselor and mentor of law students.[22] When a state university was founded, largely as a result of his efforts and plans, it had a chair of law. And with his concurrence, though not at his instigation, his nephew Judge Dabney Carr was invited to fill it.[23] These actions belie to some degree his negative words, but it is probably fair to say that his experience in the practice was a disappointment, professionally as well as financially.

Still, Jefferson's years as a trial lawyer were not lost. They honed his forensic and writing skills. They gave him a wide acquaintance with Virginians from all parts of the colony and among all classes. His encounters with the other members of the elite General Court bar convinced him that he was at least equal in intellect to any of them, including Edmund Pendleton and George Wythe.[24] At precisely the right time in the history of Virginia and America, he had acquired both the assurance to put forward his personal views as worthy of the attention of his fellow citizens and the ability to present them with force and elegance.

Appendixes

Notes

Bibliography

Index

Appendix A
Thomas Jefferson's
Bar Examination and
Admission to the Bar

In his dissertation on "The Nicholas Family of Virginia," V. Dennis Golladay discussed the role of Robert Carter Nicholas as a bar examiner. He mentioned in passing that Nicholas examined Jefferson in 1765 for fitness to practice law.[1] Golladay relied on a document headed "Acct. of fees pd. by Gentlemen examin'd to practice the Law for the use of the Examiners," in the Wilson Cary Nicholas Papers, Manuscripts Department, University of Virginia Library.[2] In view of the importance of the event in Jefferson chronology, the document warrants a critical look.

It consists of a single sheet with notes on both sides and the initials "R. C. N." at the end. At the top of the first page is the heading mentioned above. There follows a list of thirty-eight names, with an indication that each had paid the fee of £1. The sum, £38, is followed by the notation, "I paid the Gent. [the other examiners] their several Proportions of this Sum in Aprl. 1762." The dates of the examinations are not given, but the ninth name on the list is Peter Lyons, known to have been examined in 1755.[3] The names are not in alphabetical order, and the assumption is that they are in chronological order by date of examination. Thus the thirty-eight examinations were spread over a period of years. (Incidentally, Patrick Henry's name does not appear on the list, although he was examined about 1 April 1760, by Nicholas, Wythe, and the Randolph brothers.)[4]

Then, in the center of the page, is written "Octr. 1762." This date must apply to the two names that immediately follow, Thomas Gray and Thomas Robinson. Following those names are three more names, each paired with a date:

25th Sepr. 1764   Ed. H. Moseley
4th Novr.   Dabney Carr
13th Decr.   Jno. Tazewell

At this point, the lower left-hand corner of the page is torn, and the dates are partially or wholly illegible. The next two names are Isaach or Isaack Read of Lunenberg and Alexander White of Frederick. Opposite Read's name is a debatable date to be discussed below. There appears to be no date opposite White's name, and one assumes that he was examined at the same time as Read. Following White's name are those of Henry Pendleton with an unreadable date and Will Bland (name lined out) with another debatable date. Then follow the names of Edmund Pendleton, Jr., Thomas Jefferson, and four more, with the dates, if any, torn off.

On the second page are more dates and names. The first and second dates are June 1766 (William Smith) and 28 July (William Grayson). There follows a date ending in "r" but otherwise indecipherable. The remainder of this page is irrelevant for our purposes, except for notes that Colonel Randolph and Wythe had been paid their proportions of the fees that Nicholas had collected. (These notes confirm A. G. Roeber's statement that George Wythe, John Randolph, and Nicholas constituted the examining board from 1758 to 1772.)[5]

Going back to the first page of the document: the first debatable date, opposite Read's name, Golladay read as "July." My own examination left me uncertain, but I tended to agree. The second debatable date Golladay read as "1765"; I was unable to decipher it. At my request, the Manuscripts Division of the University of Virginia Library made an independent examination, and on 5 December 1983, Michael Plunkett, assistant curator of manuscripts, wrote: "We do have an effective ultra-violet lamp. We are not hand-writing experts, although all of us do have daily contact with many different manuscripts documents. I examined the document in question and solicited opinions from various staff members concerning the points brought out in your letter. It was our consensus opinion that the date given as 1765 is correct and that the last letter preceding that date was 'y'. We also agree that the date opposite Read's name was not July but probably February [Feby.]."

It would seem that Read was examined no earlier than January 1765, probably in February. Bland was examined no earlier than January and no later than July. Jefferson, then, was examined sometime between January or February 1765 and June 1766 when William Smith was examined. Does the date "June 1766" at the top of the second page imply, by naming the year as well as the month, that William Smith's examination was the first in 1766? If so, Jefferson's examination clearly occurred in 1765. But the implication is not inescapable, and all one can say with reasonable certainty, on the basis of this document, is that Jefferson was examined sometime between January 1765 and June 1766. That gap can be narrowed on the basis of other evidence, however.

The examination must have taken place after 30 May 1765, when Patrick Henry made his "if this be treason" speech before the House of Burgesses. Jefferson heard it, he recollected at age seventy-seven, while "I was yet a student of law in Williamsburg."[6] His distant recollection was sometimes faulty, but in this instance it can be trusted because Henry's oratory made such a vivid imprint on his mind that he recalled the circumstances in detail a generation later.[7]

Jefferson must have been still a student on 10 October 1765 when he bought from the *Virginia Gazette* in Williamsburg a book entitled *Grounds and Rudiments of Law and Equity* "alphabetically digested; containing a collection of rules or maxims, with the doctrine upon them, illustrated by various cases extracted from the books and records. By a Gentleman of the Middle Temple."[8] One may even speculate that he bought that particular book to help him cram for the examination.

He probably took the examination shortly thereafter. The examiners all lived in Williamsburg, so the examination must have been given there. The following spring he was at home in Albemarle. His garden book contains entries for 20 March, 6, 13, 16, and 30 April, and 4, 7, and 11 May. He left immediately thereafter on a three-month trip to Annapolis, Philadelphia, and New York.[9] Hence the examination could not have been given in the spring of 1766. It must have taken place no later than the winter of 1765. In his letter of 18 January 1790 to Dr. Thomas Walker, Jefferson spoke of his "two years in Williamsburg."[10] If, as I think, the "two years" had begun in October 1763, they would have concluded sometime around October or November 1765.

The examination in question was the one required by statute as a prerequisite for practice in the county courts. Most of the persons named in the Nicholas document, such as Gray Briggs, Paul Carrington, and Dabney Carr, practiced only in the county court during the colonial period; and those such as James Lyons and James Mercer who eventually practiced in the General Court practiced in the county courts first. So why did Jefferson, who never practiced in the county courts, take that examination?

One possibility is that he intended to practice in the county courts at the time he took it but later changed his mind. The county courts closed in the fall of 1765 as a protest against the Stamp Act, and by the time they reopened in the late spring of 1766,[11] he had decided to begin his practice in the General Court.

Another explanation, which I think the more likely one, assumes that he prepared for the bar with the intention of practicing in the

General Court. As pointed out in chapter 1, the requirements for admission to the General Court (except for those who had qualified as barristers at the Inns of Court) were (1) a license to practice in the inferior courts, granted on passing the bar examination, and (2) a one-year waiting period. Did he wait a year or more before being admitted to the General Court? Before answering that question, we need to know the date of his General Court admission, and that date is not as clear as it might be.

In his autobiographical memoir written in 1821 when he was seventy-seven years old and his memory of distant events was fallible, Jefferson said, "In 1767, he [Wythe] led me into the practice of the law at the bar of the General court."[12] On that evidence, Jefferson's biographers, beginning with Tucker in 1837, have accepted the 1767 date.[13] Unfortunately, the evidence of Jefferson's 1767 account book is not available; the earliest surviving entry is dated August 1767. If 1767 was the right year, the month had to be April. The Lyons and Tucker cases discussed in chapter 1 confirm what we would assume, that admissions took place when the court was in session, and there was no necessity for a special session in Jefferson's case as they had been in Tucker's.

On the other hand, an "epitome" of his life published in 1800 said he was admitted in 1766. The article was written by John Beckley, who knew Jefferson well.[14] We do not know what evidence was available to Beckley. It may well be that the official records of the colonial General Court were extant. Jefferson saw a reprint of Beckley's article in the Richmond *Argus* of 2 September 1800 and made a careful memorandum noting several inaccuracies but not mentioning the 1766 date.[15] If 1766 was the year, admission must have occurred at the October term of the court. [16] Jefferson accepted eleven cases (CB 1–11) in February and March 1767; would he have done so if he had not yet been admitted? Would a client consider hiring a lawyer not yet admitted to the bar? It seems unlikely.

Is a hypothesis that Jefferson was admitted to the General Court in October 1766 consistent with the theory that a one-year waiting period was required between lower court license and General Court admission? The October 1766 term began on 10 October and lasted through 6 November. If Jefferson passed his examination and was licensed by the examiners to practice in the inferior courts before 6 November 1765, such a requirement could have been met.

After spending so long a time in preparation for law practice, Jefferson must have been anxious to get started on his career as soon as possible. That he waited for a year after his examination is pretty good evidence that the waiting period was compulsory. A waiting period longer than the minimum would make no sense. The chronology suggested here is coherent and consistent with the known circumstances. I conclude that he took his examination and was licensed to practice in the lower courts in late October or early November 1765 and was admitted to the General Court bar at the October 1766 term.

Appendix B
The Myth of Jefferson's
County Court Practice

There is a myth that Jefferson had an extensive practice in the county courts while engaged in his General Court practice. It began with Henry S. Randall, who wrote in 1858:

> His register of cases . . . shows that he was employed in sixty-eight cases in 1767; in one hundred and fifteen in 1768; in one hundred and ninety-eight in 1769; in one hundred and twenty-one in 1770; in one hundred and thirty-seven in 1771; in one hundred and fifty-four in 1772; in one hundred and twenty-seven in 1773; in twenty-nine in 1774. . . . The above being confined to the General Court, does not indicate the whole amount of his business. In one of the pocket account books, it appears, for example, that he was retained as attorney or counsel in no less than four hundred and thirty cases, in all, in 1771, and in three hundred and forty-seven in 1772.[1]

James Parton in 1874 put it this way: "As the new party lines were formed, and party feeling waxed hot, he lost some practice in the General Court, but more than made up for the loss by an increase of office business and county-court cases. In 1771 he was engaged in a hundred and thirty-seven causes before the General Court; but the whole number of his cases that year was four hundred and thirty, since the politics that may have repelled the tobacco lords of Lower Virginia attracted clients in the mountain counties."[2]

John W. Davis, one of the country's most distinguished lawyers of a generation ago, addressing the Virginia State Bar Association in 1926 on "Thomas Jefferson, Attorney at Law," referred to Jefferson's General Court practice and added: "In addition he had many cases before the inferior courts, such as the county courts of Albemarle and Augusta and the Court of Oyer and Terminer at Williamsburg."

Marie Kimball went her predecessors one better when she said: "From his fee book we learn that during the five years he practiced as a lawyer he had cases in no less than 53 of the 57 counties."[3]

Dumas Malone made a more modest claim: "His business in the county courts was extensive; he had cases in forty or more of them before he got through."⁴ Clement Eaton believed with Randall that Jefferson's case book recorded only his cases before the General Court and said: "He was engaged in many lesser cases before the inferior courts which he does not register in his casebook."⁵ Finally, Page Smith, in a 1976 biography, said: "Jefferson rode the circuit with other members of the bar—to Staunton, to Culpeper, to Albemarle—handling the variety of cases that came a young lawyer's way."⁶

It is my conviction that all of these people were mistaken. Jefferson never rode circuit and never practiced in a single county court, much less forty or fifty-three of them.

The first difficulty that confronts proponents of the myth is that it was illegal in Jefferson's time for a lawyer who was not a barrister (that is, a graduate of the Inns of Court in London) to practice in both the General Court and the inferior courts. Before 1748 some General Court lawyers engaged in such dual practice. The 1748 version of "An Act for regulating the practice of Attorneys" forbade it in these words: "No attorney practising in the general court of this colony, during the time of his practising therein, shall be admitted or suffered to prosecute or defend any cause or other matter, in any county court, or other inferior court depending." The penalty for each violation was £20, half to go to the offended party and half to the informer. Barristers were exempted, and any General Court lawyer was permitted to practice in the inferior courts of Williamsburg and five neighboring counties. The 1748 prohibition was repealed in 1757 but reinstated in 1761 minus the exception relating to courts around Williamsburg but still exempting barristers.⁷ It remained in effect until the Revolution.

All but two of the writers quoted above overlooked this statute. Kimball did not, but dismissed it by saying: "This seems to have been more honored in the breach than in the observance, for Jefferson, like others, practiced in both courts."⁸ She did not say who the "others" were. Eaton also took note of the statute, saying: "The law forbade attorneys practising in the inferior courts to practise before the General Court, but this restriction was generally disregarded. Waightstill Avery was promoted to higher practise in North Carolina in November, 1769."⁹ Eaton apparently interpreted the statute to forbid an inferior court lawyer to graduate to the General Court; since such graduation occurred, he concluded that the statute was generally disregarded. His interpretation is untenable, and the invocation of the North Carolina example incomprehensible.

It is difficult to believe that the statute was generally disregarded.

The history of the legislation, the fact that it was repealed and then reenacted with one of the loopholes taken out, and the severity of the penalty all indicate that it was not to be flouted. Surely any continuous and widespread violation, such as that attributed to Jefferson, would have been punished. As a young lawyer in the process of establishing a reputation he could not afford to run that risk, even if he were so inclined.

The second difficulty that confronts proponents of the myth is Jefferson's case book. The assertion that it is only a record of his practice before the General Court is obviously untrue. The case book contains a number of instances—each listed as a "case"—where he drafted instruments: e.g., a deed (CB 375, 378, 908, 683) or a will (CB 683); and where he gave opinions (CB 614, 615, 630).

It contains a number of instances in which Jefferson rendered special services in inferior court matters but did not take them to court. For example, he drafted a pleading for the defendant in a case in Cumberland and one for a plaintiff in an Albemarle case (CB 23, 886). In another instance (CB 109) he was directed to collect a debt; he obtained a writ of attachment and gave it to John Tazewell, an attorney in the Williamsburg hustings court, to serve on Williamsburg residents who owed money to the defendant. The fact that Jefferson hired a local lawyer indicates that he respected the statutory prohibition against his direct participation in the case. The case book also contains a large number of cases in which Jefferson represented clients before the governor's council. In summary, the case book is much more than a record of Jefferson's cases in the General Court. Hence the absence of county court cases is solid evidence against the myth.

The third difficulty that confronts proponents of the myth is Jefferson's fee book. No one has ever asserted that the fee book is not a complete financial record of his practice, yet it contains no suggestion of county court business—quite the contrary. Jefferson's charges to his clients recorded in the fee book always exceeded the county court scale.

Still another difficulty with the myth is a letter that Jefferson wrote to Wythe in 1779, at a time when they, with Pendleton, were engaged in a revision of Virginia laws. He was arguing for keeping the General Court and county court practice mutually exclusive. He said:

> I think the bar of the general court a proper and an excellent nursery for future judges if it be so regulated as that science may be encouraged and may live here. But this can never be if an inundation of insects [i.e., county court lawyers] is permitted to come from the

county courts and consume the harvest. These people traversing the counties seeing the clients frequently at their own courts or perhaps at their own houses must of necessity pick up all the business. . . . Men of science [i.e., General Court lawyers] then (if there were to be any) would only be employed as auxiliary counsel in difficult cases. But can they live by that? Certainly not. The present members of that kind therefore must turn marauder[s] in the county courts; and in future none will have leisure to acquire science. I should therefore be for excluding the county court attorneys, or rather for taking the General court lawyers from the incessant drudgery of the county courts and confining them to their studies that they may qualify themselves [as] well to support their clients as to become worthy successors of the bench.[10]

This letter seems to rule out any possibility that Jefferson had ever engaged in county practice. Would he have characterized the dual practitioner as a "marauder" if he had been one?

The idea that Jefferson could have had cases in the courts of forty or fifty counties is based on a fundamental misconception of what a county lawyer's practice was like. He did not dash around the countryside, trying a case here and another there. His fees, at fifteen shillings a case, would not have covered his expenses. Instead, he regularly attended the monthly court sessions in a handful of counties. In each of those counties, he had a large number of cases in various stages of preparation for trial. The number tried at any one session would be a small fraction of the total. The time between trials was spent consulting with clients and potential clients and generally tending to cases not on the trial calendar—arranging for service of process, drafting pleadings, enforcement of judgments, and so forth.

Edmund Pendleton, before he became a General Court lawyer, rode a circuit consisting of Caroline (his home county) and five adjoining counties.[11] That was about the maximum that a lawyer practicing full-time in the county courts could handle. John Aylett in 1771 was practicing in Botetourt, Pittsylvania, Bedford, and Amherst.[12] Bartholomew Dandridge, George Washington's brother-in-law, who lived in New Kent, practiced in New Kent and Charles City counties. He advertised in Purdie and Dixon's *Virginia Gazette* on 16 June 1774 that "as soon as the courts proceed on their dockets," he proposed to add the counties of James City and York and Williamsburg hustings to his practice. St. George Tucker covered four counties—Amelia, Chesterfield, Dinwiddie, and Prince George—during the years 1783–85.[13]

How did Marie Kimball get the idea that Jefferson had cases in no less than fifty-three of the fifty-seven Virginia counties? She tells us herself—from his fee book. The only references to counties in the fee book are the county names following the names of clients. She drew the erroneous inference that Jefferson practiced in each county where a client lived. Dumas Malone must have made the same mistake in reaching his figure of forty.

Now we come to Randall and the inferences he drew from the 1771 and 1772 account books. He concluded that Jefferson was handling more business than his case book could account for and that the excess must have come from the county courts. He made two mistakes.

In that part of the account books for 1771 and 1772 where Jefferson jotted notes regarding his law practice, someone—not Jefferson, perhaps Randall—has drawn a line under each tenth note and indicated, for each such line, the cumulative number of notes. The count indicates 470 in 1771 and 347 in 1772. Randall says these books show that Jefferson was retained as attorney or counsel in no less than 430 cases in 1771 and 347 in 1772. It is difficult to escape the conclusion that he equated numbers of notes with numbers of cases. Such an equation is unwarranted. Inevitably, many cases were entered more than once.

The other mistake that Randall made was to assume that Jefferson's caseload in 1771 or 1772 consisted only of the cases that came to him that year. In the General Court, as in the county courts, a case might well go on for years. After a lawyer has been in practice for a while, his inventory of cases on hand will include some cases that came to him in the current year, some that came to him in the previous year, and some dating from even earlier years. Thus the fact that Jefferson was employed in 154 new cases in 1772, as shown by his case book, and the fact that one or more things happened that year in relation to a larger number of cases as shown in the account books, does not warrant the inference that the case book is an incomplete record of the number of new cases for that year. The larger number is simply an indication of the size of the inventory.

So the Randall inference falls, and with it falls the myth that Jefferson practiced in the county courts.

[Author's note: This appendix is an abbreviated version of an article published in July 1977 (85 *VMHB* 289–301). At that time my acquaintance with the Jefferson manuscripts described in Appendix D had scarcely begun. Subsequent study has reinforced my conviction that Jefferson never practiced in a county court.]

Appendix C
Jefferson's "Opinion" on the
Power of Courts
to Fix Fees of Court Officials

Jefferson's "opinion" is an altered version, in Edmund Pendleton's handwriting, of paragraphs 741–48 of Jefferson's legal commonplace book (see chap. 10 above). A section relating to costs and a list of fee bills going back to 1661 have been omitted here, as well as various passages indicated by ellipsis points. Angle brackets indicate words and phrases that the copyist omitted inadvertently.

At Common law none having any office concerning the administration of justice might take any Fee from the subject for the doing of his office. 2 Inst. 176, 1 Inst. 368b.[1] The sheriff was sworn, among other things "neque aliquid recipere colore aut causa officii sui ab aliquo alio quam a rege." Fortesc. c. 24.[2] No sheriff nor other officer of the king shall take any reward to do his office but shall be paid of that which they take of the king, on pain that they render double to the party and be punished at the king's pleasure. Stat. West. 1, c. 26.[3] This relates to all officers whose office does any way concern the administration of justice. 2 Inst. 209. And this was the antient Common law and was punished by fine and imprisonment, but the stat. added the aforesaid penalty. Co. L. 368b,[4] 2 Inst. 176. . . . At this day officers can take no more for doing their office than have been since the act W. 1 allowed to them by authority of parliament. 2 Inst. 210.

. . . A customary fee was condemned because the custom was unreasonable. Topsall v. Ferrers. Hob. 175.[5] (This implies that had the custom been reasonable it would have been good, and consequently that fees might be established by custom). . . . Bacon sais it is extortion for any officer to take more for executing his office than is allowed by act of parliament "or is the known and settled fee in such case." 2 Bac. abr. 464.[6] And cites 10 Co. 102a, Co. Lit. 368 (but his authorities do not justify the latter words. Both books say only that it is extortion "to take quod non est debitum, vel quod est supra debitum, vel ante tempus quod est debitum"). The same compiler sais "all fees allowed by acts of parliament become established fees and the several officers intitled to them may maintain actions of debt for them". 2 Bac. 464, and cites 2 Inst. 210, (but there is not a single word of it there. If therefore it be supposed that this passage gives to fees, which have for some time subsisted under a temporary act of legislature, the authority of custom, it must be answered that the citation is as false as it's doctrine is absurd. To say that a regulation introduced by a temporary law, shall when that law expires, continue a law under that temporary usage or custom, is to make no difference between temporary and perpetual acts.)[7] The E.of Devonshire claimed the cast away iron ordnance ⟨shot and munition as fees and avails belonging to his office of Master of the ordnance,⟩[8] and offered to prove a continuance of the custom for 60 years past. But it was answered and resolved that he could not claim them as fees or avails belonging to his office, for the said office was erected of late time to wit, by letters patent. 35 H. 8.[9] And he cannot claim them as antient fees by presciption to a new office. E. of Devonshire's ca., 4 Jac. 1, 11 Co. 90a.[10] . . . . consuetudo, Custom is one of the main triangles of the laws of England, those laws being divided into Common law, Statute law, and Custom. Of every custom there be two essential parts: Time and usage. Time out of mind; and continual and peaceable usage without lawful interruption. Co. L. 110B. If there be any sufficient proof of ⟨record or printing⟩[11] to the contrary, albeit it exceed the memory or proper knolege of any man living, yet it is within the memory of man, for memory or knoledge is twofold: first knolege by proof, as by record or sufficient matter of writing⟨. Secondly by his own proper knolege. A record or sufficient matter in writing⟩[12] are good memorials, for Litera scripta manet, and therefore it is said, when we will by any record or writing commit the memory of any thing to posterity, it is said tradere memoriae, and this is the reason that regularly a man cannot prescribe or allege a custom against a statute. . . .

. . . Bacon sais "such fees as have been allowed by the courts of justice to their officers as a recompense for their labor and attendance are established fees, and the parties cannot be deprived of them without an act of parliament." 2 Bac.464, and cites for the first part of the sentence 21 H. 7, 17;[13] Co. L. 368, and for the latter part Pr. Ch. 551. I have not seen 21 H. 7, 17, but Co. L. 368 is in these words, "such reasonable fees as have been allowed by the courts of justice of antient time to inferior ministers and attendants of courts for their labor and attendance, if it be asked and taken of the subject, is no extortion" and cites among others 21 H. 7, 17. Here then he does not say (as Bacon would make him) that fees allowed by courts of justice are established fees, but fees allowed by them of antient time are established fees. So that he must be understood as making the Custom from time immemorial to be the basis, and not the allowance by the courts). Again Pr. Ch. 551, the Chancellor only sais "if the Serjeant at arms is entitled by the ⟨antient⟩[14] course to a fee on the caption of a person in contempt, it cannot be altered without an act of parliament."[15] (So this only proves that fees established by custom, cannot be altered but by act of parliament, and not that fees allowed by courts cannot be altered but by act of parliament, as Bacon cites it.) An action by the promoter of the king (his attorney I suppose) upon the statute of extortion against an undersheriff for taking the bar fee of 20d.[16] The undersheriff gave in evidence the existence of the fee from time immemorial. The court determined it to be out of the statute, and no extortion and sais "ceo fee fuit assigne par la court pur barre fee per lour discretion in consideration del grand charge que le viscount ad in garder amesnant et in reamesnant les prisoners et in garder le number del servants de eux amesner, &c." Br. abr. Feis del court, 6.[17] (The saying "this fee was assigned by the court" is a loose expression of the reporter, or abridger, or perhaps of the court, as will appear on reflecting that the custom having existed from time immemorial, no mortal could say that it arose at first from the allowance of the court, or from what other authority. If it be supposed this origin of the custom was asserted from knolege or evidence that it was such, then it destroys their judgment, because it is no longer a custom from time immemorial, since they can give evidence how, and consequently when it arose. Hawkins states the case of the bar money and the disinction in the books that it is not for doing his office but is annexed to it; and sais there is no need for this distinction "for it cannot be intended to be the meaning of the statute to restrain the courts of justice in whose integrity the law alwais reposes the highest confidence from allowing reasonable fees for the labor and attendance of their officers." Hawk. c. 68 cites 21 H. 7, 17; 2 Inst. 176, 210; S. P. C. 49A.[18] (Here Hawkins departs from his authorities as he sais himself, and assigns a contrary reason for the position laid down by them. Those who think his authority greater than that of the books he cites, will take his and not theirs, to be the true legal reason. I am not of his school).[19] The Register in an ecclesiastical court libelled there for fees, and a prohibition "was granted, for the court has no power to compel the party to pay fees to their officers, but they must bring their Quant. meruit, or if the office be a freehold they may bring an Assize." Ballard v. Gerard, Salk. 333.[20] "Gifford was libelled against in the ecclesiastical court for fees, and upon a motion a Prohibition was granted, for no court has a power to establish fees; the judge of a court may think them reasonable, but that is not binding; but if on a Quant. mer. a jury think them reasonable, then they become established fees. Vide Hardr. 351.[21] Giffords ca., Salk. 333,[22] 5 Mod. 238.[23]

Appendix D
Jefferson Manuscripts Relating to
His Law Practice

Case Book

Jefferson's case book is a chronological record of his cases, from no. 1 dated 12 February 1767 to no. 939 dated 9 November 1774. Jefferson called it his "fair memm. book"[1] or "fair book"[2] to distinguish it from his account books, which he called his "rough books." The manuscript (HM 326) is in the Henry E. Huntington Library, San Marino, California.

The manuscript consists of 105 double-width pages. The first nine pages are an index, alphabetized by surname of plaintiff. Under each letter, the cases are not alphabetized but listed in chronological order. In the main body of the manuscript, the first 87 pages, covering the years 1767–72 (CB 1–783) have ruled lines separating the cases. The balance of the book does not.

When Compiled. The entries through 1772 appear to have been made at one time, probably copied from an earlier version of the "fair memm." book that survived the Shadwell fire of February 1770 (1770 account book, July 16). The entries with 1773 and 1774 dates were made from time to time thereafter.

Consider the first case on the first page—*Jones* v. *Lewis,* dated 12 February 1767. The entire note regarding that case, including items with various dates in 1767, 1768, 1769, 1770, appears to have been entered at one time. The second case—*Meriwether* v. *Meriwether*—lists a 1771 item before a 1770 item, a clear indication that the case note was entered no earlier than 1771. Incidentally, the 1770 entry is simply a date, "Aug. 9." Such an entry refers to a note under that date in his account book. The fourth case—*Pleasants* v. *Pleasants*—tells how Jefferson allocated a payment of £12.2. received in August 1772. This set of notes, like those of CB 1 and CB 2, appears to have been made all at one time.

A comparison of some account book entries and casebook entries bearing the same dates and concerning the same cases shows that the case book entry was in fact made after the account book entry and reflected intervening developments. For example, in *Freeman* v. *Cox* (CB 216) and *Freeman* v. *Jopling* (CB 217), the account book entry of 11 August 1768 says, "If suit brot by Freeman v. Jopling, Cox or H. Freeman, appear for def." The case book entries bearing the same date say, "Empld by def." In *Johnston* v. *Walmsley (CB 196),* the account book entry of 24 March 1769 says Jefferson was to inquire if certain documents had been filed in the land office and, if not, to bring a caveat. The case book entry of the same date says, "Enter caveat." Similar discrepancies are found in *Johnston* v. *Patterson* (CB 63 and 1767 account book, 18 Nov.) and *Brown* v. *Tullah* (CB 119 and 1768 account book, 21 June).

In *Lilly* v. *Riddle* (CB 45) and *Temple* v. *Bowyer* (CB 134), Jefferson gave brief statements in the case book, dated 5 November 1767 and 19 August 1768 respectively, and added, "See case in former book of memms." The fuller statements appear in the account books for those same dates. The references to them as "former books" indicate that the case book entries bearing the same dates were made after the years in which those account books were current. There are similar references to his "old mem book" in *Moore* v. *Hog* (CB 81, 17 March 1768) and *Harper's Case* (CB 398, 12 April 1770).

That the case book was not compiled contemporaneously with the events recorded is further evidenced by the fact that some cases are entered out of chronological order. For example, CB 194 and 195, both dated 15 October 1768, are listed after CB 193, dated 24 March 1769.

Cases Included. A number of cases are mentioned, some repeatedly, in the account books that do not appear in the case book. I have discovered no consistent pattern to rationalize the omissions.

Beckham v. *Philips* (CB 783) was a caveat that Wythe had turned over to Jefferson in June 1768. Jefferson said that he did not enter it then because he did not mean to charge anything in these cases unless the client volunteered payment. One might infer that the case book included only cases in which he expected a fee, but that clearly is not so. There are a number of cases in the case book in which he indicated at the outset that he did not intend to charge a fee, e.g., *Nelson* v. *Willis* (CB 84); and the case book omits some cases in which he collected a fee, e.g., *Wall* v. *Talbot* (1773 account book, May 3).

Several of the cases not included in the case book aborted before Jefferson had done much work on them, but so did some cases that are in the case book, e.g., *Archer* v. *McDowell* (CB 22), *Reid* v. *Will* (CB 717), *James* v. *Persons* (CB 831), *Martin* v. *Terril* (CB 855).

Number of Cases. Generally speaking, cases bear individual case book numbers, but there are exceptions. Sometimes the case book itself shows that a single number represents more than one case. *The King* v. *Cary* (CB 94) is two cases. *Reid's Case* (CB 459) is twenty petitions for lapsed lands. *Johnston's Case* (CB 367) is a bundle, but the size of the bundle is not stated; the discussion of the cases in chapter 5 shows that it was a huge bundle. Sometimes extraneous evidence shows that a case book entry which apparently indicates a single case, actually represents more than one. *Nelson* v. *Willis* (CB 84) was a bundle of five separate cases, as shown by Jefferson's copies of court dockets for October 1769–October 1772.

Case Book Information. The amount of information given about a case by the case book varies from a minimum of half a line to a maximum of eight lines or so. That brief entry usually gives the names of the parties and their counties of residence, an indication of the type of case (debt, caveat, etc.), sometimes an indication of who brought the case to Jefferson or who would be responsible for the fee, sometimes a note regarding money advanced by Jefferson for taxes or fees, usually information about payments received. In the case of caveats and petitions for lapsed lands, there is often a brief description of the property involved and the outcome of the case. In other types of cases, there is seldom an indication of the outcome or even whether the case came to trial. Nor is any indication given about pleadings, motions, or other mechanics of a case.

Fee Book

Jefferson's fee book is a chronological record of debits and credits to clients. The manuscript (HM 836) is in the Henry E. Huntington Library, San Marino, California.

The manuscript consists of fifty-five double-width pages, of which the first eighteen pages are an index, alphabetized by surname of debtor. Under each letter the cases are not alphabetized but listed in chronological order. In the pages that follow the index, debits are listed on the left side of each page, approximately twenty-five to a page, with their dates. Credits for the same range of dates appear on the facing page. Thus the first page after the index has twenty-four debits (nos. 1–24), covering the period 12 February 1767–20 August 1767. The facing page lists seven credits (nos. 25–31) made during the same period.

Like the case book, the fee book consists of two distinct parts, one relating to the six years ending 31 December 1772 and one for the two years that follow. The first part is a careful analysis of charges, advances, and receipts, with annual summaries. The second part merely lists debits and credits without bothering to calculate totals by pages, much less by years. Within the first part there are slight variations in format. For the period through May 1769, total charges, advances, and receipts are shown at the foot of each page. Thereafter only total debits and credits are shown at the foot of each page, and even the annual summaries do not break down the total debits between charges and advances.

Up until 1 June 1772 results are summarized by fiscal years. Fiscal "1767" comprises the sixteen-month period from February 1767 through May 1768. Subsequent fiscal years are twelve months each, "1771" being the twelve months beginning 1 June 1771. "1772" consists of the last seven months of calendar 1772. As indicated above, no summaries are shown for 1773 and 1774.

When Compiled. Obviously the fee book entries were not made on the dates shown. The very first entry is a debit of £3.4.0 to Gabriel Jones, under date of 12 February 1767. That was the date Jones hired Jefferson to represent him in *Jones* v. *Lewis* (CB 1). Reference to the case book shows, however, that the £3.4.0 consists of a fee of £2.10.0 and advances made on 13 April 1767 and 18 June 1768.

Further evidence that the fee book is a retrospective document, and not one kept contemporaneously, is found in items out of chronological order. For example, debit no. 58, dated 23 August 1767, is found in the midst of November 1767 items. An April 1768 item, debit no. 77, is found in the midst of March 1768 items. There are instances of the same kind in 1769, 1770, 1771, and 1773.

Fee book entries for the first several years were entered at one time. James A Bear, Jr., former resident director of the Thomas Jefferson Memorial Foundation, and Lucia S. Goodwin of the Foundation staff believe that the fee book began as a reconstruction of client accounts drawn up after the Shadwell fire of February 1770. Jefferson recorded such a reconstruction in the 1770 account book under date of 16 July. We have discussed the matter at length, and after some initial doubts, I have accepted their view. Even after that original compilation, entries in the fee book were not made contemporaneously with the transactions recorded, but the book was brought up to date from time to time.

What Included. Charges and credits to a client, noted in the case book, usually appear under the same date in the fee book. Sometimes Jefferson forgot to enter a charge in either book, e.g., *Trent* v. *Taylor* (CB 514), *Wilkinson* (CB 516), *Jameison* v. *Merideth* (CB 546), *Scott* v. *Webb* (CB 572). Some receipts and credits noted in the case book were omitted from the fee book, e.g., *Reid's Case* (CB 459), a receipt of £2.6.0 on 25 Sept. 1771; *Hughes* v. *Fontaine* (CB 496–97), a payment of £5 on 8 August 1771; *Wilkinson's Case* (CB 516), a credit of 20s. on 14 Feb. 1774; *Jameison* v. *Merideth* (CB 546), a credit of £5 on 15 Jan. 1773; *Robert Carter Nicholas* (CB 612), miscellaneous receipts aggregating £10.1.6.

Account Books

The account books are Jefferson's books of original entry, maintained contemporaneously with the events chronicled. Jefferson called them his "rough books" (*Black v. Davies,* CB 709) or "rough memorandum books" (1770 account books, 8 March).

There was an account book for each year of his practice. Those for 1767–70 and 1773 are in the Jefferson Papers at the Library of Congress. Those for 1771, 1772, and 1774 are in the Jefferson-Coolidge Papers at the Masschusetts Historical Society.[3] The record for each year is in two parts—a legal diary and a diary of personal expenditure. Some of the volumes also contain notes on miscellaneous subjects.

The account books for 1767–74 and for subsequent years are being prepared for publication as part of the Princeton edition of *The Papers of Thomas Jefferson.* The enormous task of editing and annotating the manuscripts has been performed by James A. Bear, Jr., and Lucia S. Goodwin. They call these volumes "Memorandum Books," since that is the way Jefferson referred to them. I have clung to the "account book" nomenclature used by Dumas Malone and others. Editors Bear and Goodwin have very kindly made available to me typescripts of these records. If I had been obliged to use the manuscripts for my work, it would never have progressed as far as it has. I with to acknowledge a debt that cannot be repaid.

The records for 1767–70 are in one volume. Each of the four years has its own separate diaries, and there is a "common memorandum" section that contains additional notes for 1768–70, some duplicative and some not. I have referred to these sections as the 1767 account book, 1768 account book, 1769 account book, 1770 account book, and the common memorandum section of the 1767 account book.

The 1767 diaries have been partially destroyed. The first legible entry in the legal diary (and that is only partly legible) is that of August 25.

The 1772 account book, while apparently physically intact, contains no legal entries before July 5. The diary of personal expenditures begins with 1 January, the day of his marriage. Did Jefferson simply neglect to keep his legal diary for a period of six months following his marriage? The question is debatable. At my request, Peter Drummey, curator of manuscripts at the Massachusetts Historical Society, examined the 1772 account book on 18 August 1985 and reported that there is no evidence of missing pages. He says no one can be absolutely sure without taking the book apart because, as I understand it, Jefferson's practice was to add to the published volume some blank pages to make notes on, and these are bound into the volume in a somewhat different way than the original pages; but there is no evidence of missing pages, and he does not think there are any. On the other hand, Bear and Goodwin are inclined to believe that the 1772 account book originally contained some entries for the six months, pointing out that Randall or whoever numbered the entries (see Appendix B) numbered the first extant entry "110."

Other evidence indicates that Jefferson was operating at something less than full speed for a period following his marriage but not neglecting business entirely. Though a burgess he did not attend the General Assembly session that began 10 February and ran through 11 April 1772. He made his usual trip to the Augusta County court in March but skipped the one in May. He traveled to Williamsburg for the April General Court and the mid-June meeting of the Governor's Council. His case book contains some fifty entries for the first six months of 1772, beginning with 4 March.

What Included. The legal diary includes a note made at the time each case was initiated. Sometimes the information is identical with the initial note in the case book; sometimes it is more extensive. Later notes are apt to record financial facts—advances or receipts—rather than legal events. Receipts of money may also be recorded in his personal accounts, with a note that they were for the "law fund."

Each account book from 1768 through 1771 shows a list of client balances as of 1 June. At the end of the list for 1 June 1771, Jefferson added a statement of net receipts, legal fees due, and "profits" for the first four fiscal years (1 June–31 May). There is no such computation in the abbreviated 1772 account book, but near the beginning of the 1773 book is a list of client balances (presumably as of 31 December 1772) and a computation of "profits" both for the fiscal year ending 31 May 1772 and for the remaining seven months of 1772. In the 1774 account book, under date of 11 August, he listed the client accounts assigned to Edmund Randolph, who was to take over his practice.

Opinions

Jefferson's case book lists forty-seven opinions written for clients. Of these, seven survive in the Jefferson Papers, Library of Congress. They are: *Robinson's Case* (CB 380), *Rucker's Case* (CB 384), *Snell's Case* (CB 506), *Roane's Case* (CB 559), *Ball's Case* (CB 615), *McLanahan's Case* (CB 926), and *Smith's Case* (CB 939). These are the copies Jefferson kept for his files, but three of them—Roane, Ball, and Smith—bear his signature. The Library of Congress collection includes another opinion from the period of his law practice not listed in the case book: *Hylton's Case,* dated 1771, concerning the validity of a codicil to the will of Bowler Cocke of Shirley plantation.

The opinion from the period 1767–74 that has been published is *Tucker's Case* (CB 325), quoted in a letter of 28 August 1770 from Thomas Burke to Neil Jameison (Boyd, *Papers,* 1:52–53).

After he retired from General Court practice in August 1774, Jefferson continued to write opinions for clients from time to time. A number of such opinions survive in the Library of Congress collection. Both *Smith* (CB 939) and *Patterson* were written in November 1774; the first was included in the case book and the other was not. *Muse* was written in 1775,[4] *Couch* and *Kerr* (*Birch's Will*) in 1776,[5] *Burwell's Will* in November 1777, and *Traverse's Case* in December 1778. Six—*Lyne, Freeland, Wayland, Watkins, Dabney,* and *Smith* (the same Charles Smith as in CB 939)—were written in the first eight months of 1782. His 1775, 1776, and 1777 account books mention other opinions that do not survive.[6]

The Burwell opinion and the will that the opinion concerns were published in Mary A. Stephenson, *Carter's Grove: A History* (Williamsburg, Va. 1964). The Lyne, Freeland, and Watkins opinions (strictly speaking, the Lyne document is Jefferson's notes rather than an opinion) are published in Boyd, *Papers,* 6:145–46, 151–54, 180–82.[7] The Wayland opinion was published in the *American Journal of Legal History* 9 (1964):64–68. The published Burwell and Wayland opinions were the originals delivered to the clients; the Library of Congress versions are Jefferson's copies. Some errors in the published versions can be detected by comparing them with Jefferson's copies.

The Library of Congress collection includes, in addition to the above opinions, the dates of which are known, five unpublished opinions of uncertain date: *Baker, Quarles* (2 opinions), *Wills,* and *Fleming.* They were probably written after his retirement from active practice, since none is mentioned in the·case book or in his account books for the years 1767–74.

Reports of General Court Cases

The Library of Congress collection of Jefferson manuscripts includes four reports of cases in the General Court not included in the volume of reports published after his death: *Hunt* v. *Tucker's Executors, The King* v. *Dugard, Wormeley* v. *Wormeley* (all unpublished), and *Blair* v. *Blair* (published in Dewey, "Thomas Jefferson and a Williamsburg Scandal"). The manuscript of *Wormeley* v. *Wormeley* seems to be Jefferson's original notes, whereas the other three seem to be edited versions of his original notes (see chapter 3).

The Library of Congress collection also includes a manuscript called *Carter's Case.* It is not in Jefferson's handwriting. It relates to *Carter* v. *Webb,* one of the cases (not his) included in his volume of published reports.

Commonplace Books

The manuscript of the legal commonplace book is in the Library of Congress collection. The manuscript of the equity commonplace book (BR 13) is in the Henry E. Huntington Library, San Marino, California. For a description of their contents, see Dumbauld, *Jefferson and the Law,* 15–16, 161 n. 38, 171 n. 87, 172 n. 96, 173 n. 114, 237 n. 16.

Gilbert Chinard's edition of *The Commonplace Book of Thomas Jefferson* reproduces a good part but not all of the legal commonplace book and gives some account of the remainder.

Miscellaneous Documents in the Library of Congress Collection

Most of the documents in the Library of Congress collection relating to Jefferson's law practice (except the account books and the legal commonplace book) are to be found on microfilm in reel 1 of series 1. They include:

1. The decree in *Allen* v. *Allen* (CB 86).

2. A document relating to *Harding* v. *Harding* (CB 536); it appears to be Jefferson's notes for an oral argument before the General Court.

3. Jefferson's notes on divorce (see chapter 7).

4. Documents relating to the fee bill controversy of 1774 (see chapter 10).

Argument in *Bolling* v. *Bolling*

Jefferson and George Wythe are opposing counsel in *Bolling* v. *Bolling* (CB 489). The case was presented to an arbitrator, Benjamin Waller, in writing. The manuscript of the arguments is in the Henry E. Huntington Library, San Marino, California. A lengthy summary of the argument is presented in Dumbauld, *Jefferson and the Law,* 94–120.

General Court Dockets for 1771 and 1772

In the Jefferson-Coolidge Papers, Massachusetts Historical Society, are many documents pertinent to Jefferson's law practice. Chief among these are the General Court dockets for April 1771, October 1771, April 1772, and October 1772.

Each of the dockets is in three parts. First is a page or two of "office judgments," simply listing cases without indicating what the judgments were. The "office" was the office of the clerk of the court. The progress of a case, before it graduated to the ready docket, was regulated by "rule," and a case at that stage was said to be "at the rules." Office judgments, signed by the clerk, were reviewable by the court. See CB 517, 663, 828. Typical office judgments related to special bail, abatement, sufficiency of proof of an account, and so forth.

The docket proper consists of fifty pages, more or less, somewhat larger than the modern legal-size page. The third component is an alphabetical list of chancery and common law cases commenced and writs of supersedeas and habeas corpus issued since the last court. This third component is variously called "rough docket" or "actions returnable to [date]" or "actions to [date]."

The docket proper is a register of cases ready for trial or argument. It is divided into twenty-four lists, "1st day," "2d day," and so forth, following the statutory scheme that allotted the first five days to chancery cases, including appeals, the sixth day to criminal cases, the seventh day to petitions for lapsed lands, and the remaining days to common law actions and appeals.

One might suppose that the cases listed on the third day, for example, would be tried or argued on that day. That was not the way the docket worked. New chancery cases at the trial level constituted the fifth-day list; after one appearance there, they moved to the foot of the fourth-day list, and worked their way up. New chancery appeals began their life at the foot of the third-day list and leapfrogged their way up the list. An appeal might be heard while still on the second- or third-day list, but a case at the trial level had to be on the top of the first-day list to receive attention. Altogether, about a dozen chancery cases would be heard per session.

The common law docket worked in much the same way. Cases at the trial level began life on either the twenty-third- or twenty-fourth-day list, where they languished for years. Once a case graduated to the twenty-second-day list, its progress was relatively rapid. Cases as far down the docket as the sixteenth-day list might be heard, though others not so far down might not; some sort of selection process was being used, though I have not identified it.

Common law appeals, to satisfy the letter of the statute, began their careers on the eighth- through twelfth-day lists, depending on where the appeal came from; but after a token appearance there, they were moved back, sometimes as far as the twenty-first day; progress thereafter was relatively rapid.

On each day's list, cases are shown as "references," that is, cases carried over from the previous docket, or "new causes" or "new appeals," that is, on the docket for the first time.

The Massachusetts Historical Society manuscripts are, of course, not the original court records. They are copies, appparently made for Jefferson's use. Benjamin Waller, the clerk of the court, kept one or more apprentices in his office, who, upon completing their training, became county court clerks. Several of these, seriatim, served as Jefferson's Williamsburg agent, searching for records, arranging for the issuance of writs, and the like. The copiers of the dockets clearly had been trained in the type of formal penmanship used in official documents, and it seems probable that all four of these copies were made at Jefferson's request by his agent at the time. Jefferson noted in the 1771 account book (11 May), "Pd. Steptoe for docket 26/." James Steptoe was his agent then. I have found no record of payment for the other three dockets.

Many of the pages of these four dockets are partly illegible. Where names of cases are wholly or partly unreadable, they can often be reconstructed by examining the previous or subsequent docket, since the sequences tend to be the same, with relatively few dropouts from one court to the next.

Throughout all four of these dockets are notations in Jefferson's handwriting. First, he identified all of his cases by a "p" (for plaintiff) or "d" (for defendant) in the left margin. Where he represented both parties, as he did in friendly petitions for lapsed lands, the notation was "pd." Many cases so identified as his are not recorded in his case book.

In the first three of the four dockets, someone, perhaps Jefferson, has identified the cases in which Robert Carter Nicholas was counsel of record, by "Np" or "Nd" in the left margin; "qNP," "qNd," or "qN" indicates that the annotator was not sure whether the case was Nicholas's. In many of these cases, the initials of the cocounsel also appear, for example: "E. P." for Edmund Pendleton, "G. W." for George Wythe, "T. M." for Thomson Mason, and "A. G." for Attorney-General John Randolph. "T. J." appears in some instances in the April 1771 docket but not thereafter. There were 247 of Nicholas's cases on the April 1771 docket, excluding doubtful ones, as against 305 of Jefferson's own.

Nicholas had become treasurer of Virginia in 1766; he quickly learned that he could not handle that job and his law practice, too, and turned to John Blair, Jr., for assistance. When Blair left the practice in 1770, Nicholas asked Jefferson to take over his cases, and Jefferson agreed (1770 account book, 29 Oct.). By the end of October 1771 he had changed his mind (CB 612). In the meantime, he had been monitoring Nicholas's cases and acting as necessary (see Boyd, *Papers*, 1:73).

The marginal notations identifying Nicholas's cases were continued in April 1772, even after Jefferson had declined the business; apparently he was accommodating Nicholas, who had not yet arranged for someone else to accept the responsibility. However, they do not appear in the October 1772 docket.

Jefferson also used the left margin occasionally for such notes as "spas sent"or "to be dismd" or "abated" or "agreed" (settled). In the case of petitions for lapsed lands, he used the left margin to indicate the status of service of process. "No inhab. advertd" is a common entry, meaning that the sheriff had been unable to find the defendant and that service had been made by publication.

In the body of the docket pages and on the facing pages, he made all sorts of notes. A few examples will illustrate: "dismiss at pl's costs," "spa sent by J. Ruffin, write by Colo. Bland," "account not proven," "Mason has papers and is to move for rehearing."

Jefferson made notes not only about his own cases and Nicholas's but also about some in which he does not seem to have been involved at all. For instance, he made this observation concerning a case (*Cockran* v. *Valentine*) on the October 1772 docket: "In this case it was said by GW and admitted by EP that the ct hd determd a factor's oath tho sufft proof of the articles of merchandise in the acct yet not sufft for the articles of cash, and that for these vouchers must be produced, and on argument in this case it is determd."

Partial Dockets

In years other than 1771 and 1772, Jefferson made lists of his own cases on the docket for the upcoming General Court session, which he used for note-taking purposes in much the same way as he used the 1771 and 1772 dockets. In the Jefferson-Coolidge Papers, Massachusetts Historical Society, are four of these, prepared for the October 1769, April 1770, October 1770, and April 1774 sessions.

The April 1770 document bears the heading "Court Docket, April 1770." On the MHi microfilm (reel 1) it appears at first to consist of that page and the three following pages. Another page, on the same reel but out of sequence, has been identified as the fifth page of the docket, and fragments have been identified as inserts, filling gaps in the list of petitions for lapsed lands. Another page on the same microfilm reel contains (1) a list entitled "Causes Returnable to April 1770," corresponding to the third component of the complete dockets described above; and (2) a list entitled "June 1770. List of causes as set down to October next."[8]

The October 1769 docket consists of four almost illegible pages. The title is completely illegible, but the document can be identified by relating the case names that can be made out and the court day numbers in the left-hand margin to the later lists and to the case book. Another two-page sequence, with a completely illegible title and a partially illegible list of cases, is identified as the same kind of partial docket (TJ cases only) for April 1774. It shows the granting of certificates, for instance, in *Moore* v. *Moore* (CB 652) and *White* v. *Stuart* (CB 750); the case book shows that certificates were obtained in April 1774.

Randolph Memorandum

An undated memorandum in the Jefferson-Coolidge Papers, Massachusetts Historical Society, appears to relate to Jefferson's disposition of his unfinished cases. See chapter 11 for this note, apparently addressed to Attorney General John Randolph.

Miscellaneous Documents in the Massachusetts Historical Society Collection

Lists of Motions. At each session of the General Court were days (usually Saturdays) at which motions could be presented. Typical motions were to dissolve an injunction, to appoint a commission to examine witnesses, to give notice of suit by advertisement where personal service was not practicable, to confirm an award of arbitrators, or to dismiss a suit where a settlement had been reached or where the suit had abated. Jefferson prepared lists of motions to be made in his cases. The Massachusetts Historical Society collection includes the following documents in this category:

1. A list entitled "Motions," with "memms" at the foot regarding *Freeman* v. *Jopling* and *Galloway* v. *Burnley*. Comparison of these "memms" with similar "memms" on the document entitled "June 1770. List of causes as set down to October next," mentioned above under Partial Dockets, identifies this list with the October 1770 term.

2. A page entitled "Motions to April 1771," apparently prepared in advance of the April 1771 session.

3. An untitled page appearing to be a revised version of the April 1771 motions, with notations made during or after the session.

4. A page entitled "Memorandums for October 1771," containing a short list of motions to be made at the October 1771 court.

5. A page entitled "Motions for October 1771" is a longer version of the preceding item, with some notations made during or after the session.

6. A page entitled "Motions for April 1772."

7. Two pages, the first of which is untitled and almost illegible, appear to be a revised version of the April 1772 motions, with notations made during or after the session.

8. A page entitled "Motions for October 1772."

9. Two pages entitled "Motions for October 1772," a revised version of the preceding item with notes made during or after the session.

10. A page entitled "Motions for April 1773."

A list of motions is also included in the October 1769 partial docket.

Instructions to Agent. Jefferson hired an apprentice in the office of the General Court clerk to act as his agent and sent him instructions from time to time. Many such instructions are recorded in his case book and account books.

One of the Massachusetts Historical Society documents, entitled "Instructions to Agent Nov. 1772," is a list of directions suggested by what had happened at the court session just concluded. Another, "Instructions to Agent between Octob. 1771 & Apr. 1772," appears to be a list of items to be checked with the agent on Jefferson's arrival in Williamsburg for the April 1772 court.

Precourt Checklists. On his arrival in Williamsburg for a General Court session, Jefferson examined the court docket as a check on the status of his business. For this purpose, he came armed with a list of his cases. There are four such lists among the Massachusetts Historical Society documents. One is entitled "From Octob. 1770 to April 1771," another "Causes from Octob. 1771 to April 1772," and another "Causes from Apr. 1772 to Oct. 1772." A fourth, almost illegible and with an illegible title, is clearly such a list for a period after October 1771, perhaps October 1772 to April 1773.

These lists include titles of cases not found in the case book. In "Causes from Apr. 1772 to Oct. 1772," for example, there is a series of such titles, beginning with "d. Poage v. King." Each title is followed by a date that, it turns out, is the date in the 1771 account book on which Jefferson made a related entry. In the case of *Poage* v. *King*, the date is 22 January 1771; turning to the account book, we find under that date: "Jno. Poage (Augusta) v. John King (Augusta). Should any suit be brot. to get a title to the lands caveated in McLure v. Poage or to recover damages, I am retained by the defendt." Jefferson did a lot of surveillance of this kind for which he was not paid unless a case actually materialized.

These four lists consist merely of names of cases, with a check mark at the left of each. In that respect, they differ markedly from the lists in the following category.

Postcourt Checklists. A list entitled "Memms April 1771" was prepared after the April 1771 court as a record of actions that Jefferson should take as a result of what had taken place, with a later notation (on the same line, separated by two slashes) that the action had been taken. A similar list of cases, untitled, headed by *Ball* v. *Blagg*, appears to have been prepared after the April 1772 court. A like list, entitled "Rough Memms," appears to have been prepared after the October 1772 court.

Massachusetts Historical Society Microfilms

There is no catalog or index of the Massachusetts Historical Society documents listed in this appendix. All except the account books are to be found on microfilm, reels 1 and 15. Reel 1 contains the documents pertaining to April and June 1770 in the order indicated in note 8. The following items are on reel 15, following the garden book.

First comes a list of motions for October 1771 (no. 5 of the lists of motions above), then the October 1771 docket. Next are the following items:

    Motions, April 1772 (no. 6 of the lists of motions)
    Instructions to agent, Oct. 1771 to April 1772
    Precourt checklist of uncertain date
    Motions, October 1772 (no. 9 of the lists of motions)
Then comes the October 1772 docket.[9] Between the docket proper and the alphabetical list of new cases appears "Motions for April 1773." Following the third part of the docket appear:

    The third of the precourt checklists
    The postcourt checklist of Nov. 1772
    Instructions to agent, Nov. 1772
    The first of the precourt checklists
    Motions, April 1771 (no. 3 of the lists of motions)
Then comes the April 1771 docket,[10] followed by

    Motions, October 1771 (no. 4 of the lists of motions)
    The first of the postcourt checklists
    Motions, April 1772 (no. 7 of the lists of motions)
    Motions, Oct. 1772 (no. 8 of the lists of motions)
Then comes the April 1772 docket. Between the docket proper and the alphabetical list of new cases appears the second of the precourt checklists. Following the third part of the April 1772 docket come these items:

    The second of the postcourt checklists (2 pages)
    The April 1774 partial docket
    The Randolph memorandum
    The October 1769 partial docket (4 pages)
    Motions, April 1771 (no. 2 of the lists of motions)
    Motions, Oct. 1770 (no. 1 of the lists of motions)
    The October 1770 partial docket

Notes

Notes to Chapter 1

1. See Appendix A.

2. Eaton, "A Mirror of the Southern Colonial Lawyer," 532; Dewey, "New Light on the General Court," 11.

3. Smith, "Virginia Lawyers," 306; Jacob Elligood to Thomas Burke, 21 Oct. 1772, Thomas Burke Papers; "Prince George County Records," 276; Waddell, *Annals of Augusta County*, 53, 215–16; Groome, *Fauquier during the Proprietorship*, 176.

4. *Va. Gaz.* (P. & D.), 3 Oct. 1771.

5. Lists of court dates were printed annually by the Williamsburg printers. See, e.g., *Va. Gaz.* (P. & D.), 19 Feb. 1767, and Rind's *Virginia Almanack* for 1770.

6. There is no known roster of General Court lawyers. The list as of 1 January 1767 certainly included the six named in the text. Wythe and John Randolph were bar examiners; see Appendix A. For the others, see Mays, *Edmund Pendleton*, 1:34; Drinard, "John Blair, Jr.," 437; Grigsby, *1788 Convention*, 2:217; Governor Fauquier to the Board of Trade, 3 Nov. 1765, Reese, *Fauquier Papers*, 1293. All six are mentioned in Jefferson's manuscripts regarding his practice, as are Richard Starke and Patrick Henry, who became General Court lawyers after 1 January 1767. It is assumed that if there had been others of consequence, they would have been mentioned in Jefferson's extensive records.

7. *Va. Gaz.* (P. & D.), 23 May 1766, 1 Jan. 1767, 7 Jan. 1773; biographical sketch of Wythe in the preface to vol. 4 of Call, *Reports*. That Nicholas was unable to carry out his intention of attending "the trial of every case of importance, and all others wherein my clients may desire it," may be deduced from James Parker's statement that Nicholas came "out of retirement" to participate in a 1770 argument (see chap. 6).

8. In Jefferson's published reports of eleven cases argued during his years at the General Court bar, Bland was counsel in two: *Godwin* v. *Lunan* (1771) and *Robin* v. *Hardaway* (1772).

9. *DAB*, s.v. "Randolph, Peyton"; *Va. Gaz.* (Rind), 25 Dec. 1766. John Mercer's travel diary shows that the October 1765 session of the General Court was the last one he attended (John Mercer Papers, ledger B).

10. Greene, *Quest for Power*, 29.

11. Hening, *Statutes*, 6:143, 7:124, 399.

12. Lyons's practice before the General Court was probably limited to appeals (Dewey, "New Light on the General Court," 8 n.34).

13. Letter Book of Robert Carter of Nomini Hall, 1764–68, f. 55.

14. See Appendix B.

15. "Williamsburg—The Old Colonial Capital," 37; Walker, "Officials of Colonial Williamsburg," 38, 51.

16. Mays, *Edmund Pendleton;* Drinard, "James Mercer, 1736–1793," 428; Rowland, *George Mason,* 1:72–73; McIlwaine, *JPs of Colonial Va.,* 73.

17. Hening, *Statutes,* 6:328.

18. *DAB,* s.v. "Jones, Joseph"; Tyler, *Encyc. Va. Biog.,* 1:267; Barton, *Colonial Decisions,* 188–89; Hilldrup, *Edmund Pendleton,* 9; Riely, "Paul Carrington," 451–53; Dill, *George Wythe,* 8–9; Mays, "Peter Lyons," 418; biographical sketches of John Tyler, Benjamin Waller, William Hay, and Henry Tazewell in preface to vol. 4 of Call's *Reports;* Campbell, *Patrick Henry,* 23–25.

19. Mays, *Edmund Pendleton,* 1:25–28; Dill, *George Wythe,* 10; Golladay, "Nicholas Family," 80; "Records of Charles City County," 435; biographical sketch of James Mercer in the preface to vol. 4 of Call's *Reports.*

20. Jones, *American Members of Inns of Court,* 21, 157, 178.

21. Hening, *Statutes,* 7:397.

22. A photostatic copy of the license appears in Mays, "Peter Lyons."

23. Coleman, *St. George Tucker,* 29.

24. Tucker-Coleman Papers.

25. *Va. Gaz.* (Rind), 8 Sept. 1774; James Parker to Charles Steuart, 14 Aug., 26 Oct. 1774, Charles Steuart Papers (MS 5028, ff. 242, 273); Thomas Adams to T. Hill, Nov. 1774, *VMHB* 23(1915): 178–79; Van Schreeven, Scribner, and Tarter, *Revolutionary Virginia,* 2:373.

26. It did meet to try criminals. *Va. Gaz.* (Pinkney), 20 Apr. 1775.

27. Van Schreeven, Scribner, and Tarter, *Revolutionary Virginia,* 2:374–76.

28. "Virginia Lawyers," 176.

29. Reardon, *Edmund Randolph,* 5.

30. "Virginia Lawyers," 304. See William Byrd II to Daniel Horsmanden, 25 Feb. 1736, Tinling, *Correspondence of Byrds,* 475.

31. Smith, "Virginia Lawyers," 67; chap. 9.

32. Baker to Thomas Adams, 24 Dec. 1771, *VMHB* 23(1915): 365–67; Eaton, "A Mirror of the Southern Colonial Lawyer," 532.

33. *Exec. Jour. Council,* 6:367; *Journals, House of Burgesses, 1770–72,* 139.

34. E.g., case book (CB), items 8, 18, 28, 29, 32 (for a description of Jefferson's MSS relating to his law practice, see Appendix D).

35. *Journal, House of Delegates, 1777–78,* session of 20 Oct. 1777, p. 115.

36. Biographical sketch of Blair in the preface to vol. 4 of Call's *Reports.*

37. Grigsby, *1788 Convention*, 2:223; *Journal, House of Delegates, 1777–78*, session of 20 Oct. 1777, pp. 128–30, and session of May 4, 1778, pp. 23, 27.

38. Jefferson's records show Starke was counsel in several General Court cases in 1771. He died in 1772.

Notes to Chapter 2

1. Randall, *Life of Jefferson*, 32; Boyd, "The Need for 'Frequent Recurrence to Fundamental Principles,' " 860; Garrett, *Thomas Jefferson Redivivus*, 28; Shaw, *Character of John Adams*, 25; Goebel, *Law Practice of Hamilton*, 1:47, 48; Johnson, *Papers of Marshall*, 1:41.

2. Betts, *Garden Book*, 1; Malone, *Jefferson and His Time*, 1:98–100; Bernstein, "Smallpox and Variolation"; Dumbauld, *American Tourist*, 48; Boyd, *Papers*, 1:21.

3. McIlwaine, *JPs of Colonial Virginia*, 68–69; *Exec. Jour. Council*, 6:413.

4. Sydnor, *Gentlemen Freeholders*, 81–82.

5. *Jefferson: The Road to Glory*, 78; TJ to Dr. Thomas Walker, 18 Jan. 1790, Boyd, *Papers*, 16:112.

6. Boyd, *Papers*, 1:5; Lipscomb and Bergh, *Writings*, 14:85.

7. Copy of a letter "written near 50 years ago" to Bernard Moore, with updated book recommendations, sent by Jefferson to John Minor on 30 Aug. 1814, Ford, *Writings*, 9:480–85.

8. Jeremiah Gridley, dean of the Massachusetts bar when John Adams was a novice there, told Adams that he had begun with Coke (Adams, *Diary and Autobiography*, 1:55). Adams himself read another work first, then an abridgment of *Coke on Littleton*, and then the original (ibid., 1:55, 3:271).

9. Boyd, *Papers*, 1:12.

10. Ibid., 16:112, 114.

11. Tyler, "Early Courses and Professors," 75–76; Malone, *Jefferson and His Time*, 1:73.

12. Randall, *Life of Jefferson*, 1:46n.

13. *Law Practice of Hamilton*, 1:49.

14. Boyd, *Papers*, 1:11.

15. Jefferson to William Wirt, 14 Aug. 1814, Lipscomb and Bergh, *Writings*, 14:165.

16. *Virginia Gazette* Day Books.

17. Adams, *Legal Papers*, 1:27.

18. Goebel, *Law Practice of Hamilton*, 1:46.

19. Cullen, "New Light on Marshall's Legal Education," 348.

20. Ford, *Writings*, 9:480–85. See also Jefferson to Dabney Terrell, 26 Feb. 1821, Lipscomb and Bergh, *Writings*, 15:318–22.

21. See Randall, *Life of Jefferson*, 1:32, and Kimball, *Road to Glory*, 83.

22. Malone, *Jefferson and His Time*, 1:67–68.

23. See Appendix D.

24. Lipscomb and Bergh, *Writings,* 14:85.

25. Letter to Bernard Moore, Ford, *Writings,* 9:480–85.

26. Kimball, *Road to Glory,* 86–89; Adams, *Legal Papers,* 3:326.

27. *Commonplace Book,* 7, 13.

Notes to Chapter 3

1. Adams, *Legal Papers.*

2. Barton, *Colonial Decisions,* 1:212–13.

3. Appointments of council members are recorded in the council minutes; see, e.g., *Exec. Jour. Council,* 6:34, 113, 228–29.

4. Jones, *American Members of Inns of Court,* 41–42, 125, 163; Smith, "Virginia Lawyers," 140–80; Goebel, *Law Practice of Hamilton,* 1:26n.; Morton, *Robert Carter of Nomini Hall,* 34.

5. Rankin, "General Court," 142, 147; Barton, *Colonial Decisions,* 1:221; *Va. Gaz.* (P. & D.), 11 June, 10 Dec. 1767. Because the functions of the General Court and the court of oyer and terminer were identical with respect to felonies, the distinction tended to become blurred (*Va. Gaz.* [P. & D.], 21 April, 16 June 1768).

6. Address of the council to the governor, 13 Dec. 1769, *Exec. Jour. Council,* 6:335–36. For payments "to the council," for services as judges, not as councillors, see, e.g., ibid., 6:283, 290, 305, 317.

7. Address of the Gentlemen of the Bar, *Va. Gaz.* (P. & D.), 17 Nov. 1768; Mulkearn, *George Mercer Papers,* 246.

8. Hening, *Statutes,* 6:326, 327, 328–30.

9. See *Va. Gaz.* (P. & D.), 23 April 1767, 21 April, 20 Oct. 1768, 20 April 1769.

10. See chap. 6 below.

11. Hening, *Statutes,* 5:544; opinion of Mr. Justice Roberts in *Betts* v. *Brady,* 316 U.S. 455 (1941); Scott, *Criminal Law in Colonial Virginia,* 77.

12. Beckley, *Address to the People of the United States,* 226.

13. To *Howell* v. *Netherland* (CB 345) and *Goodwin* v. *Lunan* (CB 510), both identified in the *Reports* as Jefferson cases, should be added *Allen* v. *Allen* (CB 86), not so identified.

14. *Hunt* v. *Tucker's Executors, The King* v. *Dugard, Wormeley* v. *Wormeley,* and *Blair* v. *Blair.* The argument in *Blair* v. *Blair* is referred to briefly in chap. 7; for the full text, see Dewey, "Williamsburg Scandal," 49–63.

15. Boyd, *Papers,* 6:122–24.

16. The complete set of Randolph notes, edited by R. T. Barton, was published in 1909 under the title *Colonial Decisions.*

17. See, e.g., no. 8, *Alcock* v. *Worden,* and no. 9, *Apthorp* v. *Gardiner,* Adams, *Legal Papers,* 1:171, 174.

18. No. 3, *Cotton* v. *Nye, ibid., 1:141.*

19. Dewey, "New Light on the General Court," 8.

20. Dewey, "Williamsburg Scandal," 63.

21. Dewey, "New Light on the General Court," 8.

22. Davis, "Thomas Jefferson, Attorney-at-Law," 370.

23. CB 752; *Exec. Jour. Council*, 6:505; Summers, *Southwest Virginia*, 69, 131, 133.

24. CB 767; *Exec. Jour. Council*, 6:509, 540.

25. CB 898; *Exec. Jour. Council*, 6:546.

26. CB 875; *Exec. Jour. Council*, 6:576.

27. CB 879; *Exec. Jour. Council*, 6:573.

28. Advertisement by James Hubard, *Va. Gaz.* (Rind), 11 May 1769. John Tazewell, another county lawyer, also practiced before the council (*Exec. Jour. Council*, 6:536).

29. Pp. 119–20.

30. Fee book, debit no. 605, 2 Dec. 1770, credit no. 792, 13 Sept. 1771.

31. Robert Carter III to Landon Carter, 10 Feb. 1764, Letter Book of Robert Carter of Nomini Hall, 1761–64, f. 52; Robert Carter III to Edward Hunt & Son, 29 Sept. 1767, ibid., 1764–68, f. 77.

32. See chap. 6.

Notes to Chapter 4

1. Adams, *Legal Papers*, 3:326; Shaw, *Character of John Adams*, 36.

2. Mays, *Edmund Pendleton*, 1:15.

3. Summers, *Southwest Virginia*, 56–81.

4. For Augusta, see the Augusta County Order Books. The Albemarle court met quarterly as prescribed by statute (Hening, *Statutes*, 6:201), but on the second Thursday rather than on the second Tuesday, and in March rather than February. See the court calendars in the printed parts of the almanacs in which Jefferson kept his 1771 and 1772 account books, and his records of personal expenditures.

5. Simpson, "Dabney Carr"; Jefferson to William Fleming, 19 May 1773, Boyd, *Papers* 1:97; *Records of Augusta County*, 1:127.

6. Biographical sketches of Jones are in Tyler, *Encyc. Va. Biog.*, 1:267; Barton, *Colonial Decisions*, 1:188; Grigsby, *1788 Convention*, 2:16.

7. Jefferson noted on 15 Oct. 1767 in his 1767 account book that he paid a laundry bill incurred in Williamsburg in June. Various actions taken in cases already on his books (e.g., CB 5) confirm the June visit.

8. The case book does not indicate the outcome of the case. On Jefferson's copy of the General Court docket for October 1771 (Jefferson-Coolidge Papers, Massachusetts Historical Society, hereafter MHi; see Appendix D), the case appears under the heading "14th day," with the notation "verd for def."

9. Dewey, "New Light on the General Court," 6–12.

10. Enclosure 1 to Governor Fauquier's letter to the earl of Shelburne, 20 May 1767, Reese, *Fauquier Papers,* 1449.

11. Account book entries of 20 Oct. 1767, 11 May, 9 Aug. 1771; flyleaf of 1774 account book.

12. Summers, *Southwest Virginia,* 44, 45, 82–107.

13. Malone, *Jefferson and His Time,* 1:89–92.

14. In the list of clients' debits in his 1771 account book appears Jefferson's note regarding the Shelton debt: "Patr. Henry to pay it."

15. Jefferson papers, Library of Congress (hereafter DLC); see Appendix D.

16. Meade, *Patrick Henry,* 228–32; Beeman, *Patrick Henry,* 20–22, 26.

Notes to Chapter 5

1. According to Judge Dumbauld's count, 283 of the 941 items in the case book were caveats and 146 were petitions (*Jefferson and the Law,* 157 n.5, 216 n.9). My own count is a little different, but the important point is that the case book does not list all of Jefferson's cases. The principal omissions are those described in this chapter, but there are others. See Appendix D.

2. Hening, *Statutes,* 5:424–26.

3. E.g., the penalty assessed against a General Court lawyer who violated the ban on practicing in inferior courts (ibid., 7:397).

4. Tucker, *Blackstone's Commentaries,* 4:Appendix, 161.

5. An exception: *Davies* v. *Bush* (CB 875).

6. "The Method and Expenses attending the taking up, and settling of Lands in Virginia," enclosure 13 to Governor Fauquier's letter to the earl of Shelburne, 20 May 1767, Reese, *Fauquier Papers,* 1469–71.

7. Ibid.

8. The law regarding land acquisition in colonial Virginia was a mixture of statutes, orders in council, royal instructions to the governors, proclamations by the governors, and the terms of the patents themselves (Voorhis, "Land Grant Policy").

9. There was no statute authorizing the *qui tam* caveat.

10. "Altogether there were said to be in 1754 between nine hundred thousand and a million acres possessed by people who had not completed the process for securing patents" (Voorhis, "Land Grant Policy," 177).

11. *Posey* v. *Boyd* (CB 239).

12. Jefferson to William Wood, 17 July 1772, Boyd, *Papers,* 1:94.

13. Order in council, 10 June 1725, *Exec. Jour. Council,* 4:88

14. See account books, 26 Mar. 1768 (*Witt* v. *Johnston*), 18 Aug. 1769 (*Arbuckle* v. *Brackenridge*), and 7 Feb. 1774 (*Pierce* v. *Tomkins*).

15. Mays, *Edmund Pendleton,* 1:231.

16. MHi, see Appendix D.

17. Jefferson had encountered Waterson as an opposing party (CB 27, 53, 80, 109, and 121). In the first of these cases, Waterson "improvidently . . . got the suit dismissed before I entd appearance so that my clients recover no costs." In *McCarty* v. *Buchanan* (CB 129), Jefferson observed, "Buchanan has no title yet, McC. is deceived in this by Wm. Waterson." Waterson, the messenger to whom Jefferson entrusted his 29 July 1767 letter for delivery to Williamsburg, took the money out of the letter, as well as 5s. 9d. sent to John May on another matter. Jefferson replaced the money and was later reimbursed by Madison (1769 account book, 23 Aug., 2 Sept., 15 Oct.). Apparently at the same time, Waterson also "took out of my letter Isaiah Curry's works and 22/2" (1767 account book, common memorandum section, 19 Aug. 1769).

18. Boyd, *Papers*, 1:32.

19. Mays, *Edmund Pendleton*, 1:231; Woodson, "John May," 8; Tyler, *Encyc. Va. Biog.*, 1:308.

20. The size of each of these groups, as indicated by the case book numbers, does not jibe precisely with the size indicated in the account book. Generally speaking, case book entries bearing the same dates as account book entries were made later and reflect subsequent developments.

21. Benjamin Waller, the clerk of the General Court, kept one or more apprentices in his office, several of whom became county court clerks. Jefferson used one of these apprentices as his Williamsburg agent. John May was his agent in 1767–69, when he became clerk of Botetourt County. James Steptoe served until sometime between December 1771 and August 1772, when he was appointed clerk of Bedford County. He was succeeded by John Brown, who became clerk of Mecklenburg County in 1775.

22. A petition commenced by its filing in court, a caveat by its filing in the office of the clerk of the council and taking out a summons.

23. A total of 195 summonses were issued; five of these were leftovers from *Waterson* v. *Armstrong-Bullett*.

24. The two exceptions were *Johnston* v. *Hawkins* (CB 320, 321). They involved the two largest properties in the list.

25. The reason for the three exceptions was that caveats had been filed by others that were later than Johnston's but would have been ahead of Waterson's.

26. 1769 account book, 20, 29 July, 15, 25 Sept.; 1770 account book, 21 Jan., 17 April; 1771 account book, 18 Oct.

27. See chap. 9 below.

28. In listing amounts owed him on 1 June 1769 (1769 account book), he included a charge to Waterson of £142.14.3, indicating that he expected to collect approximately full fees for the cases then in hand. But in the 1770 account book, the list of 1 June balances indicates nothing owing from Waterson. By that time it was obvious that the venture was doomed. The fee book shows no debit for the Waterson business until 27 Dec. 1772; the debit then was £55, and the corresponding credit, same date, shows the receipt of the two horses.

29. Thomas Lewis to Col. William Preston, 18 Sept. 1769, 28 Aug. 1770, Preston Davie Collection, Preston Family Papers.

30. *Journals, House of Burgesses, 1770–72*, 35, 57, 63, 72, 91, 107; Hening, *Statutes*, 8:386.

31. Preston Davie Collection, Preston Family Papers.

32. Anticipating the action of the court, Jefferson gave Waterson a list of his petitions with directions on how to give security, "to wit by bond to each def. £5 for every petn., and to inclose to me before the 7th of the court" (1770 account book, 13 Sept.). Pendleton wrote Colonel Preston on 29 April 1771: "Johnson is ruled to Security for costs as well as Waterson. . . . I understand Waterson will not get Security so his Petitions will be—dismissed when called—" (Mays, *Letters of Pendleton*, 1:64).

33. *Exec. Jour. Council*, 6:423, 426, 464, 466, 484–87, 494–96.

34. Mays, *Letters of Pendleton*, 1:64, 76.

35. CB 784–85, 852.

36. CB 575; 1767 account book, common memorandum section, 21–25 Aug. 1770.

37. E.g., CB 490–91, 508–11, 860–63.

38. 1770 account book, 19 Oct.; CB 612.

39. CB 816.

Notes to Chapter 6

1. Malone, *Jefferson and His Time*, 1:99.

2. For the riots, see Henderson, "Smallpox and Patriotism"; Watterson, "Poetic Justice"; Dabney, "Letters from Norfolk," 112–15.

3. Blanton, *Medicine in Va. in the 18th Century*, 284–85; Bernstein, "Smallpox and Variolation." See also article signed by Dr. John Dalgleish, *Va. Gaz.* (P. & D.), 14 Apr. 1768, and two articles signed "J. D.," ibid. (Rind), 2, 23 Nov. 1769.

4. Evans, "The Nelsons," 133. This smallpox outbreak appears to have been the same one reported as having occurred in Williamsburg (*Va. Gaz.* [P. & D.], 21, 28 Jan., 4 Feb., 3 Mar. 1768).

5. Tarter, *Order Book and Related Papers of the Borough of Norfolk*, 59–158; James, *Lower Norfolk Antiquary*, 1:16, 23, 117; *JPs of Colonial Virginia*, 84–85; Dabney, "Letters from Norfolk"; Read, "My Mother"; Tyler, *Encyc. Va. Biog.*, 1:191; Cross, "From the Archives," 10.

6. 1770 account book, 16 Apr.

7. Letter of Dr. Dalgleish in *Va. Gaz.* (P. & D.), 20 Oct. 1768.

8. *Va. Gaz.* (P. & D.), 9 Jan. 1772.

9. Ibid. (Rind), 22 Sept. 1768.

10. James Parker to Charles Steuart, 20 Oct. 1769, Charles Steuart Papers (MS 5025, f. 215), the collection from which all other Parker-Steuart correspondence cited in this chapter comes.

11. Boush letter, *Va. Gaz.* (Rind), 1 Sept. 1768; unsigned comment, ibid. (P. & D.), 8 Sept. 1768.

12. 1769 account book, 20 Dec.; CB 366.

13. Among the brothers of Cornelius, Maximilian, and Joseph Calvert were two named John and Jonathan; and Maximilian had a son named John. Nothing in the accounts of the riots indicates the involvement of any of them.

14. Parker to Steuart, 6 May 1769 (MS 5025, f. 128).

15. The order is appended to Cornelius Calvert's account of the 1769 riot in the *Va. Gaz.* (P. & D.), 9 Jan 1772.

16. Parker's account of the 1769 riot, particularly of the assault on his house, is found in the Charles Steuart Papers (MS 5025, ff. 123, 125, 126).

17. Ibid., ff. 138, 215.

18. Parker to Steuart, 20 Oct. 1769 (MS 5025, f. 215).

19. Boyd, *Papers*, 1:35.

20. 1770 account book, 16 Apr.

21. MS 5040, f. 96.

22. Despite Nicholas's intention to continue a full-time law practice after he became treasurer of the colony in 1766, he soon advertised that he would accept no new cases but would continue with John Blair's help to handle the business already in hand (*Va. Gaz.* [P. & D.], 21 May 1766, 1 Jan. 1767). Parker's reference to Nicholas's "coming out of retirement" seems to indicate that he was no longer active even in the cases that antedated the treasurership, although available for consultation if needed. See Freeman, *George Washington*, 3:226.

23. MS 5040, f. 97.

24. *Exec. Jour. Council*, 6:367.

25. Dec. 1770 (MS 5040, f. 118).

26. Ibid.

27. For the judgment of the court and the subsequent proceedings, see Cornelius Calvert's account in the *Va. Gaz.* (P. & D.), 1 Jan. 1772.

28. CB 410 shows that it was Parker who made the second payment. If he also made the first, that would explain why Jefferson did not apply any part of the overpayment to the fee owed by Campbell for the civil cases.

29. *Journals, House of Burgesses, 1766–69*, 269; Hening, *Statutes*, 8:371–74; Blanton, *Medicine in Va. in the 18th Century*, 285.

30. MS 5028, f. 98.

31. Boyd, *Papers*, 2:122–24; Hening, *Statutes*, 9:371–73; Malone, *Jefferson and His Time*, 1:399; Davis, *Intellectual Life in Jefferson's Virginia*, 186.

Notes to Chapter 7

1. "Early Law of Divorce in North Carolina," 605n.; Rheinstein, *Marriage Stability*, 31; Smith, *Appeals to the Privy Council*, 583-85.

2. Smith, *Appeals to the Privy Council, 583–85; Halem, Divorce Reform,* 12–17; "Early Law of Divorce in North Carolina," 606.

3. "Virginia Council Journals," 386n.; Hayden, "American Graduates in Medicine at U. of Edinburgh," 386.

4. William Lee Letter Book, 1769–71.

5. Wingo, *Marriages of Norfolk County, Va., 1706–92,* 1:5; *Va. Gaz.* (P. & D.), 23 May 1771; James, *Lower Norfolk County Antiquary,* 4:101.

6. Alden, "General Eustace," chap. 1.

7. Charles Steuart papers (MS 5025, f. 217).

8. 15 Aug. 1770, 3 May 1771, ibid. (MS 5040, f. 76, and MS 5025, f. 265).

9. John Randolph's argument in the dower case, as reported by Jefferson, in Dewey, "Thomas Jefferson and a Williamsburg Scandal," 50, 55; Coleman, *St. George Tucker,* 21.

10. The 25 May, 12 June, and 18 Nov. 1772 Parker letters quoted in this chapter are in the Charles Steuart Papers (MS 5027, ff. 159, 178, and 249).

11. Coleman, *St, George Tucker,* 13–21.

12. Tucker-Coleman Papers.

13. St. George Tucker to Dr. James Blair, 24 Sept. 1772, Tucker-Coleman Papers. All of Tucker's correspondence cited in this chapter is in this collection.

14. Ibid., 20 Sept. 1772.

15. 16 Sept. 1772.

16. Coleman, *St. George Tucker,* 22; St. George Tucker to Kitty Blair, 23 Sept. 1772.

17. *Va. Gaz.* (P. & D.), 31 Dec. 1772; *Va. Gaz.* (Rind), 7 Jan. 1773; John Randolph's argument in the dower case in Dewey, "Thomas Jefferson and a Williamsburg Scandal," 50; Hening, *Statutes,* 5:444, 445, 448.

18. 20 Feb. and 19 May 1773, Charles Steuart Papers (MS 5028 ff. 32, 73).

19. Pendleton relied heavily on Pufendorf and Milton, authorities that Jefferson had explored in preparing his notes on divorce.

20. The Jefferson report is published in full in Dewey, "Thomas Jsefferson and a Wiliamsburg Scandal."

21. Mrs. Eustace to Thomas Burke, 4 Nov. 1773, C. (Kitty) Blair to Burke, 18 Nov. 1774, Thomas Burke Papers.

22. *Va. Gaz.* (Purdie) 7 Feb. 1777; "Abstracts of Marriage License Bonds," 51; "Personal Notices from *Virginia Gazette,*" 95.

23. Shelley, "Journal of Ebenezer Hazard in Va.," 409.

24. I am indebted to Susan F. Murphy, Archivist of the Georgia Historical Society, for the Georgia information. Another indication of trouble in Kitty's second marriage is an undated deposition by John Blair, Dr. Blair's brother, in a suit in which Cuthbert was a defendant (Blair Family Papers). The plaintiff is unidentified but seems to have been Kitty, and the lawsuit

seems to have been one for separate maintenance. I wish to thank Margaret Cook, Curator of Manuscripts and Rare Books, Swem Library, College of William and Mary, for calling to my attention this deposition and the Tucker-Coleman papers referred to in this chapter.

25. Although Rind's *Virginia Gazette* reported on 22 Feb. 1770 that Jefferson had "lost all his furniture, a valuable collection of books, and what is perhaps worse, his papers" in the fire at Shadwell, Jefferson reported to John Page, Jr., on 21 Feb. that the loss "fell principally on m[y books] of common law" (Boyd, *Papers,* 1:35). By 1772 the rebuilding of his library obviously was well under way.

26. Tucker's edition of *Blackstone's Commentaries,* published in 1803, mentions three Virginia examples of legislative divorce *a vinculo matrimonii* for adultery, in 1789, 1790, and 1791 (vol. 1, pt. 2, 441n.). The implication is that these were the first in Virginia.

27. If Jefferson had persuaded the assembly to pass the bill, it would have required the governor's approval. In 1773 King George forbade royal governors to approve legislative divorces passed thereafter (Halem, *Divorce Reform,* 17). Moreover, in view of Dunmore's relationship to the Eustaces, it seems unlikely that he would have approved the divorce if Kitty opposed it.

28. Pufendorf, *Law of Nature,* bk. 2, chap. 3, sec. 1.

29. Sowerby, *Catalogue,* 2:69–70.

30. For instance, if he had read Montaigne, he would have realized that the Pufendorf citation of Montaigne, which he copied, was erroneous.

31. Sowerby, *Catalogue,* 5:168.

32. One might think from reading Jefferson's fourth note under the "Scriptural" heading that the Greek word would be found in Pufendorf, *Law of Nature,* bk. 6, chap. 1, sec. 24, n.3. In the fourth edition of Pufendorf in English, the one available to me, there is no such note; nor can I find the Greek word anywhere in chap. 1.

33. Owen, "Milton and Selden on Divorce," 242; Sowerby, *Catalogue,* 5:170.

34. Sowerby, *Catalogue,* 2:396–97. "Frederick appears to have been the first European ruler to pour the new ideas about divorce into the mold of legislation, first by an edict of 1751, and then in the great codification that was inspired by him but did not become law until 1794, eight years after his death" (Rheinstein, *Marriage Stability,* 25).

35. Pufendorf, *Law of Nature,* bk. 6, chap. 1, sec. 24.

36. After posing the question why the marriage compact should not be determinable like other voluntary compacts, "there being no Necessity, in the Nature of the thing, nor to the Ends of it, that it should always be for life," Locke added these words, "I mean, to such as are under no Restraint of any positive Law which ordains all such Contracts to be perpetual" (Locke, *Second Treatise,* chap. 7, sec. 81).

37. The caption "Blair v. Blair . . ." appears on the page of the manuscript that begins "Causes of Divorce among sev. nations." That is a larger

size page and may have been a cover. I have used the order adopted in the DLC microfilm.

38. In the manuscript the arguments "Pro" and "Con" appear in parallel columns with those headings. The first four items in the "Pro" column and the first five items in the "Con" column are taken from Hume's essay "Of Polygamy and Divorces" (Green and Grose, *David Hume: The Philosophical Works*, 2:231–39).

39. This is an almost verbatim quotation from Locke's *Second Treatise of Government*—the same passage referred to in note 36 above. Jefferson's number appears to be a page number in an edition which I have not identified.

40. A point made in Pufendorf, *Law of Nature*, bk. 6, chap. 1, sec. 10, as well as sec. 22. Hereafter all references to Pufendorf, unless otherwise indicated, are from *Law of Nature*, bk. 6, chap. 1.

41. John Milton wrote four essays urging relaxation of the English law regarding divorce. *The Doctrine and Discipline of Divorce* (1642; revised 1644), *The Judgement of Martin Bucer* (1644), *Tetrachordon* (1644/45), and *Colasterion* (1644/45). Milton later returned to the subject in *Angli pro Populo Anglicano Defensio Secunda . . .* (1654), and in *De Doctrina Christiana*, published posthumously (Wolfe, *Works of Milton*, 2:217–356, 416–79, 571–718, 719–58, 4:624–25, 6:371–81).

42. This item seems to have been taken, not from Pufendorf's summary of Milton, but directly from a passage in *Tetrachordon:* "Contentment of body they grant, which if it bee defrauded, the plea of frigidity shall divorce: But heer lies the fadomless absurdity, that granting this for bodily defect, they will not grant it for any defect of the mind" (Wolfe, *Works of Milton*, 2:623).

43. Derived from Pufendorf, sec. 22.

44. Ibid.

45. Seemingly derived from Pufendorf, sec. 10, which deals, not with divorce, but with marriage. Listing it as a reason for divorce seems to have been Jefferson's idea.

46. Paraphrasing part of Pufendorf's summary of Milton in sec. 23.

47. The first five "Con" arguments are Hume's. See note 38 above.

48. Jefferson's condensation of a passage of Hume's "Of Polygamy and Divorces" that ends: "The least possibility of a separate interest must be the source of endless quarrels and suspicions. What Dr. Parnel calls, The little pilf'ring temper of a wife, will be doubly ruinous." See Green and Grose, *David Hume: The Philosophical Works*, 2:239 and note.

49. Derived from Montesquieu, who said that "it is always a great misfortune for her to go in search of a second husband, when she has lost the most part of her attractions with another" (*The Spirit of Laws*, bk. 16, chap. 15).

50. "Woolt." has not been identified.

51. Taken from a Barbeyrac footnote (n. 4) to sec. 20 of Pufendorf.

52. The classic spelling is πορνεία. In the edition of Pufendorf available to me (the fourth English edition [1729]) the Greek word does not appear anywhere in book 6, chap. 1. The following passage appears in sec. 23,

paraphrasing Selden: "There were amongst the Jews two Sects, the Sammeans [Shammaites] and the Hillelians, who maintain'd contrary Notions on
the point before us. The former asserted, That a Man ought not to quit his
Wife, unless upon some Discovery of Baseness and Dishonesty: The latter,
That any Dislike taken of the Woman, was enough to justify a Divorce. Our
Saviour, then, as an Arbitrator between the two disputing Parties, declares
in Favour of the Sammeans; That it was not lawful upon slight Pretences, to
dissolve a Union instituted by God himself; but only upon the commission of
foul and scandalous Crimes, comprehended, according to the Genius of the
Hebrew Language, under the general Term of Fornication."

53. The suggestion seems to be that the Greek equivalents for "fornication" in the New Testament and "uncleanness" in the Old Testament were
essentially synonymous. Hence (as Milton argued) Christ's teaching, properly understood, did not repeal the Mosaic law of divorce.

54. Pufendorf quoted one Buxdorf as saying that God had permitted
divorce to the Jews because of the hardness of their hearts but had not
approved it. Milton's comment, as paraphrased by Pufendorf, was that the
argument was irreverent, "in as much as it betokens Infirmity in a Governor, to allow his Subjects in any Practice, to which he does not really give his
Approbation. And why must the Jews alone have been so notorious for
Hardness of Heart?" (Pufendorf, sec. 23 and sec. 24).

55. Seemingly derived from Montesquieu, who said it was tyrannical to
permit husbands to repudiate their wives without granting the same right to
women. "A husband is the master of the house; he has a thousand ways of
confining his wife to her duty" (*Spirit of Laws,* bk. 16, chap. 15).

56. Obviously the distinction that Montesquieu suggested, which would
define "divorce" as severance by mutual consent, has not been followed.

57. A paraphrase of a passage from Locke's *Second Treatise of Government,*
chap. 7, sec. 78.

58. Tonquin (Tonkin) is northern Vietnam.

59. The passage from Caesar is cited by Pufendorf, sec. 15.

60. This is the only reference to Locke that Jefferson could have obtained from Pufendorf without reading Locke. A Barbeyrac footnote to sec.
20 of Pufendorf paraphrases Locke on this point.

61. The story that divorces were unknown in ancient Rome for hundreds of years, until Carvilius Ruga repudiated his wife for barrenness, was
related by Pufendorf, Montesquieu, and Hume. Pufendorf and Montesquieu cited Valerius Maximus, and Hume and Montesquieu cited Dionysius
Halicarnassus. Jefferson was probably relying on Pufendorf, Montesquieu,
and Hume for these citations, though it is not inconceivable that he had
access to the Roman authors, since copies of their works were included in his
1815 library (Sowerby, *Catalogue,* 1:23, 50).

62. The Maldive Islands are in the Indian Ocean.

63. Pufendorf mentioned the "simple and irregular Marriage we may
call *Amazonian,* if any Credit is to be given to the Stories of those warlike
Dames" (sec. 9). He cited Justin among others.

64. The text at this point in the MS is arranged in two columns, the one at the left with no separate heading, and the one at the right headed "England before 4 Jac. 1."

65. The summary of the law of Romulus could have been taken from Montesquieu (*Spirit of Laws*, bk. 16, chap. 16), or Pufendorf, sec. 22; since most of the references in this part of the MS are to Pufendorf, the latter seems likely.

66. The summary of the later Roman law is taken from a Barbeyrac note to the Pufendorf text. The note cites "the law of Theodosius and Valentian."

67. The reference to Philo is taken from Pufendorf, sec. 23.

68. See note 52 above.

69. Of course, Milton was arguing what the law should be, not what it was.

70. Jefferson believed that English statutes enacted after America had been colonized could not be applied to the colonies, whether or not such application was intended, and that 1607 (the fourth year in the reign of James I) was the cutoff date. His views were shared by Virginia contemporaries. See, e.g., the arguments of Thomson Mason and John Randolph in *The King* v. *Dugard,* Jefferson's report of a case in the General Court in April 1773 (DLC).

71. *Rye* v. *Fuliambe* was a decision by the Star Chamber in the last year of Elizabeth's reign declaring that a divorce for adultery was *a mensa et thoro* (Sir Francis Moore's *Law Reports* [London, 1688], 683).

72. During the reign of James I, Thomas Hyot made an unsuccessful attempt to get the court of King's Bench to strike down the decree of an ecclesiastical court that had granted his wife separation and alimony. King's Bench held that the ecclesiastical court was the proper tribunal for the allowance of alimony and "may take order for separation or divorce if she be cruelly used" (Sir George Croke's *Law Reports* [London, 1657], 364).

73. "3.Bl." refers to vol. 3 of *Blackstone's Commentaries.*

74. "I find that by the ancient law of England, that if any Christian man did marry with a woman that was a Jew, it was felony, and the party so offending should be burnt alive" (Sir Edward Coke, *Institutes of the Laws of England,* vol. 3 ['4th ed., London, 1669], 89).

Notes to Chapter 8

1. There were at least two isolated instances of written codes in the nineteenth century, but the movement got off the ground with the adoption of the ABA Canons of Ethics in 1908. The Canons, as modified from time to time, were replaced in 1969 by the Code of Professional Repsonsibility. In 1983 the Model Rules of Professional Conduct became the ABA standard. In Virginia, the code of ethics is found in Section II of Part Six of the Rules of the Supreme Court. When the bar was made an arm of the state in 1938, the code consisted of the old canons of ethics (171 Va. xvii). They were replaced by the Code of Professional Responsibility in 1975 (215 Va. 859).

2. Biographical sketch of John Blair by Daniel Call in preface to vol. 4 of Call's *Reports;* Stanard, "The Randolph Family," 124.

3. Morris, "Legal Profession in America," 5; Hening, *Statutes*, 1:275, 302, 313, 340, 419, 482, 2:478, 498.

4. *Exec. Jour. Council*, 3:411, 420, 425–26.

5. Hening, *Statutes*, 4:360, 5:171, 345.

6. Jones, *American Members of Inns of Court*.

7. Morris, "Legal Profession in America," 18.

8. 1769 account book, Sept. 15.

9. Other cases: *Nicholson* v. *Price* (CB 409), "Use all delay"; *Nelson* v. *Willis* (CB 84), "Use every dilatory"; *Woodson* v. *Pleasants* (CB 203), "To delay as long as possible."

10. 1767 account book, Nov. 19. See also CB 803.

11. Boyd, *Papers*, 1:32; see chap. 5 above.

12. 1771 account book, Oct. 30. Another instance: *Lucas* v. *Rucker* (CB 493).

13. 1768 account book, May 17.

14. LE-IO (Informal Opinion) no. 377, *Virginia Bar News*, Feb. 1980, p. 19; *Mailer* v. *Mailer*, 455 N.E. 2d 1211 (1983).

15. Model Rules, Rule 1.9; *White Motor Co.* v. *White Consolidated Industries*, 395 N.E. 2d 1340 (Ohio App. 1978).

16. LE-IO no. 400B, *Virginia Bar News*, Feb. 1980, p. 22; no. 455, ibid., Dec. 1980, p. 43.

17. *Heathcoat* v. *Santa Fe Int'l*, 532 F. Supp. 961 (E.D. Ark. 1982).

18. *Realco Services, Inc.* v. *Holt*, 479 F. Supp. 867 (E.D. Pa. 1979).

19. Other instances: *Bibee* v. *Norrell* (CB 287), *Pleasants* v. *Bibee* (CB 892), *Witt* v. *Cribbins*, 1771 account book, Nov. 12, Dec. 21.

20. *Burford* v. *Rucker*, 1772 account book, Sept. 30.

21. LE-IO no. 591, *Virginia Bar News*, Aug. 1982, p. 61; Jefferson to White, 19 April 1769, Boyd, *Papers*, 1:25–26.

22. Copy of the opinion, including Jefferson's statement of facts, DLC; see Appendix D.

23. 1767 account book, common memorandum section, 13 Sept. 1769, Jan.–March, 1770.

24. For example, a firm that represents IBM in labor matters cannot represent IBM's opponent in an antitrust suit (*IBM* v. *Levin*, 579 F. 2d 271 [CCA-3d 1978]). A firm that represents *A* in defense of personal injury cases cannot represent *B* who thereafter sues *A* for breach of contract. (*McCourt Co., Inc.* v. *FPC Properties, Inc.*, 434 N.E. 2d 1234 [Mass. 1982]).

25. "Developments in the Law: Conflicts of Interest in the Legal Profession," *Harvard Law Review* 94 (1981): 1244, 1296.

26. Evans, *Thomas Nelson*, 26.

27. 1767 account book, common memorandum section, 21–25 Aug. 1770.

28. Hening, *Statutes*, 5:489–90, 6:326–27.

29. MacKenzie, *Appearance of Justice*, 180–83; Thode, *Reporters Notes to Code of Judicial Conduct;* 1974 *U.S. Code Cong. and Adm. News*, 6352; 28 U.S. Code, Sec. 455. The Virginia Code of Judicial Ethics is Section III of Part Six of the Rules of the Supreme Court.

30. Meade, *Patrick Henry,* 125, 128–29.

31. See chap. 6 above.

32. MacKenzie, *Appearance of Justice,* 186–87.

33. Evans, *Thomas Nelson,* 8.

34. See chap. 3 above.

35. See chap. 7 above.

36. See chap. 6 above.

37. In *Vietnamese, etc.* v. *Knights of the K.K.K.,* 518 F. Supp. 1017 (S.D. Texas 1981), it was held that a black judge, formerly local counsel for the NAACP, could properly try a case against the Knights of the Ku Klux Klan alleging the violation of the civil rights of Vietnamese fishermen. One draft of the canon provided that a judge should disqualify himself if he "had a fixed belief concerning the merits." This provision was dropped because many objected that it would bar a judge who had a fixed belief on the applicable law (Thode, *Reporter's Notes to Code of Judicial Conduct,* 61). For a discussion, see MacKenzie, *Appearance of Justice,* 207–23.

Notes to Chapter 9

1. Gustavus Scott's tenure as a General Court lawyer must have been brief, since he attended the Middle Temple 1765–71, and was a resident of Maryland in 1774 (Rutland, *Papers of George Mason,* 1:160). He is not mentioned in Jefferson's records.

2. In June and July 1773 he gave two opinions (one to William Byrd and one to a "vagrant taylor") without requiring payment at the time (CB 852, 856), and he was never paid for either. During the same months he accepted eight cases without requiring any payment on account (CB 842, 846–51, 854), and in one he advanced 5s. 9d. of his own money. After October 10 he received no payment at the time of hiring in CB 886–88, 899, 905, 906, and 911.

3. Hening, *Statutes,* 7:400.

4. Winfree, *Supplement to Hening's* Statutes, 149; Kimball, *Jefferson: The Road to Glory,* 92.

5. He charged Dr. Thomas Walker, Micajah Chiles, and James Kerr 10s. each, and David Meade £2, for drawing deeds (CB 71, 375, 378, 906); John Wilkinson, 20s. for drawing a mortgage (CB 516); Edmund Pendleton, 20s. for drawing two "bonds of arbitration" (CB 816); William Mickie, 20s. for drawing two clauses of a will and heads of a deed (CB 683); Robert and William Mickie, 21s. for drawing an instrument for division of their father's estate (CB 885). In the common memorandum section of his 1767 account book (entry of August 1770) he said that he was going to Amherst Courthouse in January 1771 to collect debts for William Nelson, and his 1771

account book shows that he went. He undoubtedly charged Nelson for this work, but what he charged and what he was paid are not recorded.

6. In addition to the instances noted in chapter 5, see CB 843, 910. Jefferson noted in his account book on 9 July 1773: "Rule. Agreed among the gentlemen who practice before the council that in future they will charge £5 in all caveats which are to stop escheat patents."

7. Two clients, two fees: CB 460. Several clients, one fee: CB 393, 435, 457, 458. Multiple fees charged to one client: CB 33.

8. The verdict is recorded, not in the case book, but on the abbreviated October 1769 docket (MHi, see Appendix D).

9. The verdict is recorded on the April 1771 docket (MHi).

10. Pp. 94–120.

11. 1770 account book, 8 Feb.

12. CB 84, 455, 456, and *Creditors of Francis Willis, Sr.* v. *Francis Willis, Jr.* (1773 account book, 11 Oct).

13. Francis Eppes of Eppington, Chesterfield County, married Elizabeth Wayles, half sister of Jefferson's wife.

14. CB 116, 845. Dumbauld, *Jefferson and the Law*, 90, gives other examples.

15. 1771 account book, 14 Feb; CB 125, 501, 507, 508, 510, 783.

16. E.g., successful petition for lapsed lands (CB 442) followed by friendly petition for same land (CB 865); successive caveats by same plaintiff for same land (CB 394, 592, 775); successful caveat followed by friendly caveat (CB 306); successive friendly petitions (CB 10, 11); revival of case abated by death (CB 47).

17. CB 916, 917.

18. CB 742, 752, 756, 757, 841, 853, 918, 919.

19. Randall, *Life of Jefferson*, 1:48. Randall apparently was not acquainted with Jefferson's fee book. He cited the "profit" figures for four years in Jefferson's 1771 account book (13 Aug.) and said that "the increase during the remaining four years must have been proportionately rapid."

20. Parton, *Life of Jefferson*, 80.

21. Schachner, *Thomas Jefferson*, 61.

22. See discussion of fee book in Appendix D.

23. E.g., CB 12, 110, 161, 459, 907.

24. CB 37, 570, 699, and 1772 account book, 13 Aug.

Notes to Chapter 10

1. Mays, *Letters of Pendleton*, 82–85.

2. Paragraph 748 of the commonplace book notes is part of the second paragraph of the Pendleton copy. Some of the abbreviated words in the commonplace book notes, such as "pl." for plaintiff, "def." for defendant, "agt." for against, "sd." for said, are spelled out in the copy. The copy omits the latter half of paragraph 744 of the commonplace book notes, apparently

by intention. Several other shorter omissions appear to have been made inadvertently.

3. Mays, *Edmund Pendleton*, 1:247.

4. P. 122.

5. In Mays, *Letters of Pendleton*, 82–85, the General Court's order of May 4 and the Pendleton opinion are grouped together under the dateline, "At a General court held at the capitol May the 4th, 1774." However, in the manuscript from which they were transcribed (Jefferson Papers, DLC), the heading and the court's order appear on one page and Pendleton's opinion begins on a separate page.

6. For the schedule of fees, adopted in 1745 and in effect until April 1774, see Hening, *Statutes*, 5:326–40. For the several statutes extending the schedule, see ibid., 6:200, 244, 7:242, 278, 384, 645, 8:186, 266, 299, 338, 515.

7. *Journals, House of Burgesses, 1773–76*, 36, 69–71.

8. Pendleton's opinion, Mays, *Letters of Pendleton*, 84.

9. *Journals, House of Burgesses, 1773–76*, 197.

10. *Va. Gaz.* (P. & D.), 21 April 1774.

11. Statements throughout this chapter regarding Jefferson's whereabouts are based on his 1774 account book and Betts, *Garden Book*.

12. In Jefferson's 1774 account book, 11 Aug., is a list headed "Judgmts &c in April 1773"; the list actually describes, for each of thirty-eight cases, what happened at the April 1774 court, as a check with his case book will verify.

13. General Court order and Pendleton's opinion, Mays, *Letters of Pendleton*, 82–85.

14. See summaries of two April 1767 judgments of the colonial General Court in actions for debt by Edmund Jenings of Great Britain against Benjamin Harrison and *Stewart* v. *Hightower*, a 1782 case in the postwar General Court (Tucker-Coleman Papers).

15. Neither Pendleton nor Jefferson mentioned a related problem concerning the power of a colonial governor to promulgate fees. The problem had arisen three times in Virginia, under governors Effingham (Mapp, *Virginia Experiment*, 1811), Dinwiddie (Smith, "Affair of the Pistole Fee"), and Dunmore (Mahan, "Virginia Reaction to British Policy," 213). The same problem had recurred in Maryland (Barker, *Background of Revolution*, 130–37, 221–27, 236, 337–54).

16. The Lee committee had failed to recommend renewal of the fee bill at the 1773 session, perhaps with the same strategy in mind. For disagreement between House and council on terms for extending the militia bill, see *Journals, House of Burgesses, 1770–72*, 291, 300–305; ibid., *1773–76*, 23,30, 34–35. For the dispute on the monetary aspect of the fee bill, see ibid., *1770–72*, 254, 266, 271, 273.

17. Reese, *Fauquier Papers*, 1293, 1363–64; Chitwood, *Richard Henry Lee*, 35–36.

18. *Journal, House of Burgesses, 1773–76*, 132.

19. "St. George Tucker," 35.

20. Washington to George William Fairfax, 10 June 1774, Fitzpatrick, *Writings*, 3:224.

21. Ibid., 223; George Mason to Martin Cockburn, 26 May 1774, Rutland, *Papers of George Mason*, 1:190; Richard Henry Lee to Samuel Adams, 24 April, 23 June 1774, Ballagh, *Letters of R. H. Lee*, 1:106, 111.

22. Van Schreeven, Scribner, and Tarter, *Revolutionary Virginia*, 1:258, 280.

23. P. 199.

24. 17 June 1774, Charles Steuart Papers (MS 5028, f. 207).

25. Ballagh, *Letters of R. H. Lee*, 1:122.

26. Van Schreeven, Scribner, and Tarter, *Revolutionary Virginia*, 1:109–65.

27. *Va. Gaz.* (Rind), 8 Sept. 1774; see also James Parker to Charles Steuart, 14 Aug. 1774, Charles Steuart Papers (MS 5028, f. 242).

28. *Journals, House of Burgesses, 1773–76*, 234–37; Mays, *Edmund Pendleton*, 1:305, 2:151; Cullen, "St. George Tucker," 44.

29. William Allason Letter Book, 1770–89.

30. An order for the Jefferson opinion from the library of Congress photo-duplication service brings a package of seventeen manuscript pages including a copy of the General Court order in Pendleton's handwriting, Pendleton's opinion, Jefferson's "opinion," a single sheet bearing the inscription in Jefferson's handwriting "On the power of the General court to establish Fees, E. Pendleton & T. Jefferson, opinons," another copy of the General Court order signed by B. Waller, and a page of notes in Jefferson's handwriting containing a list of fee bills from 1661 to 1772, and the following outline.

Analysis

Fees establd

1 by act of parl—this includes Usage.

obj[ection, i.e., an opposing argument] has been usage from 1745 to 1774. A shorter usage do in some cases than others.

ans. this would confuse temporary and perpetual acts. explain case of new cu[stom] of merchants.

2 by verd of jury

obj. Gifford's ca. Salk. [a case in Salkeld's *Reports*, cited in Pendleton's opinion] if jury find reasonable is then establd so one verd[ict] s[u]ff[icien]t

ans. absurd. every man entitled to verd.

may be one verd. by collusion.

what reason in law why one man bnd by verd where was not party?

reasonable to suppose unguarded expression of a Reporter very short

obj. Hawk. c. 68 case of bar fee assessed by court [Pendleton cited this as an instance of a fee set by a court] ans. deny it was known by whom assessed bec had subsisted from time immemorial.

obj. Salk Gifford's ca. this power in court 'defensible on Ld Holt's principles' [another reference to Pendleton's opinion]

ans strange when Ld Holt in that case expressly denies the power.

31. *Exec. Jour. Council,* 6:564–77. Jefferson's caveats can be identified from his case book and other records. The two noncaveat cases were *Davies* v. *Bush* (CB 875) and *Donald* v. *Meade* (CB 879), both decided on June 16.

32. Malone, *Jefferson and His Time,* 1:180.

33. Mays, *Letters of Pendleton,* 98.

34. Ibid., 83.

35. Jefferson's collection was the basis for Hening's *Statutes* (Dumbauld, *Jefferson and the Law,* 121–22).

Notes to Chapter 11

1. Hemphill, "Edmund Randolph Assumes Jefferson's Practice."

2. Reardon, *Edmund Randolph,* 5, 14–15. Reardon speculates that young Randolph had some experience in the inferior courts before being admitted to the General Court, but his youth makes this unlikely.

3. Jefferson-Coolidge Papers, MHi.

4. *Journals, House of Burgesses, 1766–69,* xix.

5. Presumably the understanding was that Randolph would charge no duplicative fee. It was on such an understanding that Jefferson took over George Wythe's caveat cases in 1768 (CB 167) and some of John Blair's cases when Blair quit the practice in 1770 (1771 account book, 14 Jan.).

6. The case book identifies all of the caveats except one. That one— *Sparrow* v. *Rudder* (CB 933)—is included in a list of caveats in the 1774 account book immediately preceding the entry for 27 August.

7. Betts, *Garden Book,* 54.

8. His week at court was a busy one. In his 1774 account book, under date of 11 Aug., immediately following the list of client balances prepared for Edmund Randolph, is a list of actions taken on his cases at the April 1774 court, though the date is mistakenly shown as April 1773. A case-by-case reference to the case book verifies the 1774 date, as does a two-page list of cases in Jefferson's handwriting headed "April 1774" (MHi; see Appendix D).

9. See chap. 10 above.

10. *Exec. Jour. Council,* 6:564–77.

11. 1774 account book, list immediately preceding entry for 27 August.

12. Malone, *Jefferson and His Time,* 1:180; Kimball, *Jefferson: The Road to Glory,* 238.

13. See chap. 10 above.

14. Reese, *Fauquier Papers,* 1293; *Va. Gaz.* (Rind), 8 Sept. 1774; James Parker to Charles Steuart, 14 Aug., 26 Oct. 1774, Charles Steuart Papers (MS 5028, ff. 242, 273).

15. Bartholomew Dandridge, who practiced law in New Kent and Charles City counties, advertised in the *Va. Gaz.* (P. & D.) of 16 June 1774 that "as soon as the Courts proceed on their Dockets," he proposed to extend his practice to James City and York counties and the Williamsburg hustings. See also chap. 10 above.

16. See chap. 9 above.

17. Malone, *Jefferson and His Time*, 1:161–63.

18. Ibid., 143–50; Kimball, *Jefferson: The Road to Glory*, 150–59.

19. Betts, *Garden Book*, frontispiece.

20. *Jefferson and His Time*, 6:109. See also Padover, *Life of Jefferson*, 24.

21. Lipscomb and Bergh, *Writings*, 12:355.

22. Dumbauld, *Jefferson and the Law*, xiii.

23. Malone, *Jefferson and His Time*, 6:423.

24. See chap. 10 for an instance in which Jefferson matched legal skills with Pendleton. A match between Wythe and Jefferson is described by Dumbauld in *Jefferson and the Law*, 94–120.

Notes to Appendix A

1. P. 88.

2. Misc. Accounts folder, box 13.

3. Mays, "Peter Lyons," 418.

4. Beeman, *Patrick Henry*, 8, 9.

5. *Faithful Magistrates*, 124.

6. Ford, *Writings*, 1:6.

7. Malone, *Jefferson and His Time*, 1:92–93.

8. *Va. Gaz.* Day Books. The Day Books listed this book simply as "Grounds and Rudiments of Law." The complete title is taken from the *Catalogue of the Library of Harvard Law School* (Cambridge, Mass., 1909). Thirty pages of handwritten notes on this book are bound with Jefferson's legal commonplace book, but the notes are not believed to be in Jefferson's handwriting (Chinard, *Commonplace Book*, 3).

9. Betts, *Garden Book*, 1.

10. See chap. 2 above.

11. Reese, *Fauquier Papers*, 1290–94, 1363–64.

12. Lipscomb and Bergh, *Writings*, 1:4.

13. Tucker, *Thomas Jefferson*, 42; Dumbauld, *Jefferson and the Law*, xi.

14. *Address to the People of the United States*, 226. I am indebted to John M. Hemphill II for calling the Beckley material to my attention.

15. Jefferson's notes are found on the reverse of f. 39161, ser. 1, Jefferson Papers, DLC ("Jefferson Thomas—Career, 1800 SE, Memorandum," *Index to the Jefferson Papers, Library of Congress*, p. 74). I am indebted to Paul G. Sifton of the Library of Congress for locating them.

16. The fact that Jefferson began a three-month trip north in May 1766 is fairly conclusive evidence that he did not seek admission in April.

Notes to Appendix B

1. *Life of Jefferson,* 1:47.
2. *Thomas Jefferson,* 8.
3. *Jefferson: The Road to Glory,* 90.
4. *Jefferson and His Time,* 1:119.
5. "A Mirror of the Southern Colonial Lawyer," 533.
6. *Jefferson,* 43.
7. Hening, *Statutes,* 6:143, 7:124, 399.
8. *Jefferson: The Road to Glory,* 89.
9. "A Mirror of the Southern Colonial Lawyer," 524.
10. Boyd, *Papers,* 2:235.
11. Mays, *Edmund Pendleton,* 1:28.
12. *Va. Gaz.,* 3 Oct. 1771.
13. Tucker-Coleman Papers.

Notes to Appendix C

1. Sir Edward Coke, *Institutes of the Laws of England,* in four volumes. Volume 1, also known as *Coke on Littleton,* was published in 1628; vol. 4, in 1644.

2. Sir John Fortescue, *A Learned Commendation on the Politique Lawes of England.* This work, first printed in Latin, was published in English in 1567. Coke (2:209) quoted Fortescue, and Jefferson probably was relying here on Coke rather than on his own reading of Fortescue.

3. First Statute of Westminster, a collection of statutes passed by the first Parliament in the reign of Edward I (1275).

4. *Coke on Littleton.* See note 1 above.

5. *Topsall* v. *Ferrers,* Hobart 175, 80 Eng. Rep. 323 (Common Pleas, 1618). Ferrer's wife had died in one parish but had been buried in another. The authorities of the first parish alleged a custom entitling them to the same fees as though she had been buried in their parish. The claim was rejected on the ground that the custom was unreasonable.

6. Sir Matthew Bacon's *A New Abridgement of the Law* appeared in five volumes from 1736 to 1766 (Dumbauld, *Jefferson and the Law,* 170n).

7. Jefferson is being hypercritical. Surely no one could take Bacon's meaning to be that fees allowed by act of Parliament retained their validity after parliamentary authorization had been withdrawn.

8. The words in angle brackets appear in the commonplace book version but were omitted by the copyist, presumably in error.

9. That is, the letters patent were granted in the thirty-fifth year of the reign of Henry VIII.

10. *Earl of Devonshire's Case,* 11 Coke Rep. 89a, 77 Eng. Rep. 1266 (King's Bench, 1607). "4 Jac. 1" means the fourth year of the reign of James I, i.e., 1607.

11. In his transcription of the commonplace book version, Chinard omitted these words, saying "two words erased."

12. The words in angle brackets do not appear in the Pendleton copy, presumably by error.

13. The case reported in the Year Book for the twenty-first year of the reign of Henry VII at f. 17 upheld the "bar fee" taken by the sheriff from an acquitted prisoner. The court's opinion clearly based its holding on the ground that the fee had been authorized by the court. I wish to thank Edith Henderson of the Harvard Law School treasure room for her translation of this case from law French.

14. The word "antient" appears in the commonplace book but was omitted in Pendleton's copy, probably inadvertently.

15. *Ex parte Jephson,* Precedents in Chancery 549, 24 Eng. Rep. 297 (1720). The serjeant at arms complained that certain functions, formerly exercised by him, were being exercised by the warden of the fleet, depriving him of fees to which he was entitled by ancient rules and practice. At p. 551: "The Lord Chancellor ordered the Register to look into the precedents, and to certify to him how the practice had gone, but said, that if the Serjeant at Arms was entitled by the ancient course to a fee by the caption in these cases, that it could not be altered without an act of parliament."

16. The "action by the promoter of the king" is the Year Book case described in note 13.

17. Sir Robert Brooke, *La Graunde Abridgement,* first published in 1573. The words in quotation marks must be Brooke's, because they do not appear in the text of the Year Book case.

18. "S. P. C." is Jefferson's abbreviation for Sir William Staunford, *Les Plees del Coron* (London, 1557; rept. London, 1971).

19. There is an unconscious irony here. Jefferson does not seem to realize that he has just done what he accuses Hawkins of doing. In the case of the bar fee, he has urged that the true ground of decision must be one that the court did not articulate, namely, that the custom existed from time immemorial. Hawkins's justification of the bar fee was the one voiced by the court in 21 H. 7, 17.

20. 1 Salkeld 333, 91 Eng. Rep. 293 (King's Bench, 1702).

21. *Veale* v. *Priour,* Hardres 351, 145 Eng. Rep. 492 (Exchequer, 1664) held that the defendant official was entitled to be paid the value of his services, though no fee was stipulated by the statute creating the office.

22. *Gifford's Case,* 1 Salkeld 333, 91 Eng. Rep. 293 (King's Bench, 1702). Although the page number is the same as for *Ballard* v. *Gerard* (see note 20), they are different cases. Pendleton's opinion said these cases stood for the proposition that a court could set a fee, but that the defendant had the option of taking his case to a jury. Jefferson challenged this interpretation, pointing out that in both cases the King's Bench had forbidden an ecclesiastical court to give judgment for a fee fixed by that court.

23. *Johnson* v. *Lee,* 5 Mod. 238, 87 Eng. Rep. 631 (King's Bench, 1701).

Notes to Appendix D

1. *Thompson* v. *Robertson*, 1770 account book, 8 Feb.; 1770 account book, 16 July.

2. *Dalton* v. *Lucas*, 1773 account book, 18 Jan. (personal accts.).

3. The 1775 account book (HM 590) is in the Henry E. Huntington Library, San Marino, Calif. For the location of the manuscripts for subsequent years, see Malone, *Jefferson and His Time*, 1:459.

4. 1775 account book, 26 Jan., 14 Feb.

5. 1776 account book, 10 Jan., 15 Mar.

6. The *Index to the Jefferson Papers, Library of Congress* lists (p. 75) a *Pentecost* case in 1778. The one-page document is a list of questions posed, apparently for Jefferson to answer. They concern an area claimed by both Virginia and Pennsylvania; Virginia designated it as the district of West Augusta. Each colony appointed its own officials for the disputed area, and challenged the credentials of the officials appointed by the other. Dorsey Pentecost was the court clerk appointed by Virigina (Crumrine, *The County Court for the District of West Augusta*, 16–17, 22).

7. The published version of the Watkins opinion contains an interesting error. Jefferson cites six cases in a row, giving for each the reference to his equity commonplace book, abbreviated "Com. pla." The editor has misread the citation as "Com. ple.," perhaps considering it as an abbreviation for "common pleas." This use of the equity commonplace book suggests the possibility that Jefferson used both the legal and equity notebooks as a portable law library while he was in active practice.

8. The documents described in the text appear in the following order on reel 1. First come the fragments mentioned; they appear on the front and back of the first page of a letter from John Page dated April 1770. Then follows the page described in the last sentence of the text, then the page identified as the fifth page of the April 1770 docket, then the first four pages of the same docket.

9. One page of the docket proper (containing the seventeenth- and eighteenth-day lists) is printed twice on the microfilm.

10. Four pages of the docket proper are printed twice on the microfilm: two of them are the twelfth-, thirteenth-, and fourteenth-day lists; the other two, the pages of the twenty-second-day list headed by *Jordan* v. *Johnson* and *White* v. *Anderson*.

Bibliography

See Appendix D for Jefferson manuscripts relating to his law practice.

Manuscripts (Other than Jefferson's) and Public Documents

William Allason Letter Book, 1770–89. David and William Allason Business Records, acc. no. 13. Business Record Collection, Archives Branch, Virginia State Library, Richmond.

Blair Family Papers. Swem Library, College of William and Mary, Williamsburg, Va.

Thomas Burke Papers. Acc. no. 104. Southern Historical Collection, Library of the University of North Carolina at Chapel Hill. Microfilm at Colonial Williamsburg Foundation research library.

Letter Books of Robert Carter of Nomini Hall, 1760–64, 1764–68. Special Collections, Colonial Williamsburg Foundation, Williamsburg, Va.

William Lee Letter Book, 1769–71. DuPont Library, Stratford Hall, Stratford, Va.

John Mercer Papers, Ledger B. Bucks County Historical Society, Doylestown, Pa. Microfilm at Colonial Williamsburg Foundation research library.

Wilson Cary Nicholas Papers. Acc. no. 2343. Manuscripts Department, University of Virginia Library, Charlottesville.

Order Books of Virginia County Courts. Microfilm at Archives Branch, Virginia State Library.

Preston Family Papers. Virginia Historical Society, Richmond.

Charles Steuart Papers. National Library of Scotland, Edinburgh. Microfilm at Colonial Williamsburg Foundation research library.

Tucker-Coleman Papers. Swem Library, College of William and Mary.

Virginia Gazette Day Books, 1764–66. Acc. no. 467. Manuscripts Department, University of Virginia Library. Bound photostatic copies at Colonial Williamsburg Foundation research library.

Newspapers

Richmond Argus. Microfilm at Virginia Historical Society.

Virginia Gazette. Purdie and Dixon (P. & D.), Rind, Pinkney, and Purdie. Bound volumes at Colonial Williamsburg Foundation research library.

Books and Articles

"Abstracts of Marriage License Bonds." *William and Mary Quarterly (WMQ)*, 1st ser., 1 (1892): 48–59.

Adams, John. *Diary and Autobiography of John Adams.* Ed. Lyman H. Butterfield. 4 vols. Cambridge, Mass., 1961.

——. *Legal Papers of John Adams.* Ed. L. Kinvin Wroth and Hiller B. Zobel. 3 vols. Cambridge, Mass., 1965.

Ballagh, James Curtis., ed. *Letters of Richard Henry Lee.* 2 vols. New York, 1911.

Barker, Charles A. *Background of the Revolution in Maryland.* New Haven and London, 1940.

Barton, Robert T., ed. *Colonial Decisions.* 2 vols. Boston, 1909.

Beckley, John [Americanus]. *Address to the People of the United States: with an Epitome and Vindication of the Public Life and Character of Thomas Jefferson.* 1800. Rept. in James Lyon, ed., *National Magazine; or, a Political Historical, Biographical, and Literary Repository* 2 (1800): 226–31.

Beeman, Richard R. *Patrick Henry: A Biography.* New York, 1974.

Bernstein, Solon S. "Smallpox and Variolation: Their Historical Significance in the American Colonies." *Journal of the Mt. Sinai Hospital* 18 (1951): 228–44.

Betts, Edwin M., ed. *Thomas Jefferson's Garden Book, 1766–1824* Philadelphia, 1944.

Blanton, Wyndham B. *Medicine in Virginia in the Eighteenth Century.* Richmond, 1981.

Boorstin, Daniel J. *The Americans: The Colonial Experience.* New York, 1958.

Boyd, Julian P. "The Need for 'Frequent Recurrence to Fundamental Principles.'" *Virginia Law Review,* 52 (1976): 859–71.

——, et al., eds. *The Papers of Thomas Jefferson.* Princeton, N.J., 1950—.

Bryson, William Hamilton, ed. *The Virginia Law Reporters before 1880.* Charlottesville, 1977.

Call, Daniel. *Reports of Cases Argued and Ajudged in the Court of Appeals in Virginia.* Vol. 4. Richmond, 1801; rept. Charlottesville, 1902.

Campbell, Norine Dickson. *Patrick Henry: Patriot and Statesman.* New York, 1969.

Chinard, Gilbert. *The Commonplace Book of Thomas Jefferson*. Baltimore, 1926.

Chitwood, Oliver Perry. *Richard Henry Lee: Statesman of the Revolution*. Morgantown, W. Va., 1967.

Coleman, Mary Haldane. *St. George Tucker, Citizen of No Mean City*. Richmond, 1938.

Cross, Eleanor P., and Charles B. Cross. "From the Archives." *Publications, Norfolk County Historical Society of Chesapeake* 5 (1966): 9–53.

Crumrine, Boyd. *The County Court for the District of West Augusta, Virginia, Held at Augusta Town, near Washington, Pennsylvania, 1776–1777*. Bulletin, Washington County Historical Society. 1905.

Cullen, Charles T. "New Light on John Marshall's Legal Education and Admission to the Bar." *American Journal of Legal History* 16 (1972): 345–51.

Cunningham, Noble E., Jr. "John Beckley: An Early American Party Manager." *WMQ*, 3d ser., 13 (1956): 40–52.

Curtis, George M., III. "The Role of Courts in the Making of the Revolution in Virginia." In James Kirby Martin, ed. *The Human Dimensions of Decision Making*. Madison, Wis., 1976.

Dabney, William M. "Letters from Norfolk: Scottish Merchants View the Revolutionary Crisis." In Darret B. Rutman, ed. *The Old Dominion: Essays for Thomas Perkins Abernethy*. Charlottesville, 1964.

Davis, John W. "Thomas Jefferson, Attorney-at-Law." *Proceedings, Virginia State Bar Association* 38 (1926): 361–77.

Davis, Richard Beale. *Intellectual Life in Jefferson's Viginia, 1790–1830*. 1964; rept. Knoxville, Tenn., 1972.

Dewey, Frank L. "New Light on the General Court of Colonial Virginia." *William and Mary Law Review* 21 (1979): 1–14.

——. "Thomas Jefferson and a Williamsburg Scandal." *Virginia Magazine of History and Biography (VMHB)*, 89 (1981): 44–63.

——. "Thomas Jefferson's Law Practice: The Norfolk Anti-Inoculation Riots." *VMHB* 91 (1983): 39–53.

——. "Thomas Jefferson's Notes on Divorce." *WMQ*, 3d ser., 39 (1982): 212–23.

Dill, Alonzo Thomas. *George Wythe: Teacher of Liberty*. Williamsburg, Va., 1979.

Drinard, James Elliott. "James Mercer, 1736–1793." *Proceedings, Virginia State Bar Association* 40 (1928): 423–35.

——. "John Blair, Jr., 1732–1800." *Proceedings, Virginia State Bar Association* 39 (1923): 436–49.

Dumbauld, Edward. *Thomas Jefferson, American Tourist*. Norman, Okla., 1946.

——. *Thomas Jefferson and the Law.* Norman, Okla., 1978.

"Early Statutory and Common Law of Divorce in North Carolina." *North Carolina Law Review* 41 (1963): 604–16.

Eaton, Clement. "A Mirror of the Southern Colonial Lawyer: the Fee Books of Patrick Henry, Thomas Jefferson, and Waightstill Avery." *WMQ,* 3d ser., 8 (1951): 520–34.

Evans, Emory G. *Thomas Nelson of Yorktown: Revolutionary Virginian.* Charlottesville, 1975.

Executive Journals of the Council of Colonial Virginia. 6 vols. Ed. Henry R. McIlwaine et al. Richmond, 1928–66.

Fitzpatrick, John C., ed. *The Writings of George Washington.* 39 vols. Washington, D.C., 1931–44.

Ford, Paul Leicester, ed. *The Writings of Thomas Jefferson.* 10 vols. New York, 1892–99.

Freeman, Douglas Southall. *George Washington.* 7 vols. New York, 1948–57.

Garrett, Wendell. *Thomas Jefferson Redivivus.* Barre, Mass., 1971.

Goebel, Julius, Jr., ed. *The Law Practice of Alexander Hamilton.* 2 vols. New York and London, 1964.

Green, Thomas Hill, and Thomas Hodge Grose, eds. *David Hume: The Philosophical Works.* 4 vols. London, 1886; rept. Darmstadt, 1964.

Greene, Jack P. *The Quest for Power.* Chapel Hill, N.C., 1963.

Grigsby, Hugh Blair. *The Virginia Convention of 1776.* Richmond, 1855.

——. *History of the Virginia Federal Convention of 1788.* 2 vols. Richmond, 1890–91.

Groome, Harry Connelly. *Fauquier during the Proprietorship.* Richmond, 1927.

Halem, Lynne Carol. *Divorce Reform.* New York, 1980.

Harvard Law School. *Catalogue of the Library of Harvard Law School.* Cambridge, Mass., 1909.

Hayden, H. E. "American Graduates in Medicine at University of Edinburgh." *New England Historical and Genealogical Register,* 41 (1887): 391–93.

Hemphill, John M., II, ed. "Edmund Randolph Assumes Thomas Jefferson's Practice." *VMHB* 67 (1959): 170–71.

Henderson, Patrick. "Smallpox and Patriotism: The Norfolk Riots, 1768–1769." *VMHB* 73 (1965): 413–24.

Hening, William Waller, ed. *The Statutes at Large: Being a Collection of All the Laws of Virginia. . . .* 13 vols. Richmond, Philadelphia, and New York, 1809–23.

Hilldrup, Robert Leroy. *The Life and Times of Edmund Pendleton.* Chapel Hill, N.C., 1939.

Hume, David. "Of Polygamy and Divorces." In Green and Grose, eds., *David Hume: The Philosophical Works*, 2:231–39.

Index to the Thomas Jefferson Papers, Library of Congress. Washington, D.C., 1976.

James, Edward W., eds. *The Lower Norfolk County, Virginia, Antiquary.* 5 vols. Richmond and Baltimore, 1895–1906; rept. New York, 1951.

Jefferson, Thomas. *Reports of Cases Determined in the General Court of Virginia.* Charlottesville, 1829.

Johnson, Herbert A., et al., eds. *The Papers of John Marshall*, Chapel Hill, N.C., 1974—.

Jones, E. Alfred. *American Members of the Inns of Court.* London, 1924.

Jones, Harry W., ed. *Political Separation and Legal Continuity.* Chicago, 1976.

Journal of the House of Delegates of Virginia, 1777–1778. Richmond, 1827.

Journals of the House of Burgesses, 1761–1776. Ed. John Pendleton Kennedy. Richmond, 1905–7.

Kimball, Marie G. *Jefferson: The Road to Glory, 1743 to 1776.* New York, 1943.

Kutak, Robert J. "Modern Rules of Professional Conduct: Ethical Standards for the '80s and Beyond." *American Bar Association Journal* 67 (1981): 1116–20.

Lipscomb, Andrew A., and Albert E. Bergh, eds. *The Writings of Thomas Jefferson.* 20 vols. Washington, D.C., 1903.

Locke, John. *The Second Treatise of Government: An Essay concerning the True Origin, Extent, and End of Civil Government.* London, 1690.

McIlwaine, Henry R., ed. *Justices of the Peace of Colonial Virginia, 1757–1773.* Richmond, 1922.

MacKenzie, John P. *The Appearance of Justice.* New York, 1974.

Malone, Dumas. *Jefferson and His Time.* 6 vols. Boston, 1948–81.

Mapp, Alf J., Jr. *The Virginia Experiment.* 2d ed. La Salle, Ill., 1974.

Mays, David John. *Edmund Pendleton, 1721–1803: A Biography.* 2 vols. Cambridge, Mass., 1952.

——. "Peter Lyons." *Proceedings of the Virginia State Bar Association* 38 (1926): 418–26.

——, ed. *The Letters and Papers of Edmund Pendleton, 1734–1803.* Charlottesville, 1967.

Meade, Robert D. *Patrick Henry: Patriot in the Making.* Philadelphia and New York, 1957.

Montesquieu, Baron de. *The Spirit of Laws.* Paris, 1748. Trans. Thomas Nugent. New York, 1900.

Morris, Richard B. "The Legal Profession in America on the Eve of the Revolution." In Harry W. Jones, ed. *Political Separation and Legal Continuity.* Chicago, 1976.

Morton, Louis. *Robert Carter of Nomini Hall.* Williamsburg, Va., 1941.

Mulkearn, Lois, ed. *George Mercer Papers Relating to the Ohio Company of Virginia.* Pittsburgh, 1954.

Nance, R. Earl. "Sir John Randolph." In W. Hamilton Bryson, ed. *The Virginia Law Reporters before 1880.* Charlottesville, 1977.

Owen, Elvion. "Milton and Selden on Divorce." *Studies in Philology* 43 (1946): 233–57.

Padover, Saul. *Life of Jefferson.* New York, 1922.

Parton, James. *Life of Thomas Jefferson, Third President of the United States.* Boston, 1874.

"Personal Notices from *Virginia Gazette.*" *WMQ,* 1st ser., 11 (1902): 93-98.

"Prince George County Records." *VMHB* 4 (1897): 272–92.

Pufendorf, Baron Samuel. *The Law of Nature and Nations: or, A General System of the Most Important Principles of Morality, Jurisprudence, and Politics.* Lund, Sweden, 1672. English translation by Basil Kennet. 4th ed. London, 1729.

Randall, Henry S. *The Life of Thomas Jefferson.* 3 vols. New York, 1858.

Randolph, Edmund. *Revolutionary History of Virginia.* Ed. Arthur Harvey Shaffer. Charlottesville, 1970.

Rankin, Hugh F. "The General Court of Colonial Virginia: Its Jurisdiction and Personnel." *VMHB* 70 (1962): 142–53.

Read, Helen Calvert. "My Mother." In James, *Lower Norfolk Antiquary* 1(1895): 60–61, 96–97.

Reardon, John J. *Edmund Randolph: A Biography.* New York, 1974.

Records of Augusta County, Virginia: 1745–1800. Baltimore, 1966.

"Records of Charles City County." *VMHB* 22 (1914): 433–36.

Reese, George, ed. "The Court of Vice-Admiralty in Virginia and Some Cases of 1770–1775." *VMHB* 88 (1980): 301–37.

———. *Official Papers of Francis Fauquier, Lieutenant Governor of Virginia, 1758–1768.* 3 vols. Charlottesville, 1980–83.

Rheinstein, Max. *Marriage Stability, Divorce, and the Law.* Chicago, 1972.

Riely, Henry C. "Paul Carrington." *Proceedings, Virginia State Bar Association* 39 (1928): 450–64.

Roeber, A. G. *Faithful Magistrates and Republican Lawyers: Creators of Virginia Legal Culture, 1680–1810.* Chapel Hill, N.C., 1981.

Rowland, Kate Mason. *The Life of George Mason.* 2 vols. New York, 1892.

Rutland, Robert A., ed. *The Papers of George Mason, 1725–1792.* Chapel Hill, N.C., 1970.

Schachner, Nathan. *Thomas Jefferson.* New York, 1957.

Scott, Arthur B. *Criminal Law in Colonial Virginia.* Chicago, 1930.

Shaw, Peter. *The Character of John Adams.* Chapel Hill, N.C., 1976.

Shelley, Fred, ed. "Journal of Ebenezer Hazard in Virginia." *VMHB* 62 (1954): 400–423.

Simpson, William S. "Dabney Carr: Portrait of a Colonial Patriot." *Virginia Cavalcade* 23 (1974): 5–13.

Smith, Glenn Curtis. "The Affair of the Pistole Fee." *VMHB* 48 (1940): 209–21.

Smith, Joseph Henry. *Appeals to the Privy Council from the American Plantations.* New York, 1950.

Smith, Page. *Jefferson, a Revealing Biography.* New York, 1976.

"Some Virginians Educated in Great Britain." *VMHB* 21 (1913): 196–99.

Sowerby, E. Millicent, comp. *Catalogue of the Library of Thomas Jefferson.* 5 vols. Washington, D.C., 1952–59.

Stanard, William G. "The Randolph Family." *WMQ,* 1st ser., 7 (1899): 122–24.

Summers, Lewis Preston. *History of Southwest Virginia, 1746–1786, Washington County, 1777–1870.* Richmond, 1903.

Sydnor, Charles S. *Gentlemen Freeholders.* Chapel Hill, N.C. 1952.

Tarter, Brent, ed. *Order Book and Related Papers of the Borough of Norfolk, Virginia, 1736–1798.* Richmond, 1979.

Thode, E. Wayne. *Reporter's Notes to Code of Judicial Conduct.* Chicago, 1973.

Tinling, Marion, ed. *The Correspondence of the Three William Byrds of Westover, Virginia, 1684–1776.* 2 vols. Charlottesville, 1977.

Tucker, George. *The Life of Thomas Jefferson.* Philadelphia, 1837.

Tucker, St. George, ed. *Blackstone's Commentaries: with Notes of Reference, to the Constitution and Laws of the Federal Government of the United States; and of the Commonwealth of Virginia.* 5 vols. Philadelphia, 1803; rept. South Hackensack, N.J., 1969.

Tyler, Lyon Gardiner. "Early Courses and Professors at William and Mary College." *WMQ,* 1st ser., 14 (1905): 71–83.

———, ed. *Encyclopedia of Virginia Biography.* 5 vols. New York, 1915.

Van Schreeven, W. J., Robert L. Scribner, and Brent Tarter, eds. *Revolutionary Virginia: The Road to Independence.* 7 vols. Charlottesville, 1973–83.

"Virginia Council Journals.." *VMHB* 32 (1924): 370–400.

Waddell, Joseph Addison. *Annals of Augusta County, Virginia, 1726–1871.* Bridgewater, Va., 1950.

Walker, Leola O. "Officials in the City Government of Colonial Williamsburg." *VMHB* 75 (1967): 34–51.

Watterson, John, ed. "Poetic Justice; or, An Ill-fated Epic by Thomas Burke." *North Carolina Historical Review* 55 (1978): 339–46.

"Williamsburg—The Old Colonial Capital." *WMQ*, 1st ser., 16 (1907): 1–65.

Winfree, Waverly K., comp. *The Laws of Virginia: Being a Supplement to Hening's* The Statutes at Large, *1700–1750.* Richmond, 1971.

Wingo, Elizabeth B. *Marriages of Norfolk County, Virginia, 1706–1792.* Norfolk, 1961.

Wolfe, Don M., et al., eds. *Complete Prose Works of John Milton.* 8 vols. New Haven, Conn., 1959–73.

Unpublished Studies

Alden, John R. "General John Skey Eustace." Copy at the Institute of Early American History and Culture, Williamsburg, Va.

Cullen, Charles T. "St. George Tucker and Law in Virginia, 1772–1804." Diss., U.Va., 1971.

Detweiler, Robert C. "Richard Bland." Diss., U. Wash., 1968.

Evans, Emory G. "The Nelsons: A Biographical Study of a Virginia Family in the Eighteenth Century." Diss., U.Va., 1957.

Golladay, V. Dennis. "The Nicholas Family of Virginia, 1722–1820." Diss., U.Va., 1973.

Hemphill, William E. "George Wythe, the Colonial Briton: A Biographical Study of the Pre-Revolutionary Era in Virginia." Diss., U.Va., 1937.

Mahan, Terrence. "Virginia Reaction to British Policy, 1763–1776." Diss., U. Wis., 1960.

Smith, Alan McK. "Virginia Lawyers, 1680–1776: The Birth of an American Profession." Diss., Johns Hopkins, 1967.

Woodson, E. G. "John May and His Brothers, Pioneer Plutocrats." M.A. thesis, U.Va., 1939.

Index